EVALUATION RESEARCH AND DECISION GUIDANCE

EVALUATION RESEARCH
AND
DECISION GUIDANCE

For Correctional, Addiction-Treatment, Mental Health, and Other People-Changing Agencies

DANIEL GLASER

with

EDNA EREZ

Transaction Books
New Brunswick (U.S.A.) and Oxford (U.K.)

Copyright © 1988 by Transaction, Inc.
New Brunswick, New Jersey 08903

All rights reserved under International and Pan-American Copyright Conventions. No part of this book may be reproduced or transmitted in any form or by any means, electronic or mechanical, including photocopy, recording, or any information storage and retrieval system, without prior permission in writing from the publisher. All inquiries should be addressed to Transaction Books, Rutgers—The State University, New Brunswick, New Jersey 08903.

Library of Congress Catalog Number: 87-19036
ISBN: 0-88738-137-5
Printed in the United States of America

Library of Congress Cataloging in Publication Data

Glaser, Daniel.
    Evaluation research and decision guidance.

    Bibliography: p.
    1. Social service—Evaluation.   2. Social service—
Decision making.   3. Evaluation research (Social
action programs)   I. Erez, Edna.   II. Title. [DNLM:
1. Behavior Therapy.   2. Decision Making, Organizational.
3. Evaluation Studies. WM 425 G548e]
HV41.G6   1988   362'.0723   87-19036
ISBN 0-88738-137-5

Contents

List of Tables

List of Figures

Acknowledgments

The author gratefully acknowledges permission from the publishers and publications indicated to use the following previously published material:

"Changing the Public Drunkenness Laws: The Impact of Decriminalization," by David E. Aaronson, C. Thomas Dienes and Michael C. Musheno, *Law & Society Review* 12, 3 (1979), Graph No.1 (p.416).

"The Limits of Bail Reform: A Quasi-Experimental Analysis," by Roy B. Flemming, C. W. Kohfeld, and Thomas M. Uhlman, *Law & Society Review* 14, 4 (1980), Figure No.3 (p.958).

Ted Palmer, *Correctional Intervention and Research*. Lexington, Mass.: D.C. Heath & Co., 1978, data from Table 5.1.

This volume was prepared at the urging of Saleem A. Shah and George Weber of the Alcohol, Drug Addiction and Mental Health Administration of the National Institute of Mental Health, and an early draft was reviewed by Christopher Dunn of that agency.

Part of chapter 4 was checked by Daniel LeClair of the Massachusetts Department of Correction, parts of chapter 6 by Norman Holt of the California Department of Correction, all of a not quite final version of chapters 6 and 7 by Professor Ward Edwards of the University of Southern California, and part of chapter 9 by Keith Griffiths and Elaine Duxbury of the California Youth Authority. Irving Louis Horowitz helped me reconceptualize and reorganize several chapters of the book. My wife Pearl's detailed suggestions on an early draft greatly improved its rhetoric.

To all of the above, and doubtless to many others, I am indebted for whatever virtues this work may have. I alone should be blamed for its defects.

Daniel Glaser
Los Angeles, 1987.

1

Introduction

This book is for organizations that try to change people. Prisons, probation offices, treatment centers, hospitals, clinics, and schools, for example, have clients deemed criminal, delinquent, addicted, psychotic, retarded, or simply undereducated. They try to help these people merit such labels as reformed, educated, trained, or, minimally, improved. Such an accomplishment is often called rehabilitation, treatment, instruction, or simply assistance. How well do they do it? That is the question that evaluation research is designed to answer. How can they know what decisions will probably be most effective for the achievement of their goals? That is the concern of scientific decision guidance. These are the two types of activities with which this book is concerned.

Evaluation and Evolution

As societies become affluent, and as their science and technology grow, there is an increasing concern with measuring the effectiveness of all endeavors objectively and precisely. For economic, humanitarian, scientific, and other reasons, many people want to know which types of organizations, policies, or procedures are most fruitful. This demand for rigorous assessments is part of an accelerating trend that Max Weber (1978) called the rationalization of social institutions. By this he meant that they would be guided increasingly by science and logic, rather than by subjective impressions and mystical beliefs. Computerized records, more educated officials, a more sophisticated public, as well as more probing and analytic mass media, are rapidly advancing this trend.

Efforts to provide knowledge of the effectiveness of people-changing efforts are referred to here, and in a burgeoning literature, as "evaluation research." Its pursuit thus far has been too often sporadic rather than continuous and cumulative, despite increases in the money and personnel

1

devoted to it. Scientific assessments of attempts to change people or conditions are frequently undertaken in temporary projects and produce results
that can't readily be generalized to other settings. Therefore, officials of
people-changing organizations too rarely can demonstrate how well their
programs work as compared with alternative programs or none. To increase rationality, their decisions and the judgments of those who finance
them must be based on the more adequate and logical measurement with
which this book is concerned.

What an agency regards as evaluation research frequently consists only
of gathering information on the number and variety of its clients and
services. These data are more immediately available and useful in justifying its budgets than are data on whether its services are effective. It takes
more time to determine whether the agency achieves its goals; besides, the
findings may prove discrediting. Nevertheless, commentators on people-
changing agencies increasingly assert the necessity of scientific evaluation
for policy guidance.

Legislatures, courts, and administrative agencies reach decisions daily
on the denial of liberty to individuals whose conduct has been labeled
deviant. Billions of dollars are spent annually on efforts to change these
people and to change others who come voluntarily for help. Still more
billions are spent to help schools and other community resources prevent
deviant conduct. These decisions and expenditures are made with scant
advance knowledge or later feedback on the validity of the innumerable
diagnoses, prognoses, prescriptions, and recommendations that guide
them. As two experts on our criminal justice system have asserted, "action
in ignorance imposes a moral obligation to do research" (Zimring and
Hawkins 1973:50).

Evaluation research has been called "an elusive paradise" (Glaser 1965)
because it has been promoted and initiated for over a century yet is only
now beginning to be securely established in an appreciable fraction of
people-changing endeavors. Therefore, this book provides in its next four
chapters a "how to" on evaluation, and in the remainder, a guide to giving
assessment more impact on policies and practices. It seeks to make evaluation more useful to decision makers, hence more routinely used by them.
To accomplish this, it includes two chapters on another growing aspect of
the rationalization process in organizations, the scientific analysis and
guidance of decisions. Before the concluding chapter, however, it also addresses some ethical and legal issues that arise in program evaluation.

Scientific decision guidance is an emerging field of study in schools of
business, management, and engineering, where it is increasingly applied to
people-changing efforts. This book is unique in differentiating decision
guidance into two forms.

The first of these types of guidance, presented in chapter 6, is applicable only to often repeated kinds of decisions for which researchers can compile statistics on past results. Insurance companies for many decades have analyzed the consequences of many kinds of routine activities to calculate the risks of unfavorable outcomes. Unfortunately, in courts, clinics, and other places where fateful decisions are made on people-changing efforts, the consequences of past case decisions are seldom systematically recorded and analyzed to determine the risks that are incurred by making particular kinds of decisions with different types of clients. Yet scientific risk estimation was extended in the 1920s from figuring profitable insurance rates to guiding decisions on the granting of parole or probation. This actuarial type of statistical research has consistently been shown to yield more accurate case prognoses than those offered by presumed experts on the basis of their individual impressions. However, as chapter 6 details, the routine use of risk estimation by agency officials in their case decisions has required that such estimates be recognized as only one source of guidance, rather than as the sole determinant of case actions (Glaser 1985).

The second type of decision guidance, presented in chapter 7, applies to nonroutine actions. It is based on a large and growing volume of applications in business, the armed forces, and other organizations, as well as in much everyday life activity, such as deciding what kind of automobile to buy. In all such matters, often serious and fateful choices, research has demonstrated that people tend to make too hasty decisions, with unwarranted confidence in the wisdom of their conduct. Even with scientific guidance such decisions must often be made with some uncertainty and with some reliance on subjective guesses. Multiattribute utility anaysis, the method of decision guidance presented in chapter 7, is a way of systematically identifying and weighing the relative importance of the values sought in any decision, and of employing the best types of knowledge available for estimating how well each possible alternative action would achieve these values.

Using scientific research to improve evaluations for the guidance of people-changing agencies often poses legal and ethical dilemmas. Most of these are not encountered in laboratory research with nonhuman subjects, especially in the physical sciences. Therefore, pertinent ethical and legal issues in evaluation research are discussed in chapter 8, which is written by Edna Erez, a lawyer and behavioral scientist.

This book doesn't just postulate that science can improve people-changing organizations. It also shows by numerous examples that science has already done this quite well in many matters. Chapter 9 discusses how such benefits can be made more routinely available and more fully utilized. A preliminary step, however, may be to explore some of the jargon that has developed to indicate the varieties of evaluative efforts.

Types of Evaluation

Traditionally, the sole concern of evaluation research has been to measure how well a policy, program, practice, or other action achieves specified goals. Such a definition for the term "evaluation," as generally used in applied social research, once sufficed. But a variety of somewhat inconsistently used jargon has now developed to designate evaluating activity. Assessments of how well goals have been attained are now commonly labeled either *summative, impact* or *outcome evaluation*, or *assessment. Impact evaluation* often denotes not just measurement of goal attainment, but of all of the consequences of a statute, court decision or program for the people or circumstances to which it was directed.

The term *formative evaluation* is generally used in a vague and inconsistent fashion. It designates diverse types of relatively early and usually hasty program assessments. These assessments vary greatly. They include narrative accounts of subjective impressions by outside visitors, conclusions drawn from exploratory interviews or survey questionnaires of staff, clients or others concerned with a program, or even rigorous outcome evaluations presentng "hard" statistics but based on small-scale or short-term data collection. Such studies are appropriate, indeed necessary, as pilot inquiries guiding early stages of major programs or in preparation for more conclusive evaluation research. They often result in early modifications of the design of a program, especially if it was begun hastily without much time for careful planning. They may also be the basis for plans and proposals to conduct more adequate assessments.

Frequently decisions on how to operate a people-changing agency or any of its programs must be made quickly, without waiting for the most dependable information, so that little guidance is available except from formative assessments that are not very thorough. Indeed, it has been asserted that in practice crude formative evaluations are often all that can influence officials, because an adequate outcome or impact evaluation requires followup of past clients for so long a period that before the study is completed, the agency's circumstances have altered to such an extent that the findings are obsolete (Patton 1978; Cronbach et al. 1980).

Fortunately, there are many degrees of program evaluation adequacy, and not just a sharp differentiation between crude formative and optimum summative evaluations. Knowing the optimum permits evaluators to approximate it as closely as possible with the time and resources available and to assess the limitations of suboptimum studies. There is a need to make both short- and long-term estimations of goal attainment as accurately as possible if policy is to be well-guided, for evaluation research has usually been the basis for piecemeal modification rather than termination of peo-

ple-changing efforts. This gradualism is often due to the fact that the majority of careful assessments are partially negative and partially positive in
their appraisals of existing operations, and that it is generally impossible to
replace ongoing programs abruptly or completely. The practical value of
summative or outcome assessments are repeatedly illustrated in the chapters that follow, although their limitations are also pointed out.

Evaluability assessments are investigations of the feasibility of an outcome evaluation. They make inferences as to the adequacy with which an
assessment can be completed, considering such constraints as the amount
of time and resources available, as well as the existence of relevant records,
and opposition or cooperation from those who control access to needed
information, subjects, or settings. Frequently these inquiries determine the
planning of evaluation research or constitute its planning stage.

Process evaluation or *monitoring* is the systematic observation of what
occurs in a program or of how a policy is carried out. This type of assessment is not designed to measure the ultimate attainment of a goal, but to
specify the nature of the program. A certain amount of monitoring is a
necessary first step in both evaluability and outcome assessments, because
without examining a program researchers often can't be certain of what,
exactly, they are assessing. What is called education, training, therapy,
counseling, surveillance, testing, or any other type or aspect of people-
changing activity varies tremendously. Two activities with the same designation may in fact contrast dramatically in the amount and quality of
personnel, activity, or other resources they employ for a given number of
clients, as well as in their procedures. Relying on the official label for the
activity may be highly misleading; it is necessary to check out the activity
to determine the best procedures for evaluating it, as well as to develop
hypotheses about its effectiveness or factors affecting its impact.

In studying a people-changing endeavor—the counseling of probationers, for example—a summative evaluation might compare recidivism
rates of counseled and uncounseled subjects; a process evaluation would
describe when and how the counseling occurred, who said what in it, and
what attitudes it seemed to arouse; a formative evaluation might be a crude
version of such a process evaluation, perhaps by a consultant who visited
for a few days, or it might be the findings of a questionnaire on the counseling that is distributed to clients and staff, then quickly analyzed. The
formative study would be done first, and would include some process evaluation, but more extensive monitoring might continue thereafter, and the
summative or outcome evaluation would be the last to be completed. It is
clear that all of these types of research may be useful, each in its time, but
that a combination of highly adequate summative and process evaluations
is preferable to having nothing but a crude formative study. However, if the

formative study indicates that the activities being evaluated are too negligible in dimension or quality to have much impact, this may suffice to deter further investments in evaluation until the program is improved, or to prompt termination of the program at once.

Some variations of process evaluation are called *compliance assessments, implementation appraisals, discrepancy evaluation,* or other combinations of these terms. They are concerned with monitoring programs to determine how precisely they follow laws, directives, or regulations. They tend to be sharply focused on specific details, whereas most other process evaluation employs more open-ended qualitative research methods, including participant observation or simply systematic interviewing and visiting. They note the deviations of practices from precepts and infer the subjective meanings of a program to its administrators and its clientele.

Outcome evaluations that simply measure attributes of a program's clients before and after these attributes are the targets of a people-changing effort are often said to treat each program like a mysterious black box; the input and the output of the box are compared to assess a program's effects regardless of what goes on inside. The various type of monitoring require that one crawl into the box and look around to try to determine what causes any impact or lack of effect that the outcome evaluation reports.

Cost-benefit, cost-effectiveness, and *efficiency evaluation,* the concerns of chapter 5, designate methods of expressing the results of summative evaluations in monetary terms. Thus, reducing the recidivism rates of 100 chronic juvenile offenders by 50 percent might be estimated as a benefit worth 1 million dollars to the public. If this is achieved through small-unit confinement with intensively programed work and learning incentives that cost $500,000 for 100 juveniles, the benefits are double the costs and the program is a profitable investment. However, since such estimations of the dollar values of benefits must often be highly speculative and arbitrary, the focus of these types of evaluation is frequently limited to the cost of alternative programs. Thus, if Program A is twice as expensive per client as Program B, and if they are equally effective, B is clearly most efficient. However, if Program A reduces the probability of recidivism by 20 percent more than does Program B, some estimation of the dollar value of this 20 percent reduction must be made to decide whether Program A is worth its extra cost.

The monetary thinking implied in these hypothetical examples is unavoidable in rational decisions by policy makers when they try to budget finite funds for maximum effectiveness and when many programs compete with each other for money. Unfortunately, as detailed later, the figures available for such calculations, especially on the magnitude and value of benefits, are often only very rough approximations. Evaluation research can gradually reduce the degree of roughness.

The term *comprehensive evaluation* sometimes is employed to refer to a combination of process, outcome, and cost-benefit assessments.

Conclusion

In this age of increasingly computerized record keeping and consequent speedy retrieval of information, rigorous statistical evaluations become easier. They are also more widely understood. Therefore, there is growing legislative and public demand for objective assessments of policies and for scientific decision guidance. Because this book is designed for all of the concerned public, it presents pertinent issues and logical steps in meeting these demands, and it uses little technical jargon. It avoids the use of mathematical statistics formulations, although it suggests what these might contribute on some matters, and it recommends some technical writings at these points for those who want them.

This book deals with all types of evaluations and with the scientific guidance of both routine and nonroutine decisions. It examines the ethical and legal issues in developing and using evaluations, as well as the difficulties of achieving their routine use. The problems that must be addressed initially in all these endeavors are how best to state an agency's objectives and how to measure their degree of attainment.

2

Defining and Measuring Success

As a rule, the most important assessment of a program, practice, or policy is that which measures how successful it has been. This is outcome evaluation, and it begins by identifying the goals or targets of the program, for their attainment constitutes success. Sometimes goals are readily stated and will not be disputed. In business, for example, everyone usually agrees that the main objective is to earn money, and that effectiveness is measured by profit-and-loss statements. In people-changing agencies, however, goals are frequently vague, multiple, and not measured by standard and satisfactory procedures.

Downgraders of evaluation efforts often ask, "How can we measure how successful we are if we can't define success?" A frequent ploy of those with a stake in a program, when confronting an evaluation that concludes that they failed to attain their goals, is to claim that their goals were not those upon which the evaluation was based. Indeed, officials of agencies often disagree when asked to name their goals or stubbornly argue about the relative accuracy of various overlapping verbal formulations. These stances have been called the "goals clarification game" (Patton, 1978: ch.6). They foster calls for "goal-free evaluation" (Patton, 1980:55-7), which really means to let agreement on goals be assumed rather than specified.

Such arguments about goals occur partly because every organization, like every individual, pursues a variety of goals. Frequently the pursuit of one aim impedes attainment of another, and the result is a conflict among objectives. For example, humanitarian interests of mental hospitals include keeping patients from suffering, but custodial concerns may require restrictions of patient freedoms, while therapeutic goals may be pursued by imposing emotional pain in an encounter group and even physical pain through electroshock treatment. In all organizations, the financial goal of keeping costs within a prescribed budget impedes spending for many services, supplies, or equipment that would contribute to the attainment of other goals. Importance must be attached simultaneously to therapeutic or

9

instructional, custodial, humanitarian, and economic goals in most people-changing organizations.

Additional problems in stating goals include the following: People often engage in activities because they are told to do so or because it has been the custom of their organization, without anyone knowing or clearly remembering why the practice began. In such circumstances, statements of goals are often mere speculations made later to justify the activities. Practices begun for one purpose may often be continued for another. Our language has an immense variety of words to express purpose, and these words often have overlapping and vague meanings. Administrators often have vested interests in setting attainable goals and in discrediting the goals by which their work is unfavorably evaluated.

Yet some specification of the goals sought in a people-changing effort is needed to evaluate it. Fortunately, formative evaluations and evaluability assessments, ranging in scope from brief consultations with officials to large-scale opinion polls and program monitoring, can usually attain much agreement on the most important objectives by which an effort should be rated.

A partial solution to the multiple goals problem in evaluation is simply to list the different identifiable goals and to assess the achievement of each separately. Thus, a prison's operation can be graded in terms of escape rate; number of mass disturbances; number of inmates receiving disciplinary reports; proportion of prisoners completing education or vocational training programs; productivity of institution farms and industries; postrelease recidivism rates of its inmates. Compared with the last item, the others are relatively easy to tabulate and are frequently presented in annual reports or other assessment documents.

While multiple goals may increase the completeness with which officials and other interested parties know the dimensions and conseqences of an agency's activities, there are three limitations to such efforts. The first is that multiple goals are rarely of equal importance to an agency; their relative significance must be assessed if there is to be guidance from measuring the attainment of each. Chapter 7 provides a technique—the value tree—for listing, interrelating, and weighting objectives. Closely related is the second problem, that the interaction of goals must be investigated to determine if progress toward one impedes achivement of another. The third problem is that identification of an agency's goals is itself a research challenge, for many goals are hidden.

Hierarchies of Goals and Types of Success

Both individuals and organizations rank their goals, considering some more important than others. Furthermore, the element of time makes some goals more important than others: to an individual, for example, paying bills or getting a driver's license may be the highest immediate priority, but other objectives, such as a happy marriage or a satisfying occupation, are more important in the long run. "Salience hierarchy" is the ranking of goals by their time priority, while "importance hierarchy" ranks them in long run significance (McCall and Simmons 1966).

People-changing agencies are expected to try to reduce the deficiencies of ability or the occurrence of objectionable conduct in the people who come to or who are brought to them. It is this goal of making their clientele perform differently afterward which, from the public's standpoint, should presumably be the first concern in evaluating effectiveness (of course, as chapter 5 shows, such evaluations are improved if they are related to costs). Do correctional establishments make delinquents and criminals cease trying to commit offenses? Do addiction treatment organizations help addicts become abstinent? Do vocational rehabilitation centers convert unemployables to wage earners? How much does a school's student learn?

Answers to such crucially important questions are too seldom sought by systematic research. Instead, the research staff of many agencies concentrate only on what is most salient to their administrators. For example, they tabulate statistics on the number of persons served, the number of routine actions taken, the number of admissions, releases, transfers, and discharges of clientele in specified periods. They seek separate totals on this information by geographic areas, as well as by attributes of their clientele. Such routine products of a management information system or MIS are periodically supplemented by special surveys and counts to provide any feasible quantitative answers on a crash basis to administrative questions raised by the press or by legislators, trustees, or others who control the agency's income. As the director of research of one of the nation's largest county correctional agencies expressed it, when I noted the types of interruptions we had while I visited him, most of his time is spent "helping the boss put out fires." But basic questions on effectiveness cannot be answered quickly except with questionable speculations, illustrative cases that are likely to be more dramatic than typical, and subjective impressions.

Putting out fires from critics probaby will never cease to have high priority in any organization, but making evaluation research and rational decision guidance a more readily available asset in fire quenching is the concern of this book. Evaluation is most useful in the long run the more its emphasis is on assessing an agency's achievement of its most important goals. Importance to whom? The agency as a whole or particular officials in it? The public? Is evaluation of an agency's service to the public resisted because officials fear that the results of such an assessment would discredit them? How can we identify all the goals that influence actions in an organization?

Manifest and Latent Goals

One characteristic of organizations and of individuals is what Merton (1957:199) called "displacement of goals." An agency or program originally created for one purpose frequently acquires additional functions, often unofficially, and its operation may then be guided more by the subsequently acquired objectives than by the original ones.

Official goals may appropriately be called manifest, since they are proclaimed in the legislation, directives, or formal announcements under which programs are created or policy is publicly justified. Actual goals must be inferred from the behavior of an organization's functionaries, by the objectives that they seem to be trying to attain. We can ascribe to an agency those goals that explain the decisions of its personnel, but such explanations are not always consistent with the agency's officially stated purposes. Latent goals are the interests and objectives that seem to account for an agency's or program's policy and practice, but they are different from its publicly proclaimed objectives.

As Wesley Skogan (1986) points out:

> Getting a program approved and funded is a political process, and in politics programs must be "oversold" if they are to be more attractive than other ways of spending the money. Thus, program plans usually promise much more than any real-world program possibly could deliver. Understanding this, one job of the evaluator is to steer the evaluation toward realistic goals and realistic expected effects. Only then can agreement be reached about what constitutes a "successful program."

Sometimes officials are aware of discrepancies between the goals they proclaim and the more realistic objectives that they currently seek to attain. They also know their latent concerns, above all avoiding scandals, and will admit them, at least off the record, even when they do not advertise them. At other times the directors or staffs of agencies drift into the pursuit of unofficial objectives at the expense of their proclaimed primary purposes, but they are unaware of this shift, or are loath to admit it.

The supplementation or even the displacement of manifest goals by latent goals is readily observable in many people-changing agencies. Thus, the official purposes of a parole board usually are stated in terms such as those of the National Conference on Parole (1957:66): "the protection of society on the one hand and the rehabilitation of the offender on the other," and "helping the ... offender solve his personal problems in an orderly and acceptable manner." Observation of parole board activity and analysis of the justifications that parole board members give for their decisions, however, reveal latent goals that are independent of the official objectives. These latent goals include the following: reducing disparities in the sentences received by similar offenders tried by different judges (usually reflecting different plea bargains by their prosecution and defense attorneys); maintaining order in correctional institutions by rewarding conformity to prison rules, and by not suddenly reducing the percentage paroled (which causes much inmate discontent and has been blamed for prison riots); balancing the budget, for example, by recognizing that it costs about ten times as much to confine an offender as to supervise him or her on parole (especially pertinent to the many juvenile correctional boards that are responsible for both institutional administration and parole decisions); maximizing public support by trying to avoid early parole of the most notorious and heinous offenders.

Latent goals of organizations may actually be quite justifiable. It is not the merit of different goals, but the need to be aware of all of them, that helps make an agency more effective in achieving any of them. Rationality in pursuing all goals requires that latent goals be made manifest by explicitly stating them, so that they can be defended or criticized. Only if the pursuit of a goal is recognized can the public seek evaluations of efforts to achieve it and be aware of conflicting goals.

Returning to the previous example of latent goals of parole boards, criticism of ostensible arbitrariness and inconsistency of parole boards produced many so-called reforms, especially during the 1970s, to reduce the penalty fixing powers of these boards. All that these reductions accomplished, however, was to transfer some of the parole board influence on penalties to the courts or to the legislatures. The result was that statutory or court punishments tended to be more arbitrary and inconsistent than those determined by parole boards because there are many judges acting individually in a state that has only one parole board. Also, there are insufficient checks, other than that of a parole board, on a prosecutor's power to determine charges against accused persons and to alter these charges or promise sentencing recommendations in plea bargaining agreements on penalties that many judges uncritically rubber stamp. The overzealous reformers of parole boards not only neglected the functions of these boards in reviewing sentences to reduce disparities, but also their prison-order maintenance and budget-balancing functions. Therefore, drastic reductions of parole board powers in the 1970s without giving their latent functions to other agencies often resulted in disorder and in budget crises in operating correctional institutions, crises that continue into the 1980s. Division of penalty-fixing authority among legislators, courts, and parole boards, with a limited range of discretion for each to pursue specified goals, can provide checks and balances on the rationality and consistency of penalty fixing at each level. Also, as chapter 6 shows, decision guideline research can maximize the extent and the consistency with which courts or parole boards meet these goals.

Analyses similar to the foregoing could be made of many so-called reforms in all types of people-changing organizations. Such analyses imply that evaluation of an agency's activities must measure achievement of both manifest and latent goals if it is to foster improvements in agency practices. This can be done only if latent goals are first identified and made explicit, so that they thereby become manifest. Unfortunately, there is no easy, certain, and uniform procedure for identifying latent goals in every setting. Nevertheless, the following are two broad, and generally useful procedures:

1. *Assess the relevance of the agency's actual practices to its official precepts.* To determine actual practices objectively, a researcher must get systematic and unbiased data for representative time periods and locations. Often this can be accomplished through administrative records that log and may enumerate all important actions. Personnel allocations to different tasks and budget expenditures for different functions may also reveal goals realistically. Supplementation to and checks on these types of data may come from time and motion studies, as well as from analyses of the determinants of a representative sample of case decisions. Such analyses could be undertaken either by the agency's own staff or as a process evaluation by outside researchers. Ideally they should be done by collaboration between the two in a formative evaluation aimed at identifying latent goals and including them in a total list of goals that begins with those agreed on in advance as manifest.

2. *Whenever the above first step suggests that some practices are not justified by their contribution to manifest goals, try to determine why they occur.* Often the reasons can be readily inferred; indeed, they may seem obvious. Also, those who make decisions will usually give reasons for them if asked. Either they will thereby reveal latent goals, or latent goals may become evident if administrators are pressed to explain discrepancies between their decisions and the justifications they offer. Frequently, however, the reasons given will not provide sufficient explanation for the decisions and activities observed. Alternative explanations must then be hypothesized by the investigators and tested by further probing, observation, and analysis. Such inquiry into latent goals frequently pinpoints a major source of discrepant conduct that Parsons (1951) classically identified as the dilemma of "self versus collectivity orientation."

Personal versus Organizational Goals

The private objectives of an organization's employees may be the latent goals of their work. These may supersede and even conflict with the organization's manifest goals. Such latent goals, of course, are not readily admitted by those who pursue them. Nevertheless, for evaluation research to have a continuous impact on practices in people-changing agencies, these goals should be revealed. Only with such exposure can changes be made, either in personnel or in work incentives and procedures, to make the pursuits of employees (and volunteers) more compatible with agency objectives.

There are both obvious and subtle sources of discrepancy between personal and organizational concerns of employees. Obvious personal interests, of course, include making the work easy, pleasant, and secure. This often results in staff making only minimal effort, or more subtly, in their emphasizing services that keep clients contented, such as providing fun and games at the expense of activities that require more effort but are pertinent to people-changing goals. This is evident in the passing grades and "social promotions" given in many schools to students who do not learn, if the students at least do not disturb those who want to learn. In addition, in many organizations there are allegations that activities and decisions reflect primarily the political or other career aspirations of officials, or their prejudices and biases.

A much less obvious source of discrepancy between precept and practice, often reflecting dominance of personal over organization interests, is the variation in reinforcement that different staff activities receive. This often is not intended by agency directors, but is an unanticipated consequence of human experiences in the work situation. A common example in mental (health and correctional casework is that an employee is expected to submit written diagnostic and prognostic reports and recommendations on clients, in addition to providing counseling, therapy, instruction, and other services, as well as surveillance. In this type of job there is usually much more immediate and pronounced reward for quality of report writing than for the other activities expected on the job. Written reports produce something tangible that the employee can be proud of. Reports are also the evidence of achievement and judgment most visible to supervisors, who usually do not see the counseling, assistance, or surveillance. The supervisors—whether chief probation officers, judges, wardens, parole board members, or hospital or clinic officials—make case decisions on the basis of the written reports they receive, but can assess the clarity and plausibility of a report much more readily than its validity. Even so, report-writing activities are easier to monitor than activities where staff interact with clients. Staff relationships with clientele often develop slowly and unpredictably and are not readily evident much of the time; indeed, staff who are most proficient at report-writing frequently have a background that makes them feel uncomfortable with their clients.

Differences of reinforcement for diverse parts of a job may often be revealed by studies that find a distribution of staff time incompatible with what is suggested by job descriptions. For example, there may be much more time devoted to paper work than to field work or to investigation than to supervision, in comparison with the time ratios that policies prescribe. Also, before-and-after time studies may demonstrate that when caseloads are reduced, time devoted to paperwork expands much more than time spent in other activities (cf., Glaser 1964:422-48; Glaser 1969:299-303).

Still another source of discrepancy between personal and organizational goals is an employee's primary concern with a career outside the organization. This has frequently been a serious impediment to the routinization of evaluation research in people-changing agencies when reseach staff were more concerned with completing dissertations or preparing publications to facilitate appointment to university faculties than with producing research that could guide agency practice. Occasionally, of course, research is undertaken that can serve all of these goals simultaneously. Then the personal objectives of the researchers supplement the motivation provided by organizational objectives.

Time study analyses of what staff actually do, in conjunction with assessing the relevance of their activities to agency goals, are types of process evaluation that can most readily reveal the influence of personal goals incompatible with those of the organization. Of course, the best assessment of an employee's contribution to an agency is an assessment of the quantity and value to the organization of the tasks that she or he completes. Some employees can do more for an agency than others even while they are also doing things that are purely in their own personal interest.

The solution to problems of discrepancy between personal and organizational goals will vary greatly with the agency, and with the job. The optimum solution is to make employee activities both gratifying to them and in the interest of the agency. Sometimes this can be done by dividing responsibilities that were the concern of one personnel category, as in separating investigation from assistance tasks in the duties of a correctional or mental health caseworker, so that employees specialize in aspects of what was once a single job. Sometimes this is done by a casework team that may include one or more paraprofessionals who share a common caseload with a professional; the professional's skill at writing reports and at negotiating with higher officials or other agencies is combined with the paraprofessional's stronger rapport with the clientele. In such teams each member can contribute unique types of guidance to the others, especially if no rigid caste differentiation divides them. The risk of intrastaff barriers may be reduced by facilitating and encouraging advancement from one team role to another, as from paraprofessional to professional. A group of political scientists have asserted that "the extent to which public interest goals can be reached depends largely on how well they serve the self-interests of the 12 people responsible for executing the policies in qestion" (Musheno et al. 1976).

Selecting the Types of Goal Attainment to be Measured

Confronted with myriad goals designated as guiding the activities of agency directors and staff, a first task in evaluability assessments is often to reduce the number of goals that concern the evaluator. Sometimes management can reduce discrepancies between personal and organizational objectives through sharply curtailing or eliminating tasks of little value to the agency despite staff interest in them. Thus, the preparation of long narrative case reports can be discouraged if research shows that most of their contents are not used by decision makers, their preparation consumes a tremendous proportion of staff time, and staff rewards can be more closely linked to activities more valuable to the organization.

When discredited latent personal goals are made manifest, such as providing special services to the political supporters of one's boss, such a goal is promptly disavowed, and may then be abandoned. However, many latent or personal goals, such as keeping clients contented, are often justified by officials as a means to manifest agency objectives, such as facilitating the administration of inmate housing, improving custodial security, and possibly even furthering rehabilitation or education. This leads one to a dichotomization that is suggested by Ackoff (1978:48). Goals have *intrinsic* value insofar as their attainment itself is an ideal or ultimate objective, and *extrinsic*—or one could say, instrumental—value as means to other more intrinsic objectives. To what manifest or intrinsic goals a latent or extrinsic goal contributes is, of course, a problem for evaluation research.

The attainment of a latent goal is usually measurable, once the goal is made manifest. The consequences of attaining one goal for the achievement of others can also be investigated. For example, research on the prediction of recidivism rates for young federal prisoners some years ago indicated that a good behavior record in prison was associated with less recidivism only for those who had had prior confinements. On the first confinement, inmates seemed to have difficulty avoiding violation of institution rules regardless of their postrelease recidivism prospects; only among those with two or more prior incarcerations were the inmates who still "had not learned to do time" worse recidivism risks than those who conformed to prison rules. Thus for those first incarcerated, too much stress on conformity while confined as a condition for parole might have impeded achievement of the goal of reducing recidivism rates.

One of the most useul steps for deciding which of the variety of agency attainments evaluators will measure is to classify goals by the time required to know how well thay have been achieved. Usually it is helpful to divide goals into three broad categories as immediate, intermediate, and ultimate:

Immediate goals refer to specific services that are to be provided by an agency, such as housing, medical treatment, custody, instruction, work, counseling, referral, surveillance, or any of the myriad other specific functions of various types of people-changing organizations. Evaluating attainment of immediate goals requires only compilation of statistics that show what services were provided in particular periods and perhaps for specific types of clients or in various locations. As chapter 1 indicated, this type of evaluation is the usual task of management information services, or MIS.

Most organizations were established to provide certain services, and such provision is their primary manifest goal. Many also are required by laws or other directives to provide particular services to specific types of clients. Therefore, tabulating data on the achievement of such immediate goals must be a top management priority and accounts for the ubiquity of MIS in large organizations. Palumbo and associates (1984) point out, however, that in some organizations the routinely available data do not reveal that ostensibly similar units vary greatly in the extent to which they provide many basic services, do not show differences in services for different categories of clients, or do not reveal changes over time in the quantity of particular types of services provided. In such circumstances, process evaluations can show variation in success most quickly and dramatically by gathering data on attainment of immediate goals.

Intermediate goals are the direct effects that are expected from attainment of the immediate goals of providing various services. These intermediate aims may include improved health, enhanced employment qualifications, prompt detection of serious rule violations, more favorable client or staff self-conceptions, and improved client-family relationships. Measures of the attainment of such intermediate goals include statistics on client misconduct while in custody, number of diplomas or vocational training certificates earned, increases in academic grade level, maintenance of communication or support from family, preservation of marriages, job procurement or maintenance, volume of client aid to dependents, restitution to victims, and other direct consequences sought in providing services

As chapter 9 points out, focus on intermediate goals fosters a convergence of support for evaluation research from agency administrators and the government or other officials responsible for funding their services. More extensive support from the press and the public, however, requires evidence on the relevance of these intermediate goals to more long run objectives.

Ultimate goals are traditionally formulated as the aims of a people-changing agency, its broader manifest goals, such as protection of the community and the reformation or cure of its clients. If intermediate goals are the direct effects of services, ultimate goals are the hoped-for indirect effects. Their attainment is usually measured by statistics on former clients, such as their recidivism or relapse rates, their postrelease or postgraduate earnings, promotions, marriages, home ownership, and other attainments or honors. Such statistics are essential to fully satisfactory evaluations of particular agencies, programs or services.

Following conventional usage in psychometrics and actuarial research, any measure of intermediate or ultimate goal attainment by which a program is evaluated will be referred to here as the *criterion* of program effectiveness. Our next problem is how to select criteria that are "hard" or objective, rather than "soft" or subjective; relevant to attainable goals; continuous rather than discrete statistical variables; and useful in the estimation of monetary benefits or of cost efficiency. Sometimes it is necessary to neglect one or more of these concerns and emphasize another to concentrate on what is most feasible and important with the available time and other resources for research. All four types of criteria are desirable, however, and all can usually be pursued simultaneously. All make evaluation research more clearly useful and therefore more likely to be routinely accepted and supported.

The Most Objective Criterion

In the absence of evaluation research, the effectiveness of people-changing endeavors is usually assessed by the subjective impressions of those who administer, support or oppose particular policies, practice, or programs. These people often are biased in their subjective evaluations, even when they try not to be, and frequently they do not try very hard. Many of them have devoted large amounts of time, training, lobbying, or money to get one practice adopted rather than another. Indeed, their jobs, careers, and reputations may depend upon favorable evaluation of one approach and unfavorable assessment of others. That is why, to maximize objectivity, independent evaluative research personnel are needed.

Subjective assessments tend to be biased not only by the evaluator's interests, but because they are based on observations of an unrepresentative sample of events or cases. We tend to be especially impressed by dramatic recent cases that come to our attention, whether favorably or not, and we therefore generalize about programs from such cases when they are not typical of most of the experience in the program.

Most important, perhaps, is that subjective impressions are based upon private feelings rather than on externally observable events. Our strictly personal impressions are the most quickly and easily obtained evidence of an activity's outcome; these impressions develop spontaneously, and therefore they may unwittingly be the main guidance for policies. A check against the errors of subjective impressions is perhaps the main goal of systematic evaluation research that strives to be objective.

Problems of obtaining a representative sample are not dealt with extensively here, since they are treated in much detail in other texts and journals on research methodology, but some sampling problems peculiar to evaluation of people-changing efforts are discussed in chapters 3 and 4. Even when assessments of people-changing efforts avoid sampling bias, however, they may still retain purely subjective assessments of outcome. This occurs when the statistics collected are on the personal assessments of a program by a representative sample of observers, whether outside observers agency staff, or the agency's clients. Often not much better are questions to clients on their self-conceptions, confidence, or other feelings and attitudes before and after they are in a program, since the validity of these subjective reports as indicators of subsequent behavior or ability change must still be determined. Paper-and-pencil tests or oral reports from clients or staff are never as satisfactory in evaluating a program's impact on clients as more objective evidence on the clients' performance. Indeed, questionnaire responses have often been shown to be quite irrelevant or grossly misleading as predictors of behavior (cf., Seckel 1965 and Jesness 1971, for comparisons of responses on one of the most carefully developed questionnaires on delinquent personalities—the Jesness Inventory—and actual postrelease behavior of incarcerated delinquents). Sometimes this discrepancy between word and deed occurs because subjects want to make a favorable impression on the evaluators, especially if they think the evaluators have the authority to give them freedom or other benefit. Sometimes this discrepancy has more elusive causes.

Fiedler and Bass (1959), both in studies of juveniles and in studies of military personnel, compared self-esteem scores for confined offenders, offenders released on probation or parole, and nonoffenders. These studies revealed that nonoffenders have more favorable self-conceptions than offenders, regardless of whether the offenders were confined, but that offenders confined in correctional institutions had distinctly more favorable self-conceptions than offenders released on probation or parole. Two explanations for the latter contrast were offered by these researchers. The first, from psychoanalytic theory, is that those who are confined feel better about themselves because their punishment relieves them of guilt feelings. The second explanation, from reference group theory, is that confined offenders compare themselves to other inmates, but that released offenders compare themselves to nonoffenders. Analogous research on confined and released mental patients might prove interesting.

Regardless of which of the above interpretations you accept, the implication is that self-concept tests misleadingly make any community correction program appear less successful than it actually is in comparison to an incarceration program. Similarly misleading may be evaluations of counseling and psychotherapy programs by tests of insight into psychological principles or by personality inventories. Such evaluations may be invalid because counseling or therapy often instructs clients in a "vocabulary of adjustment" needed to score favorably by verbal evidence, and in an institution or other involuntary programs, the clients treated learn that "showing insight" may hasten release. That is why so many of these programs in correctional agencies show little or no impact on recidivism rates despite their eliciting favorable impressions from clients and staff (cf., Harrison and Mueller 1964; Seckel 1965; Kassebaum et al. 1971).

Nevertheless, some acceptance of subjective criteria may be unavoidable. When prompt assessment of outcome is demanded, soft data are usually more quickly and cheaply obtainable than hard evidence. Therefore, formative evaluations based on quick surveys of clients and staff abound. It cannot be overemphasized, however, that conclusions based on soft data should always be highly qualified as tentative until knowledge is available on the validity of these types of data as predictors or indicators of objective behavior. Preliminary conclusions based on even a few dimensions of objective behavior in the community, derived from short followups on small samples, may often warrant much more confidence than purely subjective data from larger samples.

The Most Attainable Criterion

One politically astute approach of management in deciding upon a criterion whose attainment is to be assessed is to consider first the kinds of changes that an agency can most readily accomplish for a particular type of client. These changes may be immediate or intermediate goals that are presumed to be the means of reaching an ultimate end. Thus, providing a service where none previously existed may be the most readily achieved and important accomplishment for a new agency, while raising grade levels or increasing the percentage of clients attaining state trade-proficiency certificates may be the clearest gain for a new program within an existing agency. If the ultimate objective in both of these examples is to get the clients into satisfactory employment, then after demonstrating that the most attainable goals have been achieved, the agency may be pressured to show the relevance of its accomplishments by comparing subsequent employment rates or earnings of similar clients who differed markedly in the amount or quality of instruction that they received, or in the learning that they demonstrated. Thus, if immediate goals are presumed to be prerequisites to some intermediate goals, and intermediate goals to ultimate objectives, the most impressively attainable criterion is likely to be the one in this three-stage sequence that has not yet been shown to have been accomplished. A few more examples may illustrate this principle.

A large proportion of skid-row alcoholics are undernourished and debilitated. Therefore, any agency that provides them with food, shelter, and medical services, including vitamins and other prescribed food supplements for those who need them most, should be more successful in changing such clients through counseling than an agency that only offers counseling. This was shown rather dramatically some years ago by evaluation research in a pioneer alcoholic detoxification center in St.Louis (LEAA 1970).

It may seem impossible to find attainable criteria if hardly anyone is successfully changed, but it is often appropriate to subdivide a high failure-rate effort into sequential problems, each of which has close to a 50 percent favorable outcome. For example, in New York City some years ago, where addicts were assigned to treatment programs by a central referral service, it was found that less than 20 percent were in their programs a few weeks after their referral. However, observation indicated that this problem could be divided into two components, each of which had closer to a 50 percent success rate: getting the addicts to the program to which they were referred, and then getting them to keep participating in that program. Each of these problems required quite different solutions.

Part of the problem of getting addicts to program agencies was that the ex-addict staff at the referral centers were enthusiastic graduates of total abstinence programs such as the Phoenix Houses, hence were prejudiced against following instructions to send to programs of maintenance on the synthetic drug methadone those addicts who were persistent failures at all other types of treatment, and who would accept only methadone. Another part of this problem was that addicts inexperienced or unfamiliar with the programs recommended for them expected discomfort and humiliation at the agencies to which they were sent. Providing a better individual orientation for the addicts at the referral center and an escort service to take them to the recommended treatment center, whose offer of services they accepted, assured that almost everyone sent to a particular agency got started there. The completely separate problem of keeping them in treatment varied greatly with the agency and the type of client, and could be alleviated only by strategies quite different from those involved in getting them there.

A somewhat different strategy for attaining noteworthy improvement is appropriate where there already is a high success rate, as in many adult probation services with predominantly white-collar offenders. A category of such clientele often can be identified that has close to a 50 percent failure rate, and for whose distinctive needs effective programs can be developed. For example, an appreciable portion of this higher failure-rate group may consist of those whose offense closes the door to future work in their old occupation, who must concentrate on learning and procuring a new type of employment. For the remainder, who will have exceptionally high success rates once the worst risks are separated out, higher standards than nonrecidivism may be sought, such as restitution and community service, for which the achievement rate may be closer to 50 percent.

The main point is simply that one strategy in seeking continually impressive evaluation research results is to define a goal, the target of the people-changing effort, as something that is neither too easy nor too difficult to accomplish. A general principle for this purpose, illustrated in several of the forgoing examples, is to avoid adopting as an immediate objective the alteration of outcome rates that have long been very high or very low. These are what statisticians call high or low base rates, such as the high rates of relapse in alcoholism treatment or the high rate of probation success with older first offenders who have good employment records. With such cases it may be prudent for researchers to define as their problem another goal, but one for which an appreciable improvement in outcome rates can be expected from a program to be evaluated. This may mean focusing on a category of the population that has had about a 50 percent success rate without services and for whom new services will have an appreciable impact. (On base rates and outcome prediction, see the classic essay by Meehl and Rosen, 1955).

It should be pointed out, however, that there are often exceptions to the statistical rule of evaluating programs by measures of preprogram success that divide the population studied approximately in half. Therefore, no purely formal data on base rates alone will substitute for a thorough understanding of the clients, there socio-economic and cultural setting, and the programs to be evaluated.

The Most Continuous Criterion

Success is too often measured as though it were an all-or-nothing matter. It is easy to assert "you either succeed or you fail," but anyone who works at people-changing knows that success of any sort is usually a matter of degree. Recidivism, for example, is usually measured by absence or presence of one rearrest, reconviction, or reimprisonment, although those thus classified as recidivists differ tremendously in the immediacy, frequency, and seriousness of their renewed criminal behavior. Similarly, a dichotomy is made to distinguish drug addicts and alcoholics who relapse after or during treatment from those who do not, but there is great variation in the extent and in the disabling consequences of relapse. Also, those classified as not recidivating or relapsing differ in whether they have actually ceased deviant behavior or merely avoided detection, as well as in whether they achieve addtional goals, such as becoming economically self-sufficient and meeting obligations to others.

An ideal measure of the outcome of a people-changing effort would show in a continuous and equal-interval scale all variations in attaining each important goal, instead of merely classifying the research subjects as successes or failures. Continuous scales permit sensitivity to small variations in effectiveness; success-or-failure dichotomies limit evaluations much as an accountant would be limited if only permitted to tell a business whether or not it made a profit, rather than the exact amount or percentage of profit. Nevertheless, sometimes the outcomes of people-changing efforts can be expressed in some sort of a gradient rather than in a few discrete categories. This is often feasible by use of such continuous variables as time or money as indices of outcome.

Several alternative continuous measures of outcome that are functions of time can usually be formulated if one studies the goals of any people-changing effort. For example, success in promoting abstinence in addicts or alcoholics can be measured as numbers of days abstinent during a post-treatment period, thus differentiating the more immediate and persistent relapsers from those who relapse only slightly and rarely. Similarly, both those who are always abstinent and all those who elapse to any extent can be compared usefully by a continuous variable that measures attainment of some other goal, such as number of days on the job or earnings during a posttreatment period.

Murray and Cox (1979) found that chronic delinquents had a rearrest rate in Chicago of about 80 percent regardless of the penalties imposed, so that the most accurate prediction for all subgroups was that after their punishment they would be rearrested, as most were. However, 317 who were imprisoned in the state's reformatory averaged 6.3 arrests per year of freedom before their confinement but only 2.9 arrests per year of freedom during the postrelease followup. Actually, durations of prior and subsequent periods of freedom, hence of vulnerability to arrest, vary so much for this type of offender, that rates of arrest per day, week or month of freedom are often the easiest to calculate—as decimals—and these are multiplied appropriately to convert them to rates per year.

The researchers called the percentage decline revealed by this Murray and Cox comparison of pre- and postpunishment arrest rates per year in the community the "suppression effect" of the penalty. It was 68 percent for the reformatory, as compared with 40 percent for supervision and 37 percent for probation in the community. However, some special programs were about as effective or more effective than the reformatory. For example, intensive residential care in special hospitals or homes for psychological treatment had an 82 percent suppression effect, while out-of-town camps that emphasized both vocational training and recreation and had short followup programs in the community had a 70 percent suppression effect. Between the suppression effects of supervision or probation and that of the reformatory for these previously much arrested youths were rates of 52 for intensive services at home, 59 for group homes, and 47 for wilderness programs based on the Outward Bound model. Complicating this study, however, was the fact that it was what chapter 3 distinguishes as a quasi–experiment rather than a classical controlled experiment, so that there were some differences in the ages and prior criminality of those sent to these alternative treatments. This may partially have accounted for the differences in their suppression rates. Still, the reformatory appeared to be more suppressive than programs that returned highly criminalized youths without close supervision to the communities where they previously had their high arrest records, but placements in special camps or in intensive residential care away from the neighborhood were still more suppressive.

One of the most sensitive criteria of the effectiveness of any type of treatment or training for prisoners or for hospital patients is the percentage of time reconfined during a postrelease followup period. This percentage is best calculated as the number of days of reconfinement in a given number of days after release (preferably in 365 days or longer, for most studies). The average percentage of postrelease time spent in reconfinement by a group of releasees reflects the immediacy, frequency, and seriousness of their subsequent recidivism or relapses. These aspects of success or failure are not taken into account in dichotomous criteria, such as rearrested or not rearrested, rehospitalized or not rehospitalized, and so forth. The total number of days reconfined, as a percentage of the followup period for different groups of releasees, is an index of variation in the extent to which society will not tolerate the conduct of these persons.

Postrelease reconfinement time, although preferable to dichotomous criteria, is still an imperfect index, of course, because there are inconsistencies in societal reactions to deviant conduct by different individuals. Some people who continue in crime are caught while others are not, some beat the rap although just as guilty as others who are convicted, some who are convicted get shorter confinement terms than others who commit the same offense and have similar criminal records. While such diversities in the consequences of crime warrants care in conclusions on the criminality of a small number of cases, the inconsistencies of the criminal justice system can be presumed to be randomly distributed when one compares large groups of similar individuals. When appreciable numbers of similar offenders from different correctional programs are compared in a followup period, large differences in their average period of subsequent confinement as a percentage of the followup period presumably reflect contrasts in the effectiveness of the programs that they were in. Similar conclusions apply to use of reconfinement time to measure the effectivess of treatment programs for mental or other hospital patients.

The Most Support-Relevant Criterion

Perhaps the greatest advantage of reconfinement time over a dichotomous criterion is that it facilitates an estimation of public costs and benefits of alternative treatment programs. Confinement costs per day can be estimated, so that a monetary benefit of an effective program is less time per client that the government must pay for reconfinement than it spends for programs that have higher recidivism rates. If these "benefits" are related to the cost per client of the different programs, something analogous to a business's profit-and-loss statement is feasible. The history of mental hospitalization policies in the past twenty years shows that legislators and other officials charged with allocating public funds to utterly different types of programs are most easily persuaded to support those programs that can be shown to yield the greatest benefits in relation to costs. The methods of estimating costs and benefits in monetary terms are so diverse, and the problems they pose are so numerous and specialized, that it is appropriate to discuss them at some length, which is done in chapter 6.

Duration of Followup

Evaluation of a people-changing effort, if oriented to assessing attainment of intermediate or ultimate goals, requires a time lapse between conclusion of the change effort and the measurement of outcome. This is the followup period, and determining its duration frequently creates dilemmas. On the one hand, both policy makers and researchers want quick results. On the other, conclusions based upon a brief followup period may be contradicted when findings of a longer followup are available. This could prove embarrassing or even costly if the early results are proclaimed with confidence, and if policy decisions are based on them.

Early contrasts in outcome sometimes remain as time elapses, sometimes diminish, and sometimes expand. In the Provo Project, a one-year followup showed no significant difference in rearrest rates between probationers randomly selected for a special guided-group interaction program and regular probationers; the hoped for differences also failed to emerge in two, three and four-year followups. Differences between experimental and control group probationers in reduction of arrest rates, comparing each person's rate four years before entry into the experiment with his rate after entry, were significant in the first year after entry (at the .05 level) but not in the three subsequent years of followup. However, youths who normally would have been sent to a state industrial school but were instead given probation with assignment to this program had in one year a slight but significant lower rearrest rate than similar offenders on parole for a year from the state school, and this difference grew each year that the followup period was lengthened, A similar growth pattern occurred in their change of arrest rate compared with four years earlier (Empey and Erickson 1972:183-84, 210; further descriptions of this project appear in chapters 3 and 4).

Often evidence of an initial impact strongly suggests the desirability of a longer followup. Thus, in large-scale experiments in Georgia and Texas, in which a randomly selected group of parolees were given unemployment compensation if they did not find jobs, those receiving such payments worked less and were more often arrested than the unpaid parolees in the first six months out, but at the end of one year, the employment and arrest rates were about the same, and those who had received unemployment compensation had higher paying jobs. Rossi, et al. (1980) concluded that the unemployment compensation deterred parolees from seeking or accepting jobs at first, that idleness fostered crime. They also concluded, however, that the ability of the compensated parolees to defer accepting jobs until they got those they deemed satisfactory resulted in their ending the year with higher paid employment, on the average, than that held by the parolees who were not compensated when unemployed. If satisfaction with a legitimate job deters crime, it follows that a longer followup would show that the compensated parolees had a lower rearrest rate than those without this aid; unfortunately, the Department of Labor funding did not permit a longer followup in this study.

Occasionally an issue arises regarding the validity of short-term followup results that can be resolved by longer observations. Thus Lerman (1975) reported that in the California Youth Authority's Community Treatment Program, the rate of reconfinement for randomly selected and intensively

TABLE 2.1
**Monthly Rates of Arrest for Community Treatment Experimental and
Control Cases of the Two Most Numerous Types (per Palmer 1978:44)**

Followup period and Type of offense charged	TYPE OF OFFENDER			
	CONFLICTED		POWER-ORIENTED	
	Experimentals	Controls	Experimentals	Controls
Youth Authority supervision *(average 3 yrs.)*				
Moderate and severe offenses	0.034	0.080	0.055	0.066
Violent offenses	0.006	0.013	0.012	0.016
4-Year Post-*Discharge Period*				
Moderate and severe offenses	0.032	0.058	0.068	0.043
Violent offenses	0.005	0.008	0.013	0.008

supervised early releasees was lower because their parole officers less readily declared them parole violators for minor infractions than did the officers of regular parolees. He notes that the experimentals were more often detained temporarily in local arrest facilities, but less often returned to the Youth Authority's institutions as parole violators than the control group under traditional supervision.

Table 2.1 shows that in a differentiation of these parolees by type (the main point of the experiment, which Lerman largely ignores), the so-called conflicted or neurotic types in the experimental group had distinctly lower rearrest rates than those of this type in the control group of longer confined youths on regular parole, and that this difference persisted even after they were discharged from Youth Authority parole supervision. The leniency of the experimental group's intensively supervising parole officers certainly did not determine the arrest rates after these youths were discharged from parole, except perhaps indirectly, if it prevented greater criminalization by reconfinement as parole violators. On the other hand, the so-called Power-Oriented types of more enculturated and manipulative delinquents did not have significantly different arrest rates in experimental or control groups, either when under Youth Authority supervision or thereafter. This seems compatible with the already described Murray and Cox (1979) findings on advanced offenders from a high-delinquency area in Chicago.

Sometimes research is necessary to establish that conclusions from a short followup are predictive of the findings from a longer followup period, so that the longer one is unnecessary. For example, duration of followup can be a major issue in evaluating psychotherapy programs. Although many desensitization or other differential reinforcement treatments of maladaptive behaviors or feelings will eliminate neurosis or even some psychosis symptoms, advocates of deeper insight therapies claim that such "surface" treatment neglects the underlying basic causes of the ailment, so that the "disease" will manifest itself later in these or other symptoms. One of the earliest but most conclusive proofs that this criticism is of doubtful validity for neurotic anxiety cases was an experiment by Gordon Paul (1967) with the sixty students who had the highest performance anxiety scores of those who expressed motivation for treatment in a class of 380 University of Illinois students of a course on public speaking.

The students in this Illinois study were randomly divided into four groups, each with ten males and five females, with all groups equated on anxiety scores. One group received Wolpe's type of desensitization therapy, one group an attention-placebo therapy, and one group was divided into five groups of three, each assigned to one of five therapists of Rogerian or Neo-Freudian insight focus, who provided five individual therapy sessions in a six-week period (with all missed sessions rescheduled and made up). The remaining fifteen were in a control group that received no therapy at that time.

All subjects and the controls in the above experiment were rated before the six-week treatment, six weeks after the treatment, and two years after, using a large variety of behavioral, physiological, and written test measures of anxiety. In speech performance especially, and by most other measures, all groups improved somewhat over time, but the desensitization treatment group's improvement was most marked and the control group changed least by most indices at both followup points. The insight treatment group was next to the lowest in its improvements by behavioral measures, and variable on other tests, but always below the desensitized group. Reports of relapse or of new neurotic symptoms were greatest in the control group and least in the desensitization group.

Success or failure thus may or may not be a matter of time. If there is long-run persistence of early results, outcome in a brief period usefully predicts later outcome, as was revealed by the above experiment in psychotherapy, by an eighteen-year followup of federal prisoners (Kitchener et al. 1977), and by a few parole studies (Ohlin 1951: Appendix D; Kantrowitz 1977). Confidence in the relationship of short to long followup findings permits quick assessments of impact. It also enhances confidence in base expectancy analysis, an alternative to experimentation described in chapter 4, whereby data from past cases provide a pseudo-control group for assessment of followup results on current cases. Nevertheless, the optimum duration of a followup period varies somewhat with the context and objectives of an evaluation; there is no general rule for determining the optimum period.

Conclusion

Evaluation research is an effort to assess how successfully a people-changing agency attains its goals, but these goals are usually multiple and not entirely explicit. It is appropriate to estimate separately the agency's achievement of each of its distinct objectives or targets, and these goals can usefully be arranged in a hierarchy of importance, as well as in salience. Because many important goals are latent, this chapter suggested techniques for trying to make them all manifest so that their achievement can be investigated. It also discussed the incompatibility of personal goals of some staff with organizational goals, and it ascribed this in part to officials reinforcing some aspects of a job at the expense of others of equal importance.

One of the most useful distinctions in evaluation research is among immediate, intermediate, and ultimate goals. In measuring their attainment, there are advantages in employing criteria that are objective, attainable, continuous, and support relevant. When formulating conclusions from such research, the question of what constitutes an adequate followup period is complex, and the answers seem to vary greatly with the nature of the people-changing effort being assessed.

3

Evaluation Research Design and Administration: The Struggle for Internal Validity

The ideal procedure for testing the impact of an effort to change something is the controlled experiment. We learn of it in high school science courses, or earlier, especially if we are in a rural area and major in agriculture. Thus, if two adjacent garden plots are treated identically except that the experimental plot has a fertilizer added and the control plot does not, the fertilizer is the *experimental variable* (or *treatment*) that is being evaluated. If the experimental plot yields more than the control plot, we credit the fertilizer. Such a correlation assumes that the fertilizer was the only thing that differentiated the experimental from the control plot.

In this garden example, we might have reason to believe that the experimental plot also got more water, sun, insecticide, cultivation or other care than the control plot, or had different prior soil conditions. We might also be uncertain about the accuracy of the measurements of yield. Any of these doubts could lead us to question the validity of ascribing the experiment's results entirely to the fertilizer. The accuracy of findings on the impact of the treatment variable *in the research situation* is known as *internal validity*. Threats to internal validity come primarily from defects in the research methods employed, such as inaccurate observations or failure to take adequately into account the impact of other variables.

Even if there were no doubt about the internal validity of this garden plot study, skeptics could question whether the fertilizer would make as much difference under other soil or climatic conditions, or without the type of care that both the experimental and control plots received. The accuracy with which one can generalize conclusions from a study's setting to other situations is known as *external validity*. Because loss of internal validity also diminishes external validity, much in this chapter applies to both.

Theoretically, the ideal method of evaluating the impact of any people-changing effort is to treat it as the experimental variable in a controlled experiment. Practically, it is very difficult to do this with humans. In most circumstances, such experimentation is either utterly forbidden by law or is effectively resisted by influential decision makers. Even when undertaken, we usually cannot be certain that nothing but the treatment being assessed differentiates the experimental from the control persons and their settings. Contrast between the experimental and control groups in ways other than the experimental variable may account for subsequent differences between them. Therefore, although most evaluation of the impact of people-changing endeavors tries to approximate the ideal controlled experiment in as many ways as possible, it usually cannot fully achieve this ideal. Evaluation research design and administration are struggles to maximize internal validity despite innumerable obstructions.

Research Designs, Internal Validity Threats, and Defensive Strategies

The most typical sources of opinions on the relative effectiveness of different ways to try to change people are prior impressions, prejudices, vested interests, and the advice of those whose views on these matters are respected. Dramatic illustrative cases of success or failure often influence opinions about the effectiveness of a practice or policy out of all proportion to the numbers of such dramatic cases, or of how typical they are of most cases to whom conclusions from them are applied.

The minimum systematic and scientific evaluation of a people-changing effort, which is also the research design employed most often, is what the classic work of Campbell and Stanley (1966) calls a *one-shot case study* (called *one-group post-test-only design* in Cook and Campbell, 1979). This is the study of one trial of the program or practice to be assessed. It is simply an appraisal of experience in trying something out. If the results are better than expected, the evaluation is favorable. This research procedure is usually classified as nonexperimental because there is no control group, but actually any groups with which observers compare the studied group in their minds are implicit control groups. These may be groups in the past or groups elsewhere that did not experience the people-changing method that is being evaluated.

The defect of nonexperimental evaluation is uncertainty as to whether the treatment variable is all that differentiates the studied group from that with which it is compared. Although experiments are designed to avoid this problem, they do not do so if they are very imperfectly designed or administered. Furthermore, even one-shot studies may rival experiments in their scientific value if the cases studied are many and diverse, and if the statistics that they yield can be analyzed by multivariate techniques that interrelate the criteria of effectiveness with other pertinent variables (Kerlinger and Pedhazur 1973; Berk 1983). Furthermore, a one-shot study that instead of being post-test only compares a group of subjects or a situation before and after an innovation to be evaluated becomes a *pre-post comparison*. In this type of comparison that which is studied has itself before the innovation as its control. In addition, as will be elaborated later in discussing time-series analysis, if something new is introduced suddenly in an ongoing program, whatever measurable consequences it is supposed to have may be investigated by studying the change in rates of these consequences before and after the innovation.

Favorable or unfavorable impressions of any type of people-changing effort may very readily be spurious not only because of the lack of a control group, but also because of several other distinct types of threats to internal validity. Most of these were first differentiated by Campbell and Stanley (1966), and are applicable to many kinds of evaluations.

History effects are the types of invalidity in the evaluation of a people-changing method that occur because the research is done in a particular period. Thus, if a job-training program seems to increase the employment rate of its students, this may be due to a labor shortage in the area at that time rather than to the effectiveness of the training. Similarly, an apparent failure of job training to increase the employment rates of its clients may be due to an economic recession rather than to deficiencies of the training. These effects, of course, threaten external as well as internal validity. They especially threaten the conclusion of pre-post comparisons because they leave that nagging question, Did the subjects change because of their treatment or because the times changed? One way to avoid history effects is to have many studies, in diverse periods; if they all yield similar conclusions, the results presumably are not due to the date of the research.

Maturation effects are the consequences of the clients of a people-changing effort growing older, which may be confused with the effects of the attempt to change them. Thus, if high-school auto drivers whose licenses are suspended for three years when they have a serious accident seem to have lower accident rates three years later, the change may be due to their becoming more mature in judgment, driving interests, and lifestyle rather than due to the suspension penalty. Their accident rates might have diminished without the suspension. The possibility of such a maturation effect could be checked by a controlled experiment in which a randomly selected half of those having accidents is a control group that receives no license suspension (although they could receive an alternative penalty). This control group's subsequent accident rate could then be compared four or five years later with that of the experimental group that receives three-year suspensions. The difference between experimentation with plants or animals and experimentation with humans is highlighted if you imagine the protests of the license-suspended youths in the experimental group when they learn of a control group that did not get their licenses suspended!

Selection effects are those that result from the selection of subjects for the treatment or comparison group, rather than from the people-changing effort studied. Any service given only to volunteers cannot be evaluated well by comparing the subsequent behavior with that of persons who refused it, because the volunteers are a selected subgroup presumably more motivated to succeed than those who decline the service. Controlled experiments are feasible in such circumstances if the treatment or conditions to be evaluated are applied only to a randomly selected portion of the volunteers, the random residual cases being the control group, but this poses problems of external validity: conclusions from such research may be difficult to generalize to other persons with similar problems unless almost everyone volunteers or unless you can specify the types of persons who do not volunteer, to whom the conclusion may not be applicable.

Another common source of selection effects is *creaming*, the tendency of program administrators to seek the best clients, especially for new programs in which they have a personal stake, and to get rid of the worst. One of the main purposes of controlled experimentation is to avoid selection effects by comparing the subsequent behavior of a group that has the experimental variable with the later conduct of a very similar or identical group without this variable.

Mortality effect is a special type of selection effect, that of losing cases from a group being studied. If the impact of an alcoholism treatment program is assessed by obtaining a list of everyone in the program at a given time and inquiring about their sobriety a year later, the results may exaggerate the program's success because it is based only on those whose sobriety one can find out about a year later; yet the heaviest drinkers may predominate among those who are unlocatable. Sometimes there is mortality within the control group, or it may even disappear because administrators find that they cannot obtain enough cases for the experimental group to justify their budget for it, and they then insist on admitting all new cases (Empey 1980:146-47). The control group need not always be identical in size with the treatment group, but it is easier to calculate some types of statistical tests of significance if it is, and in any case, the statistical significance of findings is limited mainly by the size of the smallest group in any two or more that are being compared.

The history effect on the validity of a one-shot case study may be avoided not only by many repetitions of the case study, but also by trying a different design, a *static group comparison*. This compares the subsequent conduct rates of a group receiving some type of people-changing effort to the subsequent conduct rates of others in the same period who did not participate. Thus, if the employment rates of persons previously given vocational training could be compared to the employment rates of others who are in the job market simultaneously with them but did not receive the training, history effects threatening internal validity are avoided, since both groups are searching for jobs in the same period. Of course, history effects could still affect external validity, for changes may occur that make it invalid to generalize from the research period to a later era. Also, the results would be distorted by selection effects if the two groups compared were not similar in all respects except whether they had the vocational training. If the compared groups have a different average age, the findings may be due to maturation effects rather than to the training; presumably an older youth group would have more success in finding and keeping jobs.

Whenever the groups compared are known to be highly similar in all respects except that one experienced the treatment being evaluated and one did not, the research design has changed from a static-group comparison to some type of *experiment*. It is a *controlled experiment* if the separation of the experimental from the control group occurred before the experimental variable (or treatment), and was by random selection whereby all subjects had the same chances of being in either group. Any comparison of the experimental (or treatment) group with subjects who are not in such a randomly selected control group is a *quasi–experiment*, and these subjects are a *comparison* group.

A comparison group is usually one that is chosen because there is reason to believe that it is quite similar to the experimental group except that it has not had the experimental variable. In a classic controlled experiment, the strictly random division of a large number of subjects into experimental and control groups before the treatment variable is introduced guarantees, by the laws of probability, that the two groups are very much alike in all measured and unmeasured attributes. Yet most efforts to employ classic controlled experiments in evaluating people-changing efforts either fail to achieve random selection initially, fail to prevent changes in the composition of groups that are begun by random selection, or for other reasons are unable to keep the experimental variable clearly the only difference between treatment and control groups.

Failure to maintain controlled experiments contaminates the results, but the seriousness of this problem varies. Several sources of contamination are indicated in this chapter and in chapter 4, as well as methods of minimizing them and of estimating the direction and extent of their effects. How well evaluation research avoids contamination or threats to internal validity depends not only upon its design, but also upon how it is administered, as well as on its circumstances.

Instrumentation effects are due to deficiencies of the devices or procedures for measurement, such as a test that is either so easy or so difficult for the subjects that it hides their diversity. Chapter 2 pointed out several types of deficiencies in criteria of outcome, which it concluded should be objective, attainable, continuous, and for most research, relevant to concerns that the public supports. Especially in programs that are directed at reducing mental illness or changing attitudes, there are always serious questions about the reliability and validity of measures of states of mind, such as diagnoses or other inferences as to the subjects' current or prospective ideas and emotions.

Testing effects are changes in persons due to their being studied. These may mask or confound changes that are due to the experimental variable. Psychometricians are particularly concerned with the possibility that a test given to subjects before an effort to improve the attitude or ability that the test measures may affect the precision of future uses of this test for these persons. To illustrate, if the same or a similar ability test, attitude questionnaire, or personality inventory is used before and after a people-changing effort, improvements in performance may occur simply because the earlier experience with these measurement devices gives the subjects cues as to how to get a more favorable score the next time, or merely makes them more accustomed to test taking. Researchers can measure whether this testing effect occurs by applying what is called the Solomon Four-Group Controlled-Experiment Design. In this design the experimental and control groups are each randomly divided into two groups, only one of which is given the prior measurement. If the post-treatment measurements show no differences in scores between the groups in each pair, one pretested and one not, a logical conclusion is that there were no effects from prior testing.

Expectancy effects, whereby outcomes tend to be whatever researchers or subjects anticipate, are frequently alleged and sometimes demonstrated to be a source of invalidity in evaluations of all types. For example, it is feared that if research or program staff members know who is in the experimental and who in the control group, they will influence the findings, either intentionally or in spite of leaning over backwards to avoid having such an influence. It is alleged that if they expect or wish, either consciously or unconsciously, that the experimental service will be effective, they may not only give clients extra services and attention, but actually measure achievements more favorably than they would otherwise. Conversely, if they object to the experimental program, perhaps as a threat to their jobs or for other reasons, they may sabotage it, impede the efforts of the experimental subjects, and assess the achievements of the control cases by methods more favorable than those that they apply to the experimental group. Indeed, it is alleged that if staff members know who is in the experimental and who is in the control or comparison group, even their conscious effort to give identical services and measurements to both groups may make their conduct subtly different from what it otherwise would be. Of course, not only the staff, but also the clients, may deliberately try to make a program they favor look good or one that they oppose look bad.

An additional threat to internal validity, resembling testing effects, is that when subjects know that they are being studied, their awareness often spurs them to extra effort. This is the *Hawthorne effect*, named after a famous (but controversial) experiment on the influence of lighting on worker productivity in the Hawthorne Plant of the Western Electric Company near Chicago. In this study, workers who knew that their performance was being studied increased their productivity regardless of how their lighting was varied, from extremely dark to glaringly bright (Mayo 1933: Chapter 3). There are many other subtle interactions between researcher and subject that have been alleged or demonstrated to influence the outcome of research on people-changing efforts (see Friedman 1967).

Blinding is a method of designing and administering experimental research to prevent expectancy or Hawthorne effects from distorting results. With blinding, the persons studied are kept from knowing either that they are being studied, or their role in the experiment, for example, whether they are in the treatment or in the control group. If the experiment is *single-blinded*, only the subjects are unaware of their role in it; if *double-blinded*, even the staff is kept unaware of key features of the research, such as which are the experimental and which the control cases. This is best known in medical research to test the effects of drugs, immunization efforts, or special nutrients, in which the experimental group receives the substance being evaluated (such as a shot, pill, or capsule), and the control group receives a placebo. In a single-blinded experiment, the subjects are all given the impression that they are getting a special drug, vitamin, or immunization, but the researchers know which ones are getting the placebo. In a double-blinded experiment, all the experimental and placebo doses are identified only by code numbers and are mixed; researchers record only the numbers on the substances given to each subject, and the information needed to decode the numbers is locked up until after outcome measurements are completed on all cases, so that only then can researchers know which subjects received the tested substance and which the placebo. Sometimes a third randomly selected group is an additional control group that receives no treatment whatsoever. If the control group receiving the placebo becomes different from this neglected control group, a Hawthorne or "placebo effect" can be ascribed simply to the placebo subjects expecting that what they were given would help them.

Tranquilizers, antidepressants, and other psychoactive drugs are administered extensively to clients of mental health and correctional agencies.

They are often credited with cutting by more than half, between the 1950s and the 1970s, the number of people confined in mental hospitals in the United States, and with preventing riots in overcrowded prisons. Released mental hospital patients are expected to take these drugs on their own in the community, and to report regularly to outpatient clinics. Many do not do so, however, and it is commonly asserted that such disobedience explains the recurrence of their illnesses. Yet it is known that some patients cease taking the drugs but do not relapse, while others relapse despite regular medication. Furthermore, it has been alleged that the nonrecurrence of illness in cooperative patients may be due to factors other than the drugs.

The first efforts to test the effectiveness of psychoactive drugs in controlling mental states or ailments simply compared symptoms in patients before and after a regimen of medication. It was pointed out, however, that there might be a Hawthorne effect, that their apparent recovery with the drugs might be a response to the attention that they were receiving. Such allegations were most conclusively discredited only with double-blinded experiments, primarily in Britain. Thus, when manic-depressive and chronic-depressive patients were given lithium, but, unknown to the staff and patients, a random fraction of the individualized prescriptions were placebos, the greater reduction in mood swings in those getting lithium compared to those receiving the placebo clearly demonstrated the effectiveness of this medication. Similarly, the effectiveness of drugs in symptom control was shown by double-blind administrations of placebos and phenothiazines in treatment of schizophrenia (Leff, 1973).

The prevalence of expectancy, Hawthorne, and placebo effects makes it desirable, whenever possible, to obtain both background and treatment outcome information on subjects by what have been called *unobtrusive measures* (Webb et al. 1966). To minimize impairment of objectivity due to familiarity of researchers with subjects, we should try to supplement observations and measurements made by the researchers with pertinent statistical data on the subjects that may be available from production, education, administration, health, or other records that are compiled routinely by others for nonresearch purposes.

In most experiments to evaluate people-changing efforts as well as in nonexperimental studies, neither single- nor double-blinding is possible because the treatment to be assessed is such an obvious intrusion into the lives of the subjects that it cannot be masked. Thus, providing special housing, education, counseling, psychotherapy, early release, furloughs or job placement, or imposing surveillance, confinement or special requirements for release cannot easily be done without both subjects and staff being aware of it.

Quasi-experimental research frequently accomplishes an analog to blinding when it compares the subsequent behavior or traits of two groups of subjects who routinely were treated differently because of some events or arrangements that had nothing to do with a research plan. Thus, if a realistic work program is provided in one state's prisons (such as in Minnesota) but not in another's, the postrelease employment and recidivism rates of similar groups of prisoners in the two states can be compared. Such an assessment has the obvious risk that conditions other than the work training may account for differences in postrelease employment of prisoners in the two states; there simply may be more and better jobs available in one state than in the other. Such comparisons obviously run the risk of history effects since influential conditions may change before and after the program and may change in a different manner in each state.

All such studies or contrasts in the occurrence of a treatment variable that are the results of events other than a research plan are called *natural experiments*. An illustration may be appropriate. The late William H. McGlothlin and his associates (1977) followed up in 1974-75 about a thousand California opiate addicts who had been civilly committed many years earlier to a seven-year or longer term of state control, beginning with confinement for up to three years and followed by conditional release to aftercare with frequent—and often surprise—testing for opiates. Subjects were reconfined if testing showed they were on drugs again. One of their followup groups consisted of 292 who received such confinements for addiction in 1962-63 but were released unconditionally in a few months because a court found the then-used commitment procedure illegal; a comparison followup group of 289 committed in 1964 were similar to the earlier releases, but they had to go through the full seven-year or longer term of state control. This natural experiment in longer confinement and close postrelease supervision indicated that those released early and without controls had the most readdiction and new crime, as well as less successful employment and a higher death rate, in a followup period of the same duration as that given the longer-term state-controlled cases. Thus, state control did seem to affect postrelease behavior. (For a more technical analysis of these findings revealing stronger relationships, see Muthen and Speckart 1983).

A variation on such evaluation of natural experiments is the *interrupted time series design*. When a change in practice or policy is initiated that is supposed to affect the rates of some sort of occurrence, its impact can be assessed by comparing these rates before and after the date of the change. In the 1970s, for example, Washington, D.C. and Minneapolis decriminalized the offense of public drunkenness. An evaluation of the impact of this legislation (Aaronson et al. 1978) found that arrests for intoxication declined in both cities, as shown for Washington in figure 3.1. The researchers also checked to see whether disorderly conduct arrests increased when public drunkenness was no longer an offense in these cities. They found that Minneapolis police did somewhat increase their use of this ground for arresting drunks while Washington did not, but total arrests of inebriates declined in both cities.

A study of bail reform in "Metro City" in the Northeast (Flemming et al. 1980) found that introduction of a point system for granting recognizance only slightly accelerated what had for years been an increasing use of this mode of release. The study also found that permitting deposit of 10 percent of the bail with the court clerk instead of paying a surety bondsman, with almost all of this deposit returnable if the defendant appeared in court for all scheduled hearings, immediately cut sharply into the use of bail bondsmen, as figure 3.2 shows. Following this innovation the average amount required for bail increased at first, but only in the courts of a few judges who had opposed bail reform and were alleged to have ties to bondsmen; the amounts that they imposed eventually declined.

Powerful evaluation by an interrupted time series analysis often can be achieved when you are evaluating a short-term innovation, such as a new kind of warning, instruction, or procedure. All that is needed is a continuous record before and after the innovation, for whatever measurable rate of activity or accomplishment the innovation is supposed to affect (Horn and Heerboth 1982).

Some risk of invalid conclusions from interrupted time-series analysis may exist due to history effects if influential events occur simultaneously with the innovation to be evaluated. To check on this possibility, the authors of the above-cited study of the decriminalization of public drunkenness laws in Washington, D.C. and Minneapolis also compiled drunkenness arrest data for Houston and San Francisco, which did not then have decriminalization statutes; they found no changes in the arrest patterns for these cities. In the time-series study of bail reform, a study was also made of simultaneous trends in the severity of charges in these courts, revealing that few defendants were charged with offenses for which recognizance was likely; if there had been a change in the severity of crimes charged, this could have altered the number of cases to which the point system could be applied.

In a famous time-series study, Campbell and Ross (1968) discredited the claims of Connecticut's governor that his campaign to suspend student drivers' licenses for speed-law violations caused traffic fatalities to decline. They showed that this drop in fatalities was, instead, part of a long-term decline not only in Connecticut, but also in adjacent states. They called this trend a maturation rather than a history effect, because they believed

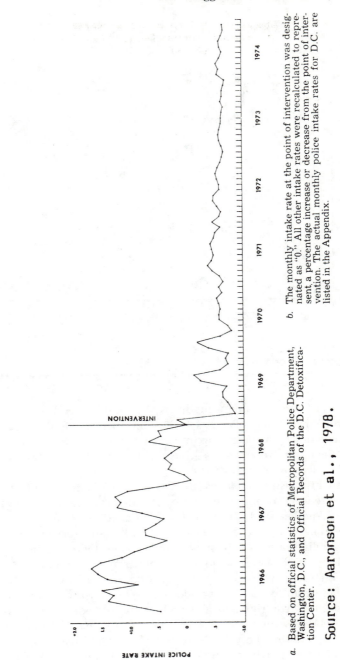

FIGURE 3.1
Monthly Police Intake for Public Intoxication[a]: Washington, D.C.[b]

a. Based on official statistics of Metropolitan Police Department, Washington, D.C., and Official Records of the D.C. Detoxification Center.

b. The monthly intake rate at the point of intervention was designated as "0." All other intake rates were recalculated to represent a percentage increase or decrease from the point of intervention. The actual monthly police intake rates for D.C. are listed in the Appendix.

Source: Aaronson et al., 1978.

FIGURE 3.2
Change in Use of Bondsmen and Cash Bail:
July 1968-June 1974

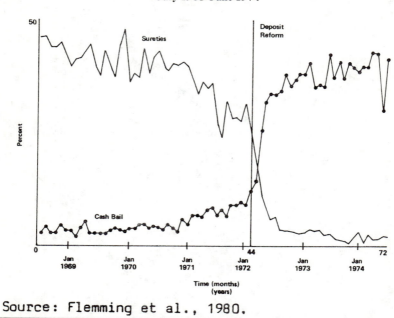

Source: Flemming et al., 1980.

that society was then maturing in its automobile use. They also showed that when the number of arrests for speeding increased following Connecticut's crackdown, the percentage of these arrestees acquitted also increased, as did the number of arrestees driving with suspended licenses, thus offsetting the effects of the arrests.

Similar time-study analyses (Ross, et al. 1970) countered a British claim to have reduced drunken driving by mandatory breathalyzer tests of arrestees. Another study (Ross 1975) discredited Swedish and Norwegian claims to have reduced drunken driving with mandatory jailing penalties. These findings are all consistent with the Ross 1960-61 essay, which observed that traffic law violations are "folk crimes," committed, like white collar offenses, by respectable people who are not stigmatized for their lawbreaking and who therefore do not evoke consistent punishment despite statutes requiring penalties and despite periodic crackdowns. Snortum (1984) has contended that the time-study analysis somewhat oversimplifies assessment of Scandinavian policies, and Ross (1984) agrees that its supplementation by research on the sociocultural context of alcohol use and law enforcement may be desirable for comparative evaluation research. More recent U.S. time-study evaluations of mandatory jailing penalties suggest that they have an impact on offense rates only as long as they are highly publicized, and that they impose tremendous work and cost overloads on police, courts, and jails (National Institute of Justice 1984).

An interrupted time-series analysis can be done simply by graphs, as in figures 3.1 and 3.2, or by the tables on which the graphs are based. If the changes that these reveal are considered large, further analysis may not be essential, but a variety of statistical tests for time-series effects are available (Campbell and Stanley 1966:37-46; Ostrom 1978; Cook and Campbell 1979, chapters 5 and 6; McCleary and Hay 1980). Here, as in other evaluation, the simplest statistics, such as graphs and tables showing trends and contrasts, are the most persuasive means of conveying research conclusions to policymakers or to the general public. More sophisticated statistical analysis is necessary to demonstrate that a weak pattern exists even when it is not clearly evident, and that whatever pattern is found could not readily occur by chance alone. When the patterns found are weak, the prospects of influencing policy with them are also weak whether or not there are enough cases to yield statistically significant results.

As indicated early in this chapter's discussion of research designs, *pre-post comparison* is a broad category of quasi-experiments in which each subject or situation studied serves as its own control, for this phrase refers to any comparison of behavior before and after a people-changing effort. The interrupted time-series design is simply a special form of pre-post comparison in which the intervention being evaluated occurred suddenly. Its application to people in whose lives interventions occurred at diverse times was illustrated in chapter 2's discussion of "the most continuous criterion," when it described the Murray and Cox 1979 use of the "suppression rate" to evaluate various types of correctional interventions into the lives of advanced delinquents. The suppression rate was the percentage reduction in arrest rates following a juvenile court's intervention, as compared with arrests during the same length of time in the community before the intervention.

Pre-post comparisons are thus easily achieved substitutes for randomized experiments in many situations where the effectiveness of two or more alternative types of people-changing efforts are to be assessed. Another example of their use was as a supplementary assessment of the Provo Project, already described in chapter 2's discussion of duration of followup. In that research, Empey and Erickson (1972) compared *changes* in criminal records of offenders after three types of penalty: regular probation, probation with special peer group controls, and state training school confinement.

The *regression effect* is a threat to validity from the fact that any unusual variation in a randomly fluctuating rate is likely to be followed by a change toward the average rate. Pre-post comparisons are especially prone to error due to regression effects. If an offender's arrests are most probable when his or her frequency of lawbreaking is greatest, and if penalties are most likely after the most frequent arrests, the regression effect alone would make it likely that arrests would occur at a lower rate after than before penalties. This was the essence of the McCleary et al. (1979) criticism of an early report of the Murray and Cox use of suppression rates. Murray and Cox rebutted this criticism by showing that about the same reduction in arrest rates occurred regardless of whether the number of postintervention arrests was compared to those immediately before the intervention or was compared to arrests in a period that ended six months before the intervention. Their implication was that for advanced delinquents with high arrest rates, offense rates do not vary randomly, but tend to increase until the occurrence of an arrest leading to an appreciable penalty, and then to decline, at least for a while.

Some Special Threats and Defenses in Experiments

As already observed, the advantage of random separation of subjects into experimental and control groups is that chance alone determines in what group any subject is placed. Therefore, people with every type of trait are likely to be as frequent in experimental as in control groups. If, on the other hand, these two groups are selected purely by the judgment that the subjects in them are similar, there is a chance that they will actually be different in some way that may account for contrasts in their subsequent behavior, regardless of the treatment that is only given to the experimental group. However, even randomly selected treatment and control groups may differ if they are so small that chance alone would make differences probable or if some conditions or events make the selection not as random as may have been assumed. As chapter 8 indicates, ethical and legal constraints are among the factors that may prevent perfect randomization, and others will be discussed in this chapter.

When experimental or control groups are small, chance alone may make them differ in composition, even with randomization procedures that would make differences negligible in proportion for large numbers of cases. There is no specific group size that guarantees matching of randomly selected groups of cases in all characteristics, measurable or unmeasurable; all that you can usually say from the mathematical laws of probability is that when all groups are randomly selected, the larger the size of the smallest group to be compared with others, the lower the probability of a significant difference among the groups. Texts in statistics provide methods of estimating this probability.

Whenever there is concern that the experimental and control groups will not be similar through chance alone, one precaution is to prevent appreciable differences between them in characteristics that are presumed to affect the outcome of whatever program or practice is being evaluated. This precaution, taken in advance of the random selection of the various groups, is known as *stratified* random sampling. It consists of first taking all cases from which experimental and control groups are to be selected and then dividing them into categories of the characteristics that should have the same proportion in all groups selected, then randomly selecting experimental and control cases from each of these categories. For example, to prevent having a higher proportion of males in one group than in another, you would first separate males from females, then randomly divide each of these gender categories into an experimental and a control group. This is stratifying by sex.

To stratify by age, you might first divide all cases into groups of nearly the same age—such as under 20, 20 to 29, 30 to 39, etc.—then randomly divide each of these age category groups into an experimental and a control group. If there are enough cases, you might stratify successively on several variables, such as sex and age. This guarantees about the same proportion of males and about the same age distribution in experimental and control groups. The random selection after stratification maximizes the probability that these two groups will also be about the same on every other variable other than the treatment that will only be given to the experimental group.

If necessary, a precaution that experimental and control groups are similar on any important dimension can also be taken after the two groups have been randomly selected. This is *edited* random selection, which is unorthodox but may be a reasonable action if one discovers before the experiment has begun that two randomly selected groups differ on some important variable. Simply select purely at random cases that one group has in higher proportion and transfer them to the other group, but also randomly select replacement cases from the other group. Continue this process until the two groups are identical. Alternatively, of course, one may weight statistics for the cases in categories that are of different proportions in the groups compared, so that statistical findings that compare the groups are corrected for these differences in the composition of the groups.

It is, of course, desirable and possibly even crucial that the division of the cases into experimental and control groups be done purely from the records, and that the random selection and editing be completed before any of the subects are notified that they will be given the experimental treatment.

Stratification and editing of random samples is simplest if a program to be evaluated begins with groups selected from a large pool of available cases. Thus, if admission to a stipend-paying vocational training program is to be offered to half of the 200 unemployed youths on a waiting list for it, or if release with methadone maintenance is to be offered to one-third of the 300 applicants who qualify for it in an institution for civilly committed addicts, stratified random selection and editing may be easy. Frequently, however, the service to be evaluated is an innovation offered only to a specified fraction of all new cases but they enter at an irregular rate that averages only a few per week.

In such *case-flow randomization*, it is often difficult to prevent staff from using personal judgment to decide what group is best for each case as it comes along. Staff may simply place each case where it seems easiest at the moment, rather than following randomization procedures in assigning in-dividuals to experimental or control groups. Therefore, it is essential that cases be assigned by research staff who use an impersonal procedure. This may be quite simple, such as giving the control group all cases with Social Security or any other previously assigned registry numbers that end in odd digits, and giving the experimental group the even ones. To assure ad-herence to such a rule, close monitoring is usually desirable. To assure the secrecy of the identity of the experimental and control groups, use of a table or a computer selection program for random numbers may be pre-ferable to use of odds and evens.

Stratification and editing procedures can also be adapted to a case-flow random assignment system. Thus, you can compare the experimental and control groups after every ten or other specified number of cases is added to them. If the two groups are found to differ on some variable deemed important, such as ethnicity or age, the group that is low on one attribute (such as having four fewer Spanish-surname members) can be given all cases with that attribute until the difference disappears. Once all groups have about the same proportions of any checked attribute, they should each resume receiving cases purely randomly until further checks reveal other significant differences.

Randomization is frequently impossible because of political or admin-istrative constraints. Thus, if there is a long waiting list for a program, it may be unethical or impolitic to ignore seniority on this list in assigning persons to a popular experimental program. Also, it may seem more effi-cent, expedient and legitimate to establish a new program first for all appropriate cases in one location rather than to have experimental and control groups. Indeed, advocates of a program often persuade officials to adopt it for everyone in their agency, but because this adoption impedes evaluation, the program's "goodness" is never rigorously demonstrated.

If assessment of a program is requested when such arbitrary methods of assigning cases exist and are unalterable, researchers cannot randomly select an experimental group to receive the program and a control group to be denied it. However, they may then have a quasi-experiment in which the treatment group comprises persons whom administrators or others selected arbitrarily for the program, and a comparison group that consists of persons from a prior time or another location who seem to match those in the treatment group as closely as possible but were not in the type of program that is to be evaluated. Similar group comparisons were discussed in the preceding section as types of natural experiment analysis, and their possible deficencies were noted.

Sometimes matching is done on a one-to-one basis. For each individual in the treatment group, a comparison person is selected who will not receive the treatments and who is the closest to this treatment individual on some salient variables, such as sex, age, ethnicity, or criminal record. But in matching on some variables one may mismatch on others. Randomization has the advantage, for large groups, of making it highly probable that all groups randomly selected are identical in their proportions of every feature that is frequent in any of them.

Even when controlled experiments are initiated with randomly selected experimental and control groups, much interference with the administration of the research design may develop that can prevent its completion as planned. Interference occurs because most evaluation of people-changing efforts does not consist of assessing one pill versus another, where one is a placebo; membership in an experimental or control group usually cannot be hidden. The treatment variables being tested may include separately, or in various combinations, such highly visible activities as vocational training, counseling, education, medication, segregation, special types of staffing, changes in procedures, diverse reward systems, job placement, concentration, or dispersion—and this list is far from exhaustive. Ideally, the experimental and control groups should differ only in that type or component of treatment that is being evaluated. However, as long as the treatment methods are visible both to the recipients and to control group members, as well as to their friends and relatives, some people will be unhappy with the distribution of services or conditions and will try to alter them.

Interference in experimental research occurs for innumerable reasons. Some people are biased in favor of particular programs and try to get them for themselves or for others whom they deem appropriate. Some people are prejudiced against a program and either try to avoid it or to get it modified in a manner contrary to that of the experimental design. Sometimes it is simply a matter of a client's geographical preference, desire to be with friends, or interest in avoiding enemies, that fosters maladministration of experiments, rather than attitudes toward particular programs. At times the interference occurs because officials at some level in an organization, high or low, resist changes, particularly those that mean more work. Because of all these and other sources of deviance of practice from precept, programs being evaluated should be monitored continuously. As this chapter's next section will elaborate, treatment, control, and comparison groups should be repeatedly monitored to be sure that their features contrast as planned, and that their membership is not drastically altered by transfer of clients before the experiment is completed.

Mortality effects, the already discussed evaluation deficiencies that result from losses of subjects during the course of a study, can occur when cases are lost from almost any type of group that is studied at any time in the course of research. These losses may be from the single set of subjects receiving a treatment to be assessed by a pre-post comparison, or from an experimental, control, or comparison group. These effects may be produced by any loss of cases after the samples are drawn and the research has begun, regardless of whether the cases are lost by transfer, escape, death, or simply by the researcher's inability to locate them or to find criterion informaton about them after the treatment is completed. If the cases lost are very numerous, especially if researchers cannot be certain that they are a representative sample of all cases in the group from which they are lost, research conclusions may be highly uncertain or totally meaningless.

Impairment of rigorous conclusions from evaluation research may also result from loss of cases before they enter the samples to be studied. This can occur if a plan to assign cases randomly as they are received fail to predict the flow of eligible cases accurately. This happened, for example, in a 1969 controlled experiment with methadone maintenance for civilly committed heroin addicts in New York that required a physician's screening before randomization at intake, to prevent admission of addicts who might be psychotic or assaultive. When a psychiatrist was hired for this task who was accustomed to middle-class patients who did not use heroin, he viewed nearly all addicts as potentially psychotic or assaultive, so that hardly any subjects came to be randomly chosen for this experiment with methadone. Another example developed when the Federal Bureau of Prisons carefully planned an experimental program for juvenile offenders to begin at its Robert F. Kennedy Youth Center in West Virginia early in the 1970s; about when it was to begin, the federal courts began to transfer to state courts most juveniles who had simultaneously broken both federal and state laws. When this occurred, there were economic pressures to use this facility and its staff for somewhat older prisoners. This type of experience with evaluation research plans going astray because of erroneous anticipations of case intake flows also has occurred in mental health, education, and many other types of people-changing efforts.

While contamination of random assignment designs may damage an experiment, the destruction need not always be complete. There are several ways of salvaging some order out of chaos. If key attributes of cases lost from the experimental or the control group are known, as well as the correlation of these attributes with outcome rates, you may be able to assess the direction and possibly the dimension of the bias resulting from case losses. For example, if mortality effects or imperfect randomization to begin with result in cases with a high risk of failure being more frequent in the experimental than in the control group, this contamination biases the research against showing favorable results for the experimental variable. If a follow-up of the two groups nevertheless reveals that the experimental group is more successful than the control group, one can conclude that the experimental effort is clearly beneficial, for the contamination's effect is to understate the actual benefts of the treatment that is evaluated. This occurred, for example, in New Haven's Residential Youth Centers, described by Goldenberg (1971:407-16), where the control group initially averaged better work attendance, more earnings, and fewer arrests than the experimental group of out-of-school and out-of-work youths, but the reverse was true six months after the experimental treatment began.

A second and simpler salvage may be possible if the lost cases are few, or if you know some of their attributes that are pertinent to prediction of outcome. You can then make reasonable assumptions about their potential impact on the experiment's findings. The most conservative assumption is that all cases lost from the control group would have been successes and that all lost from the experimental group would have been failures. A less conservative assumption is that the actual outcome for lost cases would have been the average for all cases with their known attributes. You can then calculate from the assumption chosen what the outcome rates from the total experimental and control groups would have been with no cases lost, and these rates can be compared with those actually occurring.

The final recourse in coping with contamination of randomization in a controlled experiment, to be employed if all other ways fail, is to regard the project as a pseudo-experiment, but also as a potentially fruitful one-shot case study. The criterion information (the posttreatment record of the subjects) for all or part of the sample can still usefully be compared with the same type of information on apparently similar cases not receiving the treatment. This makes it a quasi-experiment. A pre-post comparison may also be possible for the subjects in the study. Finally, it is always desirable, especially if the group studied is diverse, to conduct multivariate analyses to determine the relationships of treatment to outcome for this group when various independent variables are held constant.

Despite interference in experimental research, controlled experiments based on random separation of treatment and control cases, or good approximations to them in quasi-experiments, remain the preferred means of maximizing internal validity. As economists Stromsdorfer and Hu observe:

> Compared to other techniques of analyzing social problems and devising social programs to deal with them, the classical randomized experimental design: (a) allows one to assert cause and effect unambiguously; (b) allows one to measure the net effect of a social program without statistical bias; and, (c) is less expensive per marginal unit of information, that is, a given level of statistical precision can be achieved at a lower cost. All three of these benefits are crucial for society as it attempts to solve social problems ... (1978:324-325).

They warn, however:

> Experiments generally must remain relatively simple in order to be manageable conceptually and facilitate clear interpretation. Experiments can nevertheless be made to reflect a policymaker's definition of reality, even though this implies greater complexity. However, complex treatment on a diverse set of target groups causes a multiplicative increase in the sample size. This increases the cost considerably.

> Obviously, when the policymaker is confronted with these costs, he is forced to make choices among the policy questions he seeks to answer. This is a painful process since our experience has shown that the practical policymaker, other things being equal, would rather not have to make such choices, at least not explicitly. Likewise, the policymaker often does not understand the interrelationships between sample size, expected treatment impacts, and the statistical precision of the desired estimates he seeks. Thus, he is bound to become disenchanted with the research process, regardless of whether it is a classical experimental design. He turns naturally, then, to such methods as the case study design which promises a richness of detail for which he has a greater taste and familiarity. But what he often fails to recognize, or even asserts not to be the case, is that he has opted for much less reliable information on a greater number of facets of his problem rather than more reliable information on a smaller set of more critical facets. (1978:327)

The implication is that to increase the prospects of support for controlled experiments, as well as to reduce the risk of contamination, the research administrator's motto should be "Keep it simple!" Focus on one clear issue, if possible, in each experimental inquiry, then later explore other issues with new studies.

Several optimum circumstances and strategies to gain policymaker and client support for simple randomized experiments were suggested by

McKillip (1979). In the first circumstance, there are many more applicants for a program than it can admit. When this occurs, instead of admitting applicants according to their sequence on a waiting list, the research strategy can be to announce that applications will be received for a lottery to determine who will be admitted. With the proliferation of state lotteries, the idea of distribution by lottery may be readily acceptable. The applicants can be screened before the lottery begins to assure that all those admitted meet predetermined requirements. The lottery then selects the experimental group randomly, and the rest are the control group.

The second strategy suggested by McKillip is a variant of the first, for circumstances where all applicants can be randomly divided into cohorts numbering the maximum that can be admitted for one course of treatment; the others can be scheduled for later cohorts; or the treatment is expected to have quick effects, such as types of training or of equipment or services that should improve performance almost immediately. In these circumstances, a lottery can assign applicants to different cohorts, and the cohorts not yet treated become control groups for the cohorts treated. Thus, no one is denied the innovative treatment, and its effectiveness is soon demonstrated, which may mean that if cost-effective it can be made more widely and quickly available. But if the treatment is ineffective, there may be grounds for discontinuing the program before all cohorts are treated. While history and maturation effects may threaten validity in such evaluations, these risks are minimal if the time lapse is small.

A third strategy suggested by McKillip depends on the researcher's willingness to tolerate some selection effects from use of volunteers. With this procedure, the researcher offers applicants a choice of alternative treatments, but also offers some reward to those who state that they are willing to be assigned randomly to any of the alternatives.

Monitoring to Maximize Internal Validity

No research plan can guarantee that a program's conditions, procedures, and data collection will be as the researchers presume. Researchers must continually check that these are what they are cracked up to be rather than take them for granted. *Monitoring*, also called process evaluation, is undertaken to find out what actually happens in people-changing efforts and to check on how the data on which outcome evaluation depends are gathered. Monitoring contributes to internal validity if it focusses on how a research design is carried out and how data are derived, and it contributes to external validity (discussed in chapter 4) when it checks on whether the subjects and the treatment variable are what they are presumed to be.

Monitoring techniques may be either qualitative or quantitative, but ideally they are both. Much quantitative data should be designed to check on qualitative impressions, because too often qualitative researchers have the "Aha!" syndrome. They are carried away by a few dramatic observations of individual cases or events and then speak as though most of the people or programs that they are studying have these dramatic features. Systematic counting is necessary to determine whether or not the qualitative "most" is appropriate. Yet qualitative observations of all counting processes that are relied upon for any statistical data are needed to answer such pertinent questions as: Who or what gets counted by whom to produce the statistic? Under what circumstances? With what type of record system for accumulating the information that is counted? Who makes entries in the records, and with what care? What, in practice, determines when an instance of the phenomenon "counts" in the statistics and when it does not?

Krisberg (1980) suggests that monitoring a people-changing effort, as an adjunct to evaluating its impact, should be concerned with describing five elements: context, identification, intervention, goals, and linkages.

Study of the *context* of a people-changing effort begins with a chronicling of its history. The researcher should collect the documents that set forth the plan for the program and any statements of the goals of the planners. Process evaluators also should inquire about the expectations expressed by those who carried out the plans at various times in the history of the organization, including both the leadership and lower-level officials. If the program is long established, this information should be available from annual or other official reports and from interviews with senior or former staff. Evaluators should also procure or prepare organizational charts of the staff and of the program's relationships to other administrative or service units and their officials. Finally, the history of relevant public policy in the jurisdiction (statutes, ordinances, directives, policy statements, and so forth), and the records of the most influential policy makers, help to round out a researcher's comprehension of the context of a people-changing effort. If the research design is to determine not only the outcome of a treatment in a particular group, but also to compare it with that of one or more comparison groups, the contexts in which each of the groups was treated, or operated sans treatment, should also be studied. Such attention to the contexts from which data are gathered is needed to assess the validity of assumptions about comparability of groups that are made in designing quasi-experimental evaluation research.

Identification is concerned with who gets into an evaluated pogram, whether as client or as staff, and by what selection process. It checks also on their place and task assignments, and on their turnover or retention. If a control or comparison setting is part of the research design, the evaluator must determine the same types of facts about its participants as those that are collected about the people in the evaluated program. It is important for internal and external validity not to accept official statements about these identification matters as adequate and valid, but to observe and interview for corroboration and supplementation (see Patton, 1980, on qualitative methodology).

Intervention refers to what goes on in a people-changing effort; it is the service that is being evaluated. Included here are the full range of supporting, competing, distracting, or otherwise influential activities and social relationships that may affect these services. Thus, if the service is instruction, counseling, custody, surveillance, or job referral, a description of this intervention and of any program with which it is compared should include the social setting in which these activities occur and the attitudes of those involved.

Goal specification, as indicated in chapter 2, is also an important concern of monitoring. In the course of studying the context, participants, and interventions of a people-changing effort, researchers should seek to identify the manifest and latent goals that direct it. Most crucially, they should determine its criteria of goal attainment. As chapter 1 indicated, a formative evaluation is desirable at the outset of an impact evaluation to infer a program's guiding objectives. But it should be supplemented by a continuous process study to confirm or modify the initial conclusions.

Linkages are defined by Krisberg (1980:227) as "those formal and informal conditions and relationships that may hinder or support program operations." While this overlaps some of the concerns that come up in describing the intervention, it refers more to relationships of a program's operators to other organizations, individuals, or political forces, and to any other features of the program's organizational environment that may affect the impact of its activities.

All five of these concerns of monitoring efforts may yield information pertinent to assessing both the internal and the external validity of an outcome evaluation. They may indicate that the treatment being evaluated is not what it is presumed or supposed to be (a problem of external validity), that the experimental design was contaminated, or that the outcome data are misleading. Such conclusions should not be in absolute terms, but should specify the degree and details of any such defects. What is the program that is evaluated? What is the probable direction and extent of error in its assessment by a particular piece of evaluation research? What can we conclude about the program from analysis of both the monitoring results and those of the outcome evaluation?

Ideally, the role of evaluation in guiding the policies and practices of people-changing agencies resembles that of accounting in business and quality control in manufacturing. The function of monitoring for internal validity is analogous to that of auditing to check on the work of accountants (see Tabor 1978). Some examples of monitoring in specific studies are provided in chapter 4.

Measurement errors are threats to internal validity in all research, and monitoring is useful to discern and correct them. Evaluation data of any type—on the prior histories of the subjects, on their treatment, and on the criteria of impact—may all be partly wrong; reality may differ from what research reports it to be. Most errors are due to carelessness, which can creep into any human activity, but much error is due to use by researchers of data recorded by others for nonresearch purposes, with standards of observation and interests different from those of the researchers.

The deviation of data from what evaluators presume they represent occurs especially when reliance must be placed on information maintained by caseworkers in individual client files for clinical judgments or case decisions. Case data in such files tend not to be collected and recorded in a completely standardized manner, even when recorded on standard forms. Yet errors may also exist in official statistical reports prepared by an organization's management information system. Also, the definitions of categories in an agency's data may be different from what the researchers presume. Such problems, of course, are minimized if the same office that does the evaluation research also operates its management information system, as chapter 9 recommends for most assessments.

This section has implied the obvious: eternal vigilance is the price of internal validity. It has described a variety of problems and pitfalls in data collection, as well as ways of systematically avoiding them. Ideally, all measurement should be done independently at least twice, by different people or organizations and, when possible, from different sources of information. While this is usually not feasible, it often can be done for particular types of data and is especially desirable whenever reliability or validity are doubted. Any discrepancies between the yields of such independent measurements can then be investigated to determine which data are correct and how errors can be prevented. Practically, such checking can often be done initially until reliability appears to be highly perfect, but it should be repeated periodically in any long data collection process.

After a summative evaluation is completed, programs should still be monitored in subsequent years as a routine check on the validity of the research conclusions. If there is evidence that the context, identification, intervention, goal specification or linkages of the evaluated people-changing effort have changed markedly, inferences should be made as to whether such changes may alter the validity of assessments made in earlier studies. Thus, the qualitative and quantitative observations of prior process evaluation should be accepted as valid only when they were made and, warranting periodic replication, especially after major changes in an organization, its programs, its personnel, or its context and linkages.

Conclusion

The controlled experiments of the natural sciences are models that outcome evaluations of people-changing efforts frequently emulate, but too often unsuccessfully. The most common outcome evaluations are one-shot case studies, which can only simulate statistically the experimenter's ability to control all but the treatment and outcome variables. Quasi-experiments, natural experiments, and pre-post comparisons may more closely approximate the natural scientist's procedures, and they should produce more influential results than case study conclusions. Nevertheless, the classic controlled experiment remains the ideal method of maximizing internal validity. As Berk and associates (1985) conclude, "an intellectual case against social policy experiments is difficult to construct."

In all such research, however, there may be threats to internal validity from history, maturation, selection, mortality, testing, expectancy, Hawthorne, placebo, and regression effects, as well as from measurement errors. These difficulties may be minimized or their consequences assessed by design variations and by thorough monitoring. Their implications can often be taken into account as qualifications when findings are presented. The most serious qualifications at that point, however, are likely to deal more with external than with internal validity.

4

Sampling, Theory Guidance, and Base Expectancies: The Paths to External Validity

No matter how carefully research is administered, regardless of confidence in the accuracy of its outcome measurements and certainty that only the treatment variable differentiates the experimental from the control groups, grave doubts may be warranted as to the applicability of its conclusions. To generalize findings to other situations requires of a study not only internal validity, but a similarity of the research subjects and conditions to those in other times and places to which the findings will be applied. The question raised in considering an evaluation's external validity is, How pertinent are its results to other settings?

Concern with assessing external validity most frequently leads researchers to appraise the representativeness of research samples. Although problems of sampling are discussed here, as well as methods of alleviating them, it is contended that most important in attaining external validity is the grounding of research designs in widely tested explanatory theory. Finally, base expectancy methods of outcome evaluation are often described as more feasible than controlled experiments; in practice, therefore, they are a potential prime source of external validity that has been neglected in outcome evaluations.

Representative Sampling: Theme and Variations

Traditionally, it has been presumed that the principal way to maximize external validity is to ascertain that your research subjects are a representative sample of the persons to whom the findings will be applied, and that the research situation is typical of others to which the conclusions will be extended. Thus, testing a remedy for a plant disease ideally is done by trying it on a random sample of plants with the ailment and in a random sample of the kinds of conditions in which the disease occurs.

57

Of course, random selection from a global universe is virtually never feasible. In most evaluation research on people-changing efforts, a list or inventory of a more limited universe usually suffices. For example, you begin with a roster of all students in a school district, all inmates in a prison or a mental hospital, or all clients in particular programs. It is from such sampling frames that random selection of experimental and control cases are made. Frequently, instead of taking a sample, a researcher studies everyone in such a limited population. In either case, the research conclusions are set forth as though the subjects studied were representative of all populations of a broad category, such as students, employees, or mental health patients.

When it was proposed that the California Youth Authority's Community Treatment Program be a controlled experiment, it was assumed that there would be resistance to its plan of paroling within a month after their incarceration a random sample of the offenders who normally would be confined for an average of eight months. Athough those paroled early would be intensively supervised, it was feared that the public would object to these early releases. Victims, police, prosecutors, and judges might be chagrined to see offenders back on the street so soon after their conviction for serious crimes. This prospect of a negative public reaction was alleviated by having the Youth Authority routinely screen all incoming prisoners so that most sex offenders and others convicted of highly notorious crimes would not be included in the experiment. In practice, this generally meant that about a quarter of the males and a tenth of the females were eliminated from the pool of eligible cases from which the experimental and control groups were randomly selected (Palmer 1974).

The foregoing is an example of a *prescreened experiment* design. Because prescreening limits the range of variation in the cases studied, it probably reduces a researcher's ability to identify the full strength of relationships that prevail among the variables studied, and it makes the conclusions not apply to cases like those screened out (Berk 1983).

Nevertheless, there are numerous reasons for prescreening in the real world of evaluating people-changing efforts, and there are diverse ways of doing it. Perhaps the most common method is to provide a type of treatment only for those who apply for it or only for those who not only express a desire for it, but also are willing and able to pay for it. The reasons for such prescreening may be economic, ethical, or legal, or it could be that the treatment itself—such as psychotherapy or an addiction-reduction program—is believed by its proponents to be effective only for those who volunteer or only for those who pay or otherwise sacrifice something they value to obtain it. Conclusions from evaluating the effectiveness of a treatment for these self-selected people may not apply to others who do not strongly desire it, although experts may believe that many untreated people need the treatment more than those who receive it.

A different type of screening occurs when a treatment is deemed dangerous for the client rather than for society. This is a frequent condition when drugs are prescribed to combat an addiction or to change other behavior. When the drugs, such as methadone or tranquilizers, are themselves addictive or may have serious side effects, these drugs are restricted not only to volunteers, but also to those whom the physicians or other officials deem sufficiently in need of this treatment and unamenable to other types of treatment. Frequently these drugs are authorized only for those who are above juvenile age and who have already been treated unsuccessfully by one or more other methods.

Usually a new treatment for a serious problem, if well publicized as highly promising, will be requested for or by many more people than initially can be provided with it. Under such circumstances, officials customarily propose some type of screening, for example, supplying the treatment only to those deemed least likely to change by other methods, or to those for whom the treatment seems to involve the least risks. Whenever any screening is necessary because the demand for a program exceeds the number for whom it can be made available, *the quickest and most convincing argument for increasing its availability is rigorous proof that it is effective.* This condition of excess demand over supply provides a strong selling point for randomly dividing potential clients into experimental and control groups (not necessarily of the same size). If prescreening is done before the experiment, it is appropriate to select for the pool of eligibles only clients for whom the program is expected to have maximum impact, or the most benefits in excess of costs (see chapter 5).

One alternative to randomization is the individual *matching* of each research subject with a person of similar attributes and setting who does not receive the treatment to be evaluated. This popular type of quasi-experiment constitutes prescreening, and can impair both internal and external validity by what was described in chapter 3 as *regression effect.* Such an effect was pointed out long ago by the anthropometrist Sir Francis Galton, when he noted that children of exceptionally tall parents were likely to be shorter than their parents, and children of exceptionally short parents were likely to be taller than their parents, for all extreme variations tend to regress toward the average of the group to which they belong.

To further explain, because of regression effects, if low-scoring students in a special instructional program are matched with low-scoring students not in it, both groups will seem to improve on retest simply because both will include a disproportionate number who had pretested below their average level. Such distortion from regession effect will especially impair evaluation if, to evaluate the impact of instruction, a low-scoring group's test performance after the instruction is compared to its preinstruction record. In such a pre-post comparison design, with the experimental group providing its own control data, part of any post-instruction increase in its scores is likely to be a regression effect from individuals doing exceptionally poorly—in terms of their own normal range of variation—at the pretest. This effect varies inversely with the reliability of the test used; if it is an unreliable test in which scores normally fluctuate greatly, regression effects will be larger.

Similarly, if only high scorers on a test or clinical rating for personality defects are selected for a therapy program, part of any decrease when they are reassessed may be due to regression effects, part to testing effects, part possibly to history or maturation effects, and part to the therapy. Therefore, comparison of its post-therapy scores with those of a randomly selected control group not receiving the therapy provides the best source of externally valid evaluation of the therapy's impact. The Solomon Four-Group Controlled-Experiment design described in chapter 3 would identify testing effects, if any.

Regression effects can also occur when samples are selected by extreme scores on unobtrusive measures that are known or presumed to be correlated with the behavior that the people-changing effort is trying to alter. Both test scores and the unobtrusive measures (such as earnings, grades, number of arrests or days unemployed) have fluctuations due only to chance on which extreme variations end to regress toward a mean. Regression effects are often subtle and difficult to prevent, hence are a possible source of error in any matching. Their magnitude can sometimes be estimated by noting contrasts in shift from pretreatment to posttreatment measurements for different score ranges (see Campbell 1969:419-25).

Apart from regression effects, when matching makes the groups compared resemble each other closely, it risks making them different from populations elsewhere, thus limiting the extent to which generalizations from the matched groups will apply to other populations. Indeed, matching is a form of prescreening, and as already stated, by reducing the range of variation in the cases studied, prescreening attenuates the strength of relationships between variables that can be identified (Berk 1983).

Pre-post comparisons usually enhance confidence in both the internal and the external validity of evaluation research if available records cover appreciable time before and after the treatment. For example, in the Provo Project (Empey and Erickson 1972), for which purely postrelease data were summarized in chapter 2, pre-post comparisons were conducted on two pairs of groups, as follows:

All members of the first pair were boys whom the county's juvenile court judge decided to give probation. Before their probation was announced, they were divided randomly into an experimental group, required to participate daily in a special guided interaction and work-study program, and a control group with only traditional probation conditions.

The second pair in the Provo Project consisted of boys whom the judge decided he would traditionally have committed to the state industrial school, but whom he decided instead to place in the above experimental group of probationers. These boys were told that their special probation was in lieu of incarceration. In the original design, to which the judge had agreed, such youths were to be randomly divided, with half actually committed to the state industrial school. But after a brief period such division was terminated, and all boys newly adjudged as meriting confinement were placed in the experimental probation program. As a result, the comparison group for the experimental probationers who were originally designated for the industrial school consisted of youths sent to this school by the juvenile courts of other counties.

For each of the four Provo Project groups described above, the number of arrests per month of freedom during one year before the arrest that brought them to the project was compared with the number of arrests per month of freedom during one year after their release to the community (either on probation or on parole from state industrial school). Comparisons also were made for two-, three-, and four-year pre- and post-arrest periods.

In every one of the above-described comparisons, for each of the four groups and four durations, there were fewer arrests per month of freedom in the postrelease than in the prearrest period. This is the Murray and Cox (1979) suppression effect discussed in chapter 2. For the two randomly selected probation groups, reduction of arrests was greater for experimentals than for controls for every duration of followup, but the difference was only statistically significant (at the .05 level) during the first-year pre-post comparison. By contrast, for the comparison of potentially with actually incarcerated youths, the longer the duration of the before-and-after times studied, the greater was the reduction of arrests for the experimental group given probation than for those who were confined. This difference was only statistically significant (at the .05 level), however, for the comparison after four years. Incidentally, all of these pre-post comparisons were greater in arrests for moderate and serious offenses than in arrests for minor offenses (Empey and Erickson 1972:Chapter 10). More complex multivariate analyses provided estimates of the percentage of this posttreatment reduction in deviant conduct that could be ascribed to maturation effects or to variables other than the treatment and the percentage that could be ascribed to the program (*Ibid*:Chapter 11).

The prescreening, matching, and pre-post-comparison problems discussed here reflect the fact that evaluation research must often be based on whatever subjects are available. The researchers may categorize these subjects by some attributes, and they may specify that their conclusions apply only to persons similar to those studied. But what attributes are relevant when making such qualifications on the external validity of the findings? By what features should the larger population that the research subjects are presumed to represent be described? These questions are often neglected, yet their answers may greatly influence both the prospects of finding a large impact from a people-changing effort and the validity of generalizations from whatever impact is discovered.

Administrative Versus Theory-Guided Sampling

Researchers frequently adopt an administrator's perspective in trying to make their studies acceptable to officials. Therefore, they design evaluation research to fit administrative categories of clients, such as students classified by current grade, patients by ward, probationers by district, or prisoners by housing unit. Using these modes of description in selecting research subjects can be called *administratively guided sampling.* The objective in this sampling commonly is to obtain a purely random selection of an appreciable number of subjects, with little or no subsequent losses of those selected. If this is accomplished, the researchers and officials can reasonably assume that the subjects studied are representative of the administrative category from which they are drawn. Of course, a check on the validity of this assumption should be made by comparing the sample with the population on all attributes for which objective data are readily available, such as age, race, grade level, or number of prior commitments.

Differences between sample and population attributes are called *sampling bias*, and if they are small it is assumed that the research has high external validity. But there may be several serious errors in such an assumption. One source of error is the variation over time in how clientele are classified by a people-changing organization, that often results from changes in staff or in the types of clients received. The intake of such an agency often shifts following alterations in legislation, administrative policies, or court rulings, as well as after economic recessions and demographic changes in their "catchment areas." These sources of instability frequently make the subjects in a particular administrative category when and where evaluation research was done differently from those to whom the research findings may be applied.

Not only are there changes over time in one place, but evaluations done in one area usually are not intended for that locale alone, but instead are disseminated for application almost everywhere, including locations thousands of miles away with quite different populations. Thus, most relevant to the external validity of a sample is often not its sampling bias, but its *application bias*, which is the difference between the research subjects and any population to which the findings are applied.

Application bias can be minimized, and prospects of finding useful knowledge increased, with *theory-guided sampling*. This means selection of research subjects on the basis of validated hypotheses deduced from scientific principles to explain *why* an effort to change certain categories of people should work. Evaluation findings can then be qualified as applying to these categories of people, whenever or wherever they are found, rather than to an administrative category. Making such a theory-guided specification requires development and validation of a theory as to why a certain kind of effort should have an impact on a particular type of person.

Evaluation researchers with theory-guided sampling typically test a people-changing effort on the kinds of people for whom they have deduced that it will be most effective; alternatively, or in addition, they may also test it on the kinds of subjects for whom they infer from theory that it will be least successful. Such studies thereby test not only this change effort, but also the abstract principles from which their sampling-guidance deductions were made. If this inference is from an already widely validated scientific generalization, such as the laws of learning in psychology or the law of sociocultural relativity in sociology and anthropology (that social separation fosters cultural differentiation), the chance that the hypothesis is valid is enhanced (Glaser 1980).

Theory is frequently set forth in research proposals to explain why particular results are anticipated, but it is then largely neglected in selection of subjects because administrative categories facilitate access to an agency's clients or to their records. However, well-grounded theories as to the kinds of people that a people-changing effort should affect indicate the kinds of research subjects that are most fruitfully studied.

Most important for external validity is that if an evaluation reveals marked impact from some sort of intervention into the lives of clients, the theory-derived specifications of the attributes of the most changed clients provide categories that are unlikely to change in time or place as much as do administrative designations. It is the relative stability of theory-derived categories of subjects, as compared to administrative categories, that enhances the external validity of conclusions from research with theory-guided sampling.

Theory, however, may sometimes indicate that certain administrative categories are more amenable than others to change by a particular type of effort. That is, certain administrative distinctions among subjects may correspond fairly closely to pertinent theory-derived distinctions. Thus, both the differential association and control theories of crime causation imply that counseling should reduce recidivism most in offenders with appreciable stake in conformity who have not had extensive success in crime or been much influenced by other lawbreakers (Glaser 1980:126-29). This theory implies that such offenders are most likely to be conflicted about their crime. It follows that intensive counseling should be more effective in reducing recidvism rates for first offenders on probation than for recidivist probationers, prisoners, or parolees. Indeed, the Lipton, Martinson, and Wilks survey found that counseling was effective in reducing recidivism almost exclusively for young first offenders on probation (1975:223-229), and not for other categories of lawbreakers. Furthermore, such theory implies that these research findings would be more marked, and that their application bias when applied to diverse times or places would be reduced, if the evaluation had been for the effects of intensive individual counseling on such a theory-derived rubric as "first offenders on probation" rather than on such an administrative category as "juvenile probationers."

The theory pertinent to sample selection will sometimes vary with the criterion of successful outcome that is employed. Thus, in operating halfway houses to which mental hospital or prison inmates are transferred before discharge or parole, three somewhat contrasting goals may be of interest, and appropriate theory suggests a different kind of sample for each. To minimize public antagonism to halfway houses, one criterion of effectiveness is a low rate of visible deviant behavior by the residents, especially a low rate of violent or disorderly conduct. For this goal, validated theory suggests the selection of older persons without histories of violent behavior in or out of the institution. This *minimum risk* type of case election is customary when community residences are first established or when they can hold only a small percentage of the total institutionalized population, for this policy minimizes opposition to the continued use and expansion of halfway houses.

A second goal when considering release of confined prisoners or patients through halfway houses is to protect the community from offenses by anyone who must eventually be allowed to go free. If a hospital or prison inmate released by discharge or transferred to aftercare or parole begins a spree of misconduct, officials are unlikely to know of it until days or weeks later. On the other hand, if an inmate is released through a halfway house, officials will quickly observe or suspect any major misconduct because residents permitted daily or weekend leave from the house must sign out and indicate time, destination, purpose, and probable time of return. Where there is great concern about their possible misconduct, as in halfway houses for criminals awaiting parole, still closer surveillance often occurs: residents are checked in the community to verify their reports of job search, employment, or other approved outside activity; they are also given surprise urine or breath tests for drugs or alcohol; they are severely limited in the duration and purposes of departure from the house until they establish a good conduct record; increasingly they are even monitored electronically with a variety of new devices that often are fastened to the resident's ankle or arm and that signal the resident's location to a central monitoring station (Ford and Schmidt 1985).

With any of these types of surveillance, a halfway house resident's failure to return on schedule, failure to be at a stated destination, failure on drug or alcohol tests, or suspicious behavior in the residence will prompt officials to impose more restriction, even reconfinement in an institution. Therefore, a theory-focused evaluation of halfway houses as agencies to *maximize control* might select as a treatment group releases with appreciable prospects of relapse to intolerable conduct, and would compare their immediate postrelease behavior with that of similar subjects in a control or comparison group released by discharge, aftercare, or parole.

A third goal in releasing someone from total confinement through halfway houses is to reduce relapse or recidivism rates by crisis-intervention or other rehabilitative assistance during initial reentry into the community. This is the goal of *maximizing rehabilitation.* For this purpose, theory suggests the transfer to halfway houses of those inmates with the least prior successful experience in a conventional life, but with any record of constructive activity during their confinement, for example, completing vocational training courses well or earning academic diplomas or degrees. Their legitimate self-support in the community may be easier in the halfway house because they don't have to worry about finding food, shelter, and someone to talk to in their leisure time. They can therefore concentrate on finding and holding a job. House staff can also provide immediate counseling or other aid, as well as immediate controls should residents be tempted to seek sexual, alcoholic, or other pleasures in a manner that impedes their employment prospects.

For this goal of maximizing rehabilitation, the optimum subjects for release through a halfway house are youths with little prior success at either legitimate pursuits or crime, despite the fact that as youths they still have higher than average recidivism rates. Indeed, several studies find that it is for such high-risk cases that the contrast in recidivism rates is greatest between halfway house residents and comparison cases released directly from a prison or jail by discharge or parole (Hall et al. 1966; Beha 1977; Beck 1979). (These studies are discussed further in chapter 7.)

Unfortunately, programs are often administered to maximize administrative ease rather than client benefits. Thus, vocationally instructive activities are assigned to patients or prisoners already proficient at them rather than to those likely to benefit most by learning a trade. When this practice prevails, theory-guided sampling research may not find sufficient subjects to test a theory on maximizing rehabilitation.

Theory-Guided Monitoring

The external validity of an evaluation may be jeopardized at any stage if a theory-guided research design is imprecisely carried out. Such contamination is frequently caused by deviations of experimental, comparison, or control programs from what the researchers expect or assume them to be. The only way to be aware of these deviations is by continuous and thorough monitoring to locate differences from theory-prescribed practices or conditions in the program to be evaluated and to ascertain that control or comparison programs have the features assumed in the research design. This monitoring for external validity requires methods of process evaluation somewhat similar to those discussed in chapter 3 for assuring internal validity, but focused on the observations that are pertinent to the theory on which the evaluation research sampling design and procedures are based.

Contamination of designed experimental procedures that affects external validity, and that could only be detected by monitoring, was revealed by Gilham and associates (1979) through tape recording and content analyzing a training program. Their evaluation of this program was guided by the simple theoretical principle, well-validated in communication research, that behavior tends to conform to the pattern fostered by the most frequently received messages. The training was for persons who work with delinquent youth. The evaluation used a variation of the McKillip (1979) two-cohort design described in chapter 3 (which resembles what Campbell and Stanley (1966) call the "randomized post-test-only control group design"): trainees were randomly assigned to either an experimental or a control group with the experimentals first to receive the training, so that the two groups could be compared when only one was trained. The control group was trained at a later date.

In this Gilham et al. study, the organizations that were to send employees for training were randomized rather than the individual trainees, so that the experimentals and the controls would be unlikely to be in contact as coworkers. A long questionnaire given both groups (when only one had been trained) was focused on eight types of behaviors that the training was supposed to affect (such as their positive reinforcement of youths or their contact with the parents of their assigned youths). The results showed that only on five of these eight behaviors did the experimentals differ significantly from the controls, and in the direction expected. However, for the three types of behaviors on which the results were not as anticipated, the monitoring showed that: one type was rarely mentioned in the training; one type was discussed primarily in a manner quite contrary to that planned (which explains why the impact of training on this behavior was in the direction opposite to that sought); the third type was ambiguous both in the instruction and in its impact.

It is often because of a lack of theory guidance in research design and sampling that contamination that destroys external validity is ignored by researchers in proclaiming their results. Such insufficiently or inappropriately qualified conclusions are especially likely if research is focused on testing a prevailing practice rather than a theory on why such a practice should be effective, and for whom. This was well illustrated by Kassebaum, Ward, and Wilner (1971) in reporting an experiment in which California prisoners, mostly recidivist offenders who had already been repeatedly incarcerated, were randomly assigned for housing in four large units of a new prison that had these physically identical units somewhat segregated from each other. The following program variations were designed by the researchers, in consultation with officials, to achieve what they thought would be a rigorous assessment of group counseling:

(1) In one unit inmates were invited to *volunteer* for one hour of counseling per week in groups of ten to twelve, led by a custodial or other staff member who had received some training in the use of nondirective counseling with no special focus. The nonvolunteers were to remain in this housing but were not to participate in the counseling.

(2) All inmates in a second unit were *required* to participate in group counseling for two one-hour sessions per week, each with a specially-trained staff member.

(3) Another unit was divided into areas housing 50 men, each area with its own dayroom where they were all required to meet for counseling in four one-hour sessions per week attended by three specially trained staff of diverse background. On the fifth day they split into three smaller groups, each with one of these three staff.

(4) The fourth unit had no special counseling program.

To assess the counseling in the first unit, the researchers compared the parole outcome rates of the volunteers with those of the nonvolunteers there. To evaluate the two units with mandatory counseling, their parole outcome rates were compared with those of the inmates in the unit with no special counseling.

Process evaluation, by observation, interviews, and questionnaire, showed that the major incentive for volunteering for any group counseling in this prison was the inmate belief, promoted by staff, that participation would be viewed favorably by the parole board. Prison sentences in California at that time were highly indeterminate, and the board (then called the Adult Authority) had tremendous power to decide the duration of an inmate's confinement. While this condition encouraged inmates to volunteer for the counseling, the researchers described the interaction in the counseling sessions as typically passive, with neither staff nor prisoners taking much initiative in it or having much confidence in its value.

Clearly, the comparison of outcome rates for volunteers and nonvolunteers from the same unit was probably much influenced by selection effects. Evaluation of the mandatory counseling was biased from mortality effects created by nonrandom transfer of many prisoners to different units while the experiment was underway. This study, however, has much more serious external validity problems from lack of guidance by a theory on conditions of counseling effectiveness. The counselors had few training sessions, their attendance at these was poor, and the training reflected no clear theory on what counseling techniques could alter recidivism rates for what kinds of offenders. Indeed, from the standpoints of any of the most influential crime-causation theories—differential association, control, opportunity or differential expectation (Glaser 1980)—this counseling alone would not be expected to reduce recidivism of the repeatedly arrested and incarcerated young adult male offenders who comprised most of these prisoners. In fact, the counseling was found to have no impact for any of the groups compared or for any category of inmate distinguished within them.

If this evaluation had been guided by differential association and opportunity theories (which in the 1960s, when this project began, were the leading explanations for crime), it would have tried to compare the counseling's impact with that of other modes of intervention, such as intensive vocational training linked to rewards for learning and postrelease job assistance. It would have prescribed more vocational and reintegration counseling, would have compared such counseling for parolees in the community with counseling in the institutions, would have recommended individual rather than group counseling for advanced offenders, might have sought former offenders as counselors, but would have expected reduction in recidivism from such programs to be greatest in the less advanced offenders with most association with anticriminal persons.

However, because California correctional officials then had been naively sold on counseling by a great diversity of psychiatrists, clinical psychologists, and social workers of diverse perspectives, they were especially persuaded to expand these services when the federal government provided grants for counseling programs. Judging from the defensive expressions of blind faith in counseling by their staffs when I criticized these programs as a consultant to their youth and adult correction departments in 1961, it is unlikely that they then would have supported and facilitated a theory rather than an administratively guided assessment. However, the disappointing subsequent results from evaluation research on California's theoretical prison counseling programs discouraged its officials and many academic criminologists from promoting rehabilitation efforts of any type. They equated all such efforts with counseling to the extent that they became unwilling to develop the types of theory-guided vocational and reintegrative programs that research now indicates can reduce recidivism.

Today, when behavior modification theory guides so many people-changing efforts, especially for juveniles, it is especially important to monitor these efforts to assess the extent to which positive reinforcements are made contingent on approved conduct by the subjects, and negative reinforcements are contingent only on behaviors that the program wishes to extinguish. Too often people in authority who become angered by a client's conduct persist in applying negative sanctions or expressing hostile attitudes even when the client's conduct improves; or, conversely, they give attention or other rewards most to clients who become conspicuous by their misconduct.

Too often, efforts to apply differential association or control theory in a halfway house, recreation, gang intervention, or other treatment program in the community focus on attachments of clients to program staff and to peers in the program, but fail to investigate and try to affect attachments of their clients to others in the community when they are away from the program. This was noted, for example, in Steiner's (1985) monitoring of the Youth Work Project, a halfway house for young adult federal offenders in an inner-city neighborhood in Los Angeles, which contracted for administration of its main counseling program by staff from the Boy's Republic, a suburban establishment for unadvanced juvenile offenders.

Research design and sampling based on widely validated theory, combined with vigilant monitoring to insure that practice conforms with theoretical principles, can produce much more cumulative practical knowledge on people–changing than evaluation research has yielded thus far. This conclusion is implied by the fact that scientific knowledge is theory that has been well-tested, in enough times and places, with clearly consistent findings for designated varieties of circumstances, to inspire confidence in its validity. Scientific people–changing requires knowledge about what types of intervention succeed for specified kinds of people, as well as on what types do not affect particular types of subjects.

Base Expectancy Rates as Alternatives to Experiments

Insurance companies have repeatedly demonstrated that predictions based upon actuarial statistics result in fewer errors than predictions by case-study judgments. This conclusion has also been confirmed by college admission officers, banks, the military, and many other types of organizations that base their case decisions on experience in predicting the behavior of many individuals. Of course, actuarial tables are developed by statistically testing ideas that emerge from case studies. There is thus an interaction among different types of research that produces an optimal research mix, whereby: (1) casework experience and prior theories generate hunches as to how various types of interventions will work with different kinds of people; (2) statistical prediction studies indicate what the probabilities of various outcomes have been in prior experience with specific types of cases; (3) knowledge of these findings reduces practitioners' errors in case study assessments; (4) hypotheses about other statistical patterns are stimulated by practitioners' case analyses that are then tested by new statistical studies (Sawyer 1966).

Prediction tables produced by such statistical studies in corrections and mental health can be used to classify each prospective release, on the basis of demonstrably predictive attributes, into a category with a given probability of postrelease success or failure. Indices of prior conduct are the attributes that best predict future behavior. Thus, among the best predictors of recidivism by released lawbreakers are number or prior arrests, total duration of prior incarceration, and—as an inverse predictor—longest job ever held. Age, marital status, and history of drunkenness or drug addiction also are good predictors of postrelease conduct. Research has shown that predictions based on the few variables that add most to the multivariate prediction of subsequent behavior are as accurate or more accurate than predictive scores calculated from a large number of variables, many of which are likely to be intercorrelated, and each of which may add erroneous information.

Statistical prediction research for correctional prognoses dates back to the 1920s (Simon 1971; Glaser 1985), but did not become widely applied until the 1970s, when its impact grew rapidly in sentencing and parole guidelines. These guidelines, as chapter 6 shows, reduce disparity of penalties by recommending a duration of confinement based on statistical analysis of past decisions in order to "make the punishments fit the crimes" more consistently. They also reduce the prospects of new crimes by releases through actuarial prediction of recidivism risks. An example of a purely predictive table based on statistical analysis of experience with federal offenders is the salient factor score of the U.S. Parole Commission. It classifies prisoners by seven predictive factors, from each of which it assigns a score to the prisoner based on multivariate statistical studies. The scoring is as follows:

ITEM A: Prior convictions (adult or juvenile)
          None = 3; one = 3; two or three = 1; four or more = 0

ITEM B: Prior incarcerations (adult or juvenile)
          None = 2; one or two = 1; three or more = 1
ITEM C: Age at first commitment (adult or juvenile)
          26 or older = 2; 18-25 = 1; 17 or younger = 0
ITEM D: Current commitment offense
          Did not involve auto theft or check forgery/larceny = 1;
          Involved auto theft or checks = 0
ITEM E: Prior parole or probation record
          Never had parole revoked or been committed for a new of-
          fense on parole, and not now a probation violator = 1;
          Had parole revoked or was committed for a new offense while
          on parole, or is now a probation violator = 0
ITEM F: Heroin or opiate dependence
          No history of heroin or opiate dependence = 1;
          Otherise = 0
ITEM G: Work or school record
          Verified employment (or full-time school attendance) for a
          total of at least 6 months during the last 2 years in the com-
          munity = 1;
          Otherwise = 0
TOTAL SCORE ...._____

Over 90 percent of federal prisoners with salient factor scores totalling 9 or more have favorable outcomes in their first year on parole, as do about 75 percent of those scoring 6, 7, or 8, around 63 percent with 4 or 5, and about 55 percent with 3 or fewer points (Hoffman and Beck 1980).

Configuration tables are sources of predictions without addition of numeric points. These tables specify the particular combination of variables that produces the best classification of subjects for predictive purposes. This is illustrated by table 4.1. The table was developed by a computer program that cross-tabulates with postrelease conduct all inmate attributes for which standard information is available, to identify the attribute that divdes the cases into the two groups for which the difference in recidivism rates most exceeds chance probability (by chi square test). In LeClair's (1977) Massachusetts research, on which table 4.1 is based, this process indicated that the most significant difference in recidivism rates between two groups of releasees was achieved by dividing them into one group with twelve or more recoded court appearances and the other with eleven or less. In applying this computer program then to each of these two groups to determine which of the other variables dichotimized them into groups with the most statistically significant contrast in recidivism rates, Table 4.1 shows, a different age-group split was optimum for each of the two groups classified by their recorded court appearances. This process of successive

TABLE 4.1
Configuration Table for Risk Classification (from LeClair 1977)

Total Sample (Reci- divism rate = 25%)	Twelve or more prior court appearances (Recidivism rate = 29%)	Age 27 or younger at time of release (recidivism rate = 48%)	
		Age 28 or older at time of release (Recidivism rate = 23%)	
	Eleven or fewer prior court appearances (Recidivism rate = 20%)	Age 25 or younger at time of release (Recidivism rate = 24%)	Total no. of charges 7 or more (Recid. rate = 32%)
			Total no. of charges 6 or less (Recid. rate = 14%)
		Age 26 or older at time of release (Recidivism rate = 6%)	

dichotimizations is continued until no further split yields categories with statistically significant differences in recidivism rates. The table is then applied to another sample of past releasees, and any splits that do not yield statistically significant contrasts in recidivism rates for both samples is dropped. This process, in the research that produced table 4.1, led to deletion of further splits for the age-group categories other than twenty-five or younger.

The additive-score method of constructing prediction tables from regression analysis (illustrated by the federal salient factor score), and the configuration method (demonstrated in Massachusetts), seem to yield predictions of similar accuracy (Babst et al. 1968).

In the late 1950s, Leslie T. Wilkins persuaded the British Home Office and the California Departments of Corrections and Youth Authority to apply prediction tables to the evaluation of treatment programs when random assignment to experimental and control groups is not feasible. The tables are used to calculate what Wilkins called the "base expectancy" of recidivism or of parole failure or any other outcome criterion for any particular group of inmates in a program to be evaluated.

When applying the prediction table to determine the base expectancy of recidivism for a sample of prisoners (or for an entire population of prisoners in a particular institution or program), classify them by the score groups or by the configuration of categories in the prediction table to determine the number of recidivists that would be expected for those in each category if they were part of the cross-section of prior cases on which the prediction table was based. Add up these numbers of recidivists in the total sample, and express them as a percentage of the sample to get the sample's expected recidivism rate (or a larger population's rate, if it is applied to all of them).

If the actual behavior rates of the subjects in a particular program then prove better than the expected rates, the program is credited with improving their conduct; if their actual conduct is worse than predicted by the table, the program is assumed to be deleterious. Thus, the prior sample or population on which research was done to develop the prediction table provides what Blumstein and Cohen (1979) call a pseudo-control group for the evaluation of a specific current program. Selection effects from the choice of prisoners for assignment to the program that is evaluated are automatically taken into account when you determine from the prediction table what the expected outcome would be for the particular combination of prisoners that the program received. This, of course, assumes that the predictions of these tables are highly valid. If they are continually tested, and the data on which they are based is as theoretically pertinent and as accurate as the state of research and knowledge permit, you can be confident that assessment by this method is the best that can be done without an optimum controlled experiment.

The Massachusetts Department of Corrections probably has been using the base expectancy method of assessing its policies and practices more thoroughly and consistently than any other people-changing agency. They began using this method during the 1960s with Francis Carney's (1967, 1969) evaluation of special counseling projects, in which he used a rather complex configuration table. It continues today in the department's regular assessment of the recidivism-reducing effects of most of its separate facilities and procedures. Table 4.2, derived from table 4.1, lists recent Massachusetts base expectancy categories and their predictions. *These predictions are not used to guide release decisions, but rather to assess facilities or programs.*

By classifying all prisoners paroled from a particular facility or program into the five categories of table 4.2 (most easily done by sorting them in the sequence indicated by table 4.1) an *expected* recidivism rate is calculated for the total mix of inmates assigned there. If their *actual* rate is less than this expected rate, their correctional assignment is considered recidivism reducing, as compared with the assignments of the "pseudo-control group" of prisoners with similar expected rates in the population of past releasees from which tables 4.1 and 4.2 were derived.

Application of the base expectancy method in the Massachusetts De-

TABLE 4.2
Massachusetts Base Expectancy Risk Categories (from LeClair 1977)

Category Number	Description	Recidivism Rate
I	Age 27 or younger at time or release, 12 or more prior court appearances	48%
II	Age 25 or younger at time of release, 11 or fewer prior court appearances, and total number of charges 7 or more	32%
III	Age 28 or older at time of release, 12 or more prior court appearances	23%
IV	Age 25 or younger at time or release, 11 or fewer prior court appearances, and total number of charges 6 or less	14%
V	Age 26 or older at time of release, 11 or fewer prior court appearances	6%

partment of Corrections since the early 1970s has been guided by a theory of *reintegration*, which its researchers distinguish (perhaps debatably) from a theory of rehabilitation. Daniel LeClair (1985a, 1985b), prominent in the department's effort, contends that a principal reason for the widespread failure to find recidivism-reducing effects from traditional rehabilitation programs in prison is that the impact of these programs is offset by the impact of prisonization, which fosters criminality. The focus of the department, therefore, has been to counter prisonization by reintegrative efforts, which, it presumes maximize the influence on inmates of law-abiding persons in the community and minimize the influence of the most prisonized convicts. The practices deemed reintegrative include home furloughs from prison, daily release to attend school or work in the community, halfway houses (called prerelease centers), liberal visiting privileges, coed institutions, and movement of inmates through institutions in descending order of security level and size.

Applying the Massachusetts base expectancies (table 4.2) to all inmates released from their prisons in 1973, LeClair (1981) found that those who had received one or more furloughs had an expected one-year followup recidivism rate of 24 percent, but an actual recidivism rate of 16 percent, while those who had no furloughs had both an expected and an actual recidivism rate of 27 percent. Sixty-one percent of that year's releasees were in the furloughed group. But in 1974, when 73 percent of the releasees had been furloughed, the nonfurloughed prisoners had an expected recidivism rate of 26 percent and an actual rate of 31 percent, while the furloughed group showed little change: their expected rate was 24 percent and actual rate 14 percent. This contrast between the two groups remained about the same in subsequent years.

Table 4.3 indicates the relationship of security level at release to recidivism rates. These figures strongly support the Department of Correcton's policy of combatting prisonization by moving inmates to lower-security units as they approach their release date. It also reveals the fact that the total inmate population's recidivism rates declined after the department initiated the reintegration program, a decline that has continued since the data for table 4.3 were gathered (LeClair 1981). It also suggests the need to revise the base expectancy tables periodically to take into account any possible changes in the optimum combination of factors for such tables, as well in the outcome rates that they predict.

One problem with using actuarial prediction tables in people-changing organizations is that their application makes them become obsolete. This has been demonstrated in medical and other professional school admission tests, I have been told by psychometricians prominent in such testing. The problem arises because the initial replacement of impressionistic case judgments by predictive test scores to determine admission increases the percentage of students who complete these schools satisfactorily. Their higher success rates mean that revised admissions tests based on what predicts their record in the professional school are derived from student performance records with less variance than existed when the first admission tests were developed from the records of students admitted less scientifically; predictions based on cases with less variance are likely to have less predictive power than those based on a more diverse population. In addition,

TABLE 4.3
Expected and Actual One-Year Recidivism Rates of 1974
Massachusetts Department of Corrections Male Releasees by
Security Level of Institution from Which Released
(from LeClair 1977)

Security Level	Number of Releasees	Recidivism Rates		Significance of Difference*
		Expected	Actual	
Maximum	418	28%	26%	Not significant
Medium	130	21%	19%	Not significant
Minimum	81	22%	9%	.01
Halfway House (Prelease Centers)	212	21%	12%	.01
Total Releasees	841	25%	20%	.001

*by Chi Square test

there is an elevation of performance grading standards at a school when it becomes more selective in its admissions, so that scores on older admission tests that once predicted passing grades later indicate a higher probability of failure.

It follows that if theory-guided applications of base expectancy tables are effective in correctional and mental health institutions, success rates may initially increase, because this would lead to briefer retention or even diversion of the better risk cases and to longer confinement of those with high failure rates. Revised tables should then be sought for the inmates, however, in case those for whom retention is determined by the old tables differ in important ways from the population on which the old tables were based, and in case changes in the communities to which they are released also alter the accuracy of predictions by the old tables.

There has not yet been enough experience with base expectancy applications in these agencies to warrant confident forecasting of such effects; all that has become clear is the need to retest base expectancy tables continually, and to revise them whenever the tests show that a different table would make more contrasting yet accurate predictions. Frequent repetition of prediction research to identify factors not consistent in predictive significance in different periods, and deleting such factors from base expectancy tables, is a means of reducing the history effects suggested by the foregoing discussion.

As another alternative to experimentation when base expectancy tables are not available for an entire agency population, Blumstein and Cohen (1979) suggest discriminant analysis by multiple regression to determine from available data what variables best predict the selection of clients for a program that is to be evaluated. With such information, the researchers can apply these variables to clients not selected for the program, and may thus identify a pseudo-control group released in the same period. Outcome rates of the treated group can then be compared with those for the pseudo-control group to assess the impact of the treatment.

Theory-guided controlled experiments, when feasible, are still preferable to base expectancy and discriminant analysis for outcome evaluation of people-changing efforts. A major reason for this is the possibility that there are influential selection effects from variables not taken into account by the base expectancy tables or discriminant analysis, and that these selection effects may largely account for the success or failure of particular programs. Thus, those with a vested interest in programs that evaluations show are ineffective may claim that they had worse risk cases than base expectancy tables indicate. Random assignment of cases to large experimental and control groups, if done rigorously and not subsequently contaminated by mortality effects, assures by the laws of probability that an experimental evaluation is unaffected by known or unknown selection factors.

Conclusion

To assure external validity in the evaluation of people-changing efforts, it is customary to try to assess a representative sample of a designated universe of clients. Prescreened random selection of experimental and control groups, pre-post designs, and other procedures that reduce barriers to obtaining permission to conduct a treatment experiment also have some effects that impair external validity. In addition, such procedures may make it difficult for the researcher to identify the full strength of relationships among relevant variables. Furthermore, when administrative categories for differentiating clients are the basis for sample selection in evaluation research, the conclusions may lose their external validity over time and place as the attributes of clients placed in these categories often vary.

Theory-guidance of sampling and other aspects of evaluation research maximize the prospects of finding effective people-changing methods and minimize loss of external validity from application bias. These benefits occur because such research generalizes its findings not to administrative categories of clients, but to the kinds of people and conditions that the theory indicates will be most amenable to change by the treatment being evaluated. These prospects are especially good if the hypotheses that underly the research design are derived from widely validated theory. However, theory may also indicate the administrative categories of clients for which the treatment has the most favorable or unfavorable prospects.

Perhaps the greatest threat to external as well as internal validity is deviation of treatment or research procedures from what the researchers intend and assume them to be. As elaborated in chapter 3 and repeated here in somewhat different formulation, vigilant monitoring of the people-changing efforts being evaluated is necessary to discover and to correct promptly or to take into account any serious deviations of practices from the research plan. Theory that explains why a particular type of intervention into the lives of clients should be effective, and for whom, will also indicate what kinds of differences between treatment plans and their execution will make the intervention ineffective. Such theory will also show what types of selection effects in evaluating an intervention will most impede the accurate assessment of its effectiveness.

Prediction research permits the development of base expectancy tables that are useful alternatives to experimentation when random selection of treatment and control groups is unfeasible. With such tables, expected outcome rates can be calculated for the people in a program to be evaluated, and then their actual outcome rates can be compared with those that were expected.

While base expectancy assessment is not as ideal as the most perfectly controlled experiment, it is one of the most widely feasible of the rigorous outcome evaluation procedures available. As has been demonstrated by the Massachusetts Department of Corrections, it is especially practical when it is well institutionalized in a large organization with many programs or aspects of programs than can be evaluated by a single base expectancy table. Almost all agencies could gain much if they used this procedure routinely, but it is important that they continually retest the prediction tables from which their expected outcome rates are calculated. Such agencies would gain even more if they used the resulting outcome evaluations as the basis for cost-effectiveness and cost-benefit analysis.

5

Costs and Benefits: The Increasingly Decisive Assessments

Money and other resources are always limited. Funds used for one program are not available for another. Therefore, once it is shown that a people-changing effort works, the question remains, is it worth its cost? Indeed, the best way to gain consensus on policies, to get conservatives and liberals to agree, is to demonstrate that the dollar value of an outcome exceeds its cost. But how can this be done in people-changing organizations?

Even if we can precisely total a program's costs as so many dollars per case, and even if we have a summative evaluation of the program's effects, how can we assess, except arbitrarily, the money value of the benefits it produces? What is it worth to change a delinquent into a nondelinquent, a paranoid into a normal, an alcoholic into an abstainer? Or with only partial success, what is it worth to reduce the frequency and severity of relapse, hence the number of days of reconfinement per followup year? What is the cost of reducing postrelease failure rates by ten percent? What is the added cost of a second ten percent reduction, for a total of 20 percent? Is this cost greater than the cost of achieving the first 10 percent gain?

Once you can estimate with some confidence which programs change what types of people and to what extent, the first step in estimating whether the effort is financially worthwhile is to find out how much must be spent to obtain it. The *cost-effectiveness* of a people-changing effort is its estimated cost per unit of the change achieved.

Obviously, if cost-effectiveness figures are available for alternative ways of achieving a given people-changing objective, policy makers can select that program that produces a particular change at the lowest average cost. This knowledge is more easily obtained for intermediate goals, such as assuring that clients earn high school diplomas, than for ultimate goals, such as reducing recidivism. If correctional officials know the dollar cost of educating various types of prisoners through high school by traditional classroom methods, and the cost by using teaching machines with token rewards for achievement, they can select the method of education that is cheaper. But what if this cost, even by the most cost-effective method, seems too expensive for some types of inmates?

Cost-benefit analysis assigns an estimated dollar value to a people-changing accomplishment, such as education through high school, and relates this benefit's value to the cost of achieving it, per person changed. The results of such analyses are customarily expressed in either of two ways: as *benefits minus costs* per case, which will be called *profit* here, or as the *ratio of benefits to costs*, which will be called *efficiency*.

Some publications use the phrase "benefit-cost." It refers to exactly the same thing as "cost-benefit" in other publications. Also, some writers use these expressions in the plural ("costs-benefits"), while others almost always use the singular for one or both terms. Regardless of what such analysis is called, it makes evaluations more influential, both because of what chapter 1 (following Weber) calls the increasing rationalization of our institutions and because of the pressure for budget cuts whenever government deficits are large, which is a recurrent if not chronic condition. That is why chapter 2 calls a cost-benefit conclusion "the most support-relevant criterion."

Of course, society's cost in anguish from mental illness, crime, and other social problems, and its benefit from reducing it, can never be fully represented by money (indeed, neither can these feelings ever be adequately communicated in words). Also, moral gains or losses (such as those from success or failure in reducing incest or child molestation) cannot be monetized satisfactorily. Yet all types of human feelings are regularly equated with sums of money by courts to settle civil suits for emotional damages, or to determine how large a fine would be a just-deserts penalty for a particular offense. Most people regard this court work as useful even if there is often debate as to whether the judgments are too harsh or too lenient. Furthermore, Ellickson and Petersilia (1983) found that the belief that benefits clearly outweigh costs was the best predictor that a criminal justice innovation would be fully adopted by policy makers.

For these reasons, an argument can be made for attempting monetary evaluations of people-changing efforts despite the unavoidable fact that the precise dollar conclusions will not be proved absolutely valid. Generally some initial consensus can be achieved on the approximate value of different types of accomplishment, as well as on their average costs, and these first assessments can gradually be made more accurate. There are many methods of making such estimations. Each approach offers some advantages and some disadvantages. Discussion here begins with the simplest methods, then examines more complex procedures. None is too diffcult to comprehend, and all can be very useful.

Supplemental Cost-Effectiveness: The Easiest Assessment

The easiest costs to estimate are the extra funds needed to add a service to an ongoing program. For example, if a new kind of staff specialist, such as a trade teacher, tutor, or psychologist is added at a group home, clinic or correctional institution, it is much easier to estimate what this increment costs—including salary, office space, equipment, and perhaps secretarial and administraive services—than to determine the total cost of operating the entire establishment. Such a cost estimate is a first step both to getting approval and to evaluating such a supplementary service. Indeed, in justifying budgetary decisions, officials must usually assess the merit of each specific recent or contemplated addition rather than the worth of their entire establishment. The accuracy of estimates subsequently tends to be reviewed by appropriation agencies, which often make cost data on proposed or recent additions to services readily available to evaluators.

The simplest type of cost-effectiveness analysis is to calculate total costs per unit of service provided. Thus, in Gilbert McKee's (1978:638) assessment of vocational training at a California prison early in the 1970s, he estimated the hourly cost of training per inmate for the various trades as follows: shoe repair, $.67; sheet metal, $.64; machine shop, $.57; masonry, $.57; welding, $.53; offset printing, $.51; office machine repair,$.49; landscape gardening, $.49; bakery, $.47; auto mechanics, $.40; electronics, $.40; auto body and fender, $.39. Similarly, cost of psychotherapy could be calculated per hour of service, presumably with a cheaper rate per patient for group than for individual therapy.

The cost figures per unit of service become cost-effectiveness assessments for achieving the intermediate goal of directly altering the clients when you can estimate the number of units of service required to make a measurable degree of change. Thus, as a rough estimate from his postrelease data, McKee assumed that at least 1,000 hours of trade training in prison were necessary to improve markedly a prisoner's prospect of satisfactory employment after release. This suggests that auto mechanics, electronics, and body and fender trade training are much more cost-effective than shoe repair training because they are cheaper. Actually, the postrelease data showed that shoe repair training had little effect on postrelease job improvement regardless of how extensive the training, while a thousand hours in most of the other trades had a signficant effect. A more refined cost-effectiveness analysis would probably estimate a different total number of hours in each of the various trades as necessary to qualify the average trainee for employment.

Cost-effectiveness analysis is even more valuable as a contribution to rational policies if it can be expressed as the cost per unit of obtaining an ultimate goal, such as reducing recidivism. This requires followup of the service recipients to determine how much their subsequent rates of un-desirable conduct or desired behavior differ from those of a control or comparison group, or from their expected rates according to a base expec-tancy analysis.

The process of moving from supplementary costs to estimating the more ultimate cost-effectiveness of trying to reduce reimprisonment can be illus-trated by hypothetical data on the addition to a prison's resources of a unit to provide relatively intensive psychotherapy (as opposed to the usual pri-marily diagnostic and crisis intervention services of prison psychiatrists and psychologists). Let us suppose that a psychiatrist is hired at $80,000 per year, a clinical psychologist at $35,000, a psychiatric social worker at $30,000, a secretary at $20,000, and a clerk-typist at $15,000, with $200,000 required for their fringe benefits, supplies, and other expenses, including annual cost of office space, equipment, and furnishings, so that the unit's total budget is $380,000. If the unit provides its psychotherapy for 380 clients in the course of a year, the average cost of this service is $1,000 per client per year.

TABLE 5.1
Supplementary Costs and Cost-Effectiveness in a Five-Year
Followup Period for a Psychotherapy Unit ("PsU") for Various
Types of Clients in a Correctional Agency (Hypothetical Figures)

Cost-Benefit Items	Type of Client			
	Child molest-ers	Rapists with no prior of-fense record	Rapists with prior offense record	Unspecia-lized offenders
Psu service costs:				
average duration	1.5	1	1.5	1
year	years	year	years	year
Cost per client	$1,500	$1,000	$1,500	$1,000
Subsequent confinement:				
Expected without	3	6	2	3
PsU Services	years	months	years	years
Expected With PsU	1	3	2	4
	year	months	years	years
Time Saved by PsU	2	3	zero	− 1
	years	months	years	year
Cost-Effectiveness	$750	$4,000	zero	− $1,000
(cost per year of later confinement saved)				(loss)

Table 5.1 combines these estimates of cost with hypothetical outcome data suggested by available research on psychotherapy's possible effectiveness in reducing reconfinement rates (from parole violation or recidivism) for various types of prisoners. Of course, the actual effectiveness of such therapy can only be known well by experimental or quasi-experimental followup studies. Research thus far suggests that the best current psychotherapeutic programs would help rehabilitate most sex offenders who have committed little or no other kinds of serious delinquency or crime (Doshay 1943; Brecher 1978). However, enculturated offenders, especially unspecialized chronic lawbreakers involved in crime since early adolescence, probably would exploit the relatively permissive and purely verbal psychotherapy programs, and these programs would diminish the suppressive effect of traditional confinement on them (Murray and Cox 1979). Psychotherapy for them might well increase their reconfinement rates, and thus be negatively cost-effective, as intensive community supervision was for California's Community Treatment Program when provided as an alternative to confinement for its "power-oriented" youths (Palmer 1974). Types of benefits other than reconfinement might also be credited to psychotherapy, such as improved prison adjustment and less confinement in disciplinary cells or protective custody. These savings can readily be monetized, but for the sake of simplicity they will not be considered here.

As has already been suggested, cost-effectiveness analysis is feasible for a supplemental service whenever two types of data are available: an outcome evaluation for this type of service, indicating the rate at which it achieves its immediate, intermediate or ultimate goals; and the cost per client of adding this service.

Naturally, the precision with which supplementary costs can be estimated varies. For example, while exact salaries may be known, overhead costs such as building space, equipment, and administrative services usually must be estimated imperfectly, with arbitrary guesses on some items, such as depreciation. Also, the cost estimates per case always assume a given workload for a facility and its staff, but these are seldom exactly predictable. Therefore, if there are fewer clients, but no cuts are made in staff, cost per case increases; conversely, when a unit must handle more clients than planned, the cost per case usually declines, but the effectiveness may also be altered. These accounting and budgeting problems, of course, are not peculiar to people-changing agencies; they are shared by almost all businesses and other organizations.

More Comprehensive Cost-Effectiveness Estimates

Many legislative, judicial, and administrative decisions on people-changing efforts consider more contrasting alternatives than whether or not to provide a supplementary service. There are decisions of incarceration versus supervision in the community, of confinement in a maximum security institution or placement in a minimum security camp, of parole or probation with only infrequent contact required as against close supervision or even mandated residence in a halfway house. In mental health services it may be a question of inpatient versus outpatient treatment, which usually have quite contrasting costs to whoever pays the bill (the state, the patient, or an insurance company).

Determination of costs for such contrasting facilities and services requires a tabulation of the total annual expenditures in operating each, to be done as completely as possible including depreciation of buildings and equipment (or rental charges) as well as the administrative costs that the agency creates for offices of higher authority, or for various advisory boards.

An interesting example of such cost-effectiveness estimation was provided by the Patuxent Institution, as it formerly operated. This unique establishment under Maryland law confined adults convicted of serious crimes whose behavior showed "a propensity toward criminal activity" due to "intellectual deficiency or emotional disorder." This judgment was made by a board of medical examiners, and if a court accepted it, the accused was committed to Patuxent for intensive psychotherapeutic treatment until the institution staff decided that he or she was "cured;" if the court disagreed with the board as to the cause of the subject's criminality or its amenability to treatment, the accused received a traditional prison sentence. Judges often did not concur with the psychiatric recommendation that an offender be sent to Patuxent.

A cost-effectiveness analysis by Bloom and Singer (1979) found that offenders sent to Patuxent were confined an average of 6.8 years before parole, with 76 percent of the parolees rearrested within four years, and the average time after release of these arrests was 2.3 years. Offenders deemed to meet the criminality standards of Patuxent by examining psychiatrists but nevertheless sent by the court to prison were confined an average of 4.8 years, with 84 percent rearrested within a four-year followup period, averaging 1.3 years before rearrest. Controlling for many predictive factors such as age and prior record that differentiated the two groups, the researchers calculated by a rather complex curvilinear multiple regression formula that Patuxent deferred reimprisonment for its typical offender by one year, as compared with prison. To estimate the cost to the state of achieving this one-year deferral, they collected the data presented in table 5.2, which has separate figures per inmate for the state's three maximum security prisons when filled to their designed capacity, as well as in their actual overcrowded condition.

TABLE 5.2
Estimated Costs of Commitment for Similar Offenders to Maryland's
Patuxent Institutions and to Its Maximum Security Prisons, Per Inmate
(In 1976 Dollars; from data in Bloom and Singer 1979)

Type of Cost	At Patuxent and its Reintegration Centers & Services	IN REGULAR PRISON & PAROLE:	
		Prisons full to capacity	Prisons overcrowded
Incarceration, per yr.:			
Capital Costs	$5,300	$5,300	$3,370
Security	6,250	3,750	2,310
Food	850	600	600
Plant Maintenance	1,120	1,070	670
Housekeeping	360	290	290
Administration	830	460	280
Therapy	1,130	200	200
Other Treatments	700	590	590
Total Annual Cost	16,540	12,260	8,310
Cost for Average Term	112,472	58,848	39,888
(6.8 years in Patuxent; 4.8 years in prison)			
Diagnoses and Committee Decisions:			
At Entrance	5,520	2,440	2,440
Later Formal Hearings	54,450	—	—
Reintegration Services:			
Patuxent Prelease Center	170	—	—
Halfway House	1,970	—	—
Parole	2,900	190	190
Total Costs per Inmate:	$128,482	$61,478	$42,518

Table 5.2 indicates that in 1976, to defer further crime by its serious offenders, Maryland spent $85,964 per inmate for confinement in Patuxent. As Nelson (1975) points out, costs (and benefits) may be estimated from the standpoint of government (as is done for costs in table 5.2), from the standpoints of clients and their families, and from the standpoint of society. Costs to the client and kin include their expenditures because of government actions (such as legal costs), possible loss of earnings by the client (opportunity costs), and unmeasurable costs, such as humiliation and degradation. Government losses, in addition to those of table 5.2, include the loss of taxes from the client's lost earnings. Costs to society encompass the government's costs, which are a diversion of resources from other societal needs, the loss of potential contributions to national production by the client, and the offender's damage to the general moral climate.

In addition to calculating government costs, Bloom and Singer (1979) estimated offenders' greater loss of earnings due to longer confinement if sent to Patuxent rather than to Maryland prisons. They offered several figures, each based on a different arbitrary assumption, but ranging from $8,000 to $13,000. This was a societal loss added to the government costs indicated in table 5.2. Thus, the cost of sending someone to Patuxent rather than to prison was well over $90,000 (in 1976 dollars). Assuming that their thoughtful calculations are approximately correct, and that society's benefits from this expenditure were one year of additional incapacitation plus somewhat lower lifetime recidivism of these serious offenders, were these benefits worth their cost? Such a question leads to the challenging problem of benefit analysis, of monetizing the gains that may or may not compensate for the cost of a people-changing effort.

Monetizing Benefits

The simplest benefit to measure, and to relate to costs, is one that can be expressed immediately and directly in money. The possible benefits from people-changing efforts, in a sequence that approximates the decreasing ease and directness with which they can be monetized, include: (1) the client's increased legitimate earnings; (2) the government's taxes on these earnings; (3) the public's decreased monetary losses from crime or from other deviant behavior that is changed; (4) decreased government expenditures for apprehending, adjudicating, confining, and caring for clients; (5) decreased need for protection from crime or other deviance (such as guards and locks); (6) less physical and emotional pain.

Cost-benefit analysis relates such gains to the cost of getting them. Thus, if mental patients, delinquents, or criminals who never had a legitimate income are able to hold a job after being in a program that seems to have changed them, the program's profit or efficiency can be appraised by comparing the client's earnings (or the taxes the government collects on these earnings) to the program's cost.

While the studies presented thus far have monetized costs but not benefits, some research monetizes benefits but not costs, as in the Mayer and Butterworth (1979) experiment on prevention of violence and vandalism in Los Angeles schools. It was based on a theory, derived from behavioral psychology, that violence and vandalism are caused by a combination of instructional material inappropriate for the students' reading skills; inappropriate punishment (such as violent, nagging, or boring penalties); poor modeling of appropriate behavior by teachers; the teachers' ignoring student violence; direct reinforcement of violence (sometimes by sponsoring violent play, erroneously deemed cathartic of aggression); and misusing behavior management procedures by lack of sensitivity to the subtle ways in which reinforcement get linked to conduct.

Seventy-three schools that routinely maintained vandalism records (covering damage or theft of school property, with cost estimates, reported monthly to the school board) were invited to apply for participation in the experiment, if they agreed to send staff to ten workshop meetings. Twenty schools were selected from twenty-five that applied, and these were randomly divided into ten experimentals and ten controls; however, one school withdrew when it learned that it was in the control group, and one of the experimental schools also withdrew later, leaving five elementary and four junior high schools in each group.

At each experimental school, with the aid of the principal, two "model" teachers were selected who had what the researchers described as desirable attributes and who agreed to cooperate. In addition to these models, two other teachers were randomly selected at each experimental school to serve as barometers of spillover effects; this was to determine how much these barometers were affected by the model teachers, principals, and school psychologists who attended the workshops, and by the researchers and trainers who visited each school and invited all faculty and staff to consult with them. Data on the behavior of all these teachers and of six students in each of their classrooms were collected during randomly sampled time periods in which ten-second moments for observing a particular teacher or student were followed by five seconds for recording on standardized check-off forms. These observations were done during a preprogram baseline period in November and an evaluation period in the following May, with around 90 percent interobserver agreement. It revealed a significant reduction of disruptive student behavior, an increase in student attendance, and improved teacher reinforcement practices in the experimental schools.

The directly monetized benefit of this experiment was the change in cost of vandalism in dollars. During the 1976-77 school year, when this project was conducted, the cost of vandalism in the experimental schools dropped 57 percent from the preceding year, declining from an average of $1,793 to $763 per school. Meanwhile, in the control schools, the cost of vandalism increased 320 percent, from an average of $1,410 in the preceding year to $5,926 in the project year. Extension of the program of other schools yielded similar results (Mayer and Butterworth 1981; Mayer et al. 1981). It is unfortunate that the cost of the special training and monitoring program in the experimental schools could not be estimated as though it were a routine activity, but it may involve little or no new expense once well established. The improvements in student conduct might also have been monetized to estimate the school system's net profit from such staff training.

Do We Need Discount Rates?

Cost-benefit analysis began in the United States in the 1930s when Congress required evidence that every government flood control and soil conservation project produce benefits in excess of its cost. Later this requirement was extended to many other types of public expenditures (see Mishan 1976; Sassone and Schaffer 1978:3-5). Economists recruited to make these analyses had an investment frame of reference from the business world, where profits are expressed as a rate of compound interest on the original capital investment, so that one investment's yield can be compared to another's.

This percentage-return perspective is appropriate for a construction project or for a piece of military equipment for which an expected duration of usefulness must be estimated. How well the expected total benefit from such items will repay the costs obviously varies with their longevity. A project's return of benefits per year of usefulness is related to its cost by economists, and the percentage of costs returned per year is compared by them with the interest charges that the government takes off in advance (or discounts) when it invests money as a loan, notably in Federal Reserve loans to banks.

The rates of return calculated by economists in cost-benefit analysis are called discount rates by them, since they are comparable to rates of return on investments. Even the simplest and clearest new texts on cost-benefit analysis, which are the ones that focus especially on people-changing efforts (notably on health-care projects, such as Thompson 1980), are by economists who have the discount-rate frame of reference. They express the present value of a project in terms of its estimated total future yield as an investment at compound interest for which a particular discount rate is obtained.

In evaluating many people-changing policies and practices, especially in mental health and criminal justice agencies, cost-benefit relationships are not so usefully expressed as a rate of compound interest earnings for a given duration. These organizations usually have little control over their case intake, and they cannot shift their resources to another type of business if their current activities are unprofitable. Their policies or practices, when adopted, are usually for continued use until something else seems better, rather than for a specific number of years. Their administrative rationality can best be assessed through simple estimates of costs and benefits from supplemental or alternative services, as this chapter shows, without converting the costs and benefits estimated into a discount rate compounded for the expected duration of the practice or policy. With programs of diverse duration, as in the Patuxent versus prison cost-comparison presented here, a comment on the longer investment in high-cost activities in one program might be an interesting supplement to the conclusions. Yet differences in length of treatment will be reflected in total costs of the various programs anyhow, if costs are totalled for a length of time that encompasses the duration of treatment.

As has been repeatedly implied here, assessments based on both benefits and costs, rather than either separately, are the most useful. The conclusions of such assessments can be expressed as benefits-minus-costs or as a benefit-cost ratio, which can appropriately be labeled profit and efficiency, respectively. If the presentation of these findings is not complicated by a discount rate analysis, its message will be much easier for the public and for most officials to comprehend. Such simplicity is certainly justifiable if, as is shown here for assessments of people-changing efforts, simplicity can be gained without any loss of validity or utility.

Four Simple Types of Cost-Benefit Analysis

Cost-benefit analyses vary tremendously, depending especially on the types of information available for estimating the monetary value of benefits and on the duration of followup that is feasible when estimating benefits. Four examples will illustrate some of these variations:

Quick Assessent of a Program That Shows Results Quickly.

Stuart Nagel (1983) argues from hypothetical data that managers with immediate budget constraints would be influenced more by estimating profits (benefits minus costs) than by figures on efficiency (benefits-to-costs ratio). He suggests that the benefits-cost ratio is more pertinent to long run policy planning than to prompt decisions regarding the specific supplementary services that are usually designated as separate programs. Profits or losses from suplementary programs can be assessed quickly if the benefits can be estimated soon after the program is provided.

Ann Solberg (1983) provides a very good example of a quick profits assessment, based on only a sixty-day followup of a special program to improve immediate postrelease adjustment of mental hospital patients. Her data come from hospital and outpatient billing records, where every pill or service that a patient receives is regularly recorded, with charges entered by the computer at a rate that includes overhead costs, so that insurance or Medicare can be billed (at the high rates that usually shock patients and their families, who do not take overhead into account when they compare these charges to what they view as the staff time or material received).

At the Fresno County Acute Psychiatric Unit, patients released to the community for ninety-day evaluation periods had previously been found to have their highest rate of rehospitalization during the first two weeks that they were out. Therefore, an experimental "assertive approach to followup" was provided by assigning extra social workers to a randomly selected experimental group for thirty days after the patients' release. This staffing was in addition to the aftercare services routinely available to every releasee, including those in the randomly selected control group. The supplemental social workers provided a prerelease interview and a large number of postrelease personal contacts and phone calls to the patients, the patients' families, and other relevant persons, particularly during the first two weeks that the patient was out of the hospital. The extra social workers also took an active role in case management, so that the experimental cases used more of the regularly available aftercare services than did those in the control group.

The control group cases in this Fresno experiment were found to average about 2 1/2 times as many days of rehospitalization as the experimentals in their first sixty days out of the hospital, and they required more services if rehospitalized, so that their total days of rehospitalization averaged over three times that of the experimental cases. Therefore, the savings in rehospitalization costs even in these first 60 days more than repaid the cost of the supplemental services and of the greater use of regular outpatient services during the first thirty days out. It would be interesting to know if there were still greater long run savings from less rehospitalization during a longer followup period.

Known Money Benefits and Costs from Vocational Training

In McKee's (1985) analysis of vocational training in California prisons, from which hourly costs for the various trades have already been presented, average annual earning rates were procured by an eighteen-month followup of vocationally trained parolees and an untrained comparison group, using state unemployment insurance records. Zero earning periods of unemployment or reconfinement were counted, but parolees from both groups who had no recorded earning in four or more different quarters of the six quarter-years of followup were excluded from the analysis.

The trainees averaged $215 more per year than the nontrainees. The average cost of training was $627. Because of the trainees' lower recidivism rates and their cumulative expertise and seniority in their trades, there is reason to believe that the difference between trainee and nontrainee earnings would increase in subsequent years. Therefore, it is probable that in a few years the government recovered more than its cost of training from the higher tax payments of trained releasees and by saving costs of arrest, adjudication, and reconfinement.

Average income of trainees varied greatly by trade, being about seven times as high in machine shop, and over four times as high in welding, offset printing, sheet metal, auto body and fender, auto mechanics, electronics or meat cutting, as in the lowest paid trade, shoe repair (which, it was noted, had the costliest training). Number of training hours completed was especially significant as a predictor of earnings for the top four trades, but in these especially, there was an inverse relationship between earnings and the time period between termination of training and release. Over 60 percent of the parolees with prison machine shop training and no previous experience in that trade had initial postrelease employment in and over 80 percent were employed in it by a year after release. The corresponding figures in other trades were as follows: welding, initially, and also a year later, about 50 percent; auto body work, 35 percent initially and 50 percent by the end of the year; but in auto mechanics, 40 percent both initially and by the end of the year. No other trades were as successful in placements as these.

Gilbert McKee (1978:641) estimated that the subsequent income gained in this eighteen-month followup period from each hour of training was $2.97 for general shop training, $1.48 for silk-screen printing, $1.18 for office machine repair, $1.07 for electronics, $.82 for welding, $.77 for auto mechanics, and $.63 for body and fender work. If, from such estimated increases in earnings due to training in prison, you estimated total government returns from its investment in vocational training, the benefits would include not only more taxes paid by higher earners, but also decreased welfare payments to their dependents and decreased criminal justice costs for recidivists. Also, of course, lowering recidivism rates reduces the public's cost and suffering from crimes. Persistence in accumulating such more ramified cost-benefit data could show which types of prisoners gain most from each kind of training, a knowledge useful for both the correctional system and the trainees.

Unfortunately, McKee's research was a doctoral dissertation project in economics rather than a government-conducted or sponsored study to guide policy. California Department of Corrections officials approved his study, but never saw the finished product. I heard about it, had to procure a copy from *Dissertation Abstracts*, and then to persuade McKee (now involved in other pursuits) to write the 1978 article and to permit the 1985 publication of parts of his thesis.

If the directors of people-changing agencies had a rational perspective toward maximizing both government and societal benefits, they would have their staff routinely conduct studies such as McKee's, and with increasing thoroughness. This would enable them to design and adjust their programs to maximize benefits in relation to costs, as well as to sell the programs to legislators on the basis of cost-benefit evidence. Although agency officials usually deplore their limited funds, they have hardly begun to pursue the elemental kinds of data collection and analysis needed to justify their expenditures.

Known Costs and Benefits from a "Work Relief" Program.

Public cost and benefit can also be estimated for very limited programs. For example, the Vera Institute of Justice in New York City, aided by government grants, established the Wildcat Service Corporation which, during most of the 1970s, employed ex-addicts from treatment programs, of whom about three-fourths were on methadone. They started at a weekly wage of $95 that rose to $115 maxmum for merit. They performed diverse tasks on over a hundred contracts procured by the corporation, ranging from painting curbs red next to fire hydrants and making portable barriers for the police, to operating some of the state's off-track betting offices.

The objective of the corporation was to supply supportive work at a reasonable but low wage for as long as the recipients wanted it, but with hopes that they would eventually find better employment elsewhere. For each of the first 300 jobs, Wildcat management named two qualified applicants, and the researchers randomly selected one of the pair as an experimental to get the job, but followed up the other as a control. These were predominantly minority group members; three-fourths had not completed high school, and they averaged 4.5 criminal convictions before entering this project. Data on subsequent conduct of experimental and control cases came from records of Social Security offices, the welfare department, the police, and interviews by the researchers (Friedman 1977).

The average experimental employee worked two-thirds of a year for Wildcat, earning $3,247 and $1,154 elsewhere in the rest of the year; the average control case earned only $1,112 during the year, but received $1,797 more than the average experimental from welfare. The experimentals were arrested slightly less often than the controls were. It was estimated that the cost of supported work to the taxpayer was $6,131 per experimental man-year, but that the benefits included:

Public goods and services	$4,519
Welfare reduction	1,797
Increased income tax collection	311
Savings from crime reduction by: Less criminal justice expenses	86
Less crime victimization	207

These total $6,920, a profit of $789 over costs, and a benefit-cost ratio of 1.13 (Friedman 1977). The cost-benefit analysis suggests the merit of institutionalizing supported work in a large variety of forms for different sorts of people now largely dependent on welfare, with research focused on determining which types of work assistance are most efficient for which kinds of clientele.

A specialized technical literature has developed in economics on the cost of crime per offender of various types, and thus on the money value of any benefits achieved for society by reducing crime (e.g., Higgins 1977; Gray 1979). This permits monetary estimation of the value of reduced crime victimization, such as that above in the Wildcat example.

A General Model for Selection of Clientele and Estimation of Cost Benefits in Any Deviance Prevention Effort

If *deviance* designates whatever conduct you want to diminish (for example, student misconduct in school, drunken driving, nonpayment of alimony, or any other deplored behavior), a general model for estimating costs and benefits is suggested by Mark Lipsey's (1984) evaluation of delinquency prevention efforts in Los Angeles. On the basis of his approach, you can assert that in any deviance-reduction effort for a particular set of subjects, who will be called here the *clientele*;

Efficiency (Benefit/Cost Ratio) $= R \times S \times C$

where:

R $=$ the deviance *risk* factor, defined as the proportion of a specified clientele who are likely to engage in the deviance if no prevention effort is made,

S $=$ the *success rate*, defined as the proportion of the clientele likely to engage in deviance for whom at least some subsequent deviance is prevented by the evaluated effort, and

C $=$ the *cost differential*, defined as the ratio of the average benefits from preventing a case of the deviance to the average cost of the deviance prevention efforts for those cases in which it is prevented.

Accordingly, if the potential deviants in a particular clientele are only 40 percent (R $= .4$), and if a deviance prevention method is successful for half of these clientele (S $= .5$), then the proportion of these clientele for whom deviance can be prevented is (R X C) $= .5 \times .4 = .2$, or one-fifth. If the benefit from one case of deviance prevention is worth $2,500, and the deviance prevention effort costs $500 per case, then $C = 5$. In these circumstances:

Efficiency $= R \times S \times C = .5 \times .4 \times 5 = 1$

For such a clientele, with these values for the three variables, the benefits of prevention equal the costs. If either R, S, or C increased, however, without reducing the others, efficiency would exceed unity, and the prevention effort would be profitable. Let us now examine how you estimate the parameters with which to apply this general model, using Lipsey's study as an example.

The first task is to sort the potential clientele into risk groups in order to estimate the value of R. Estimation of risk is the central concern of chapter 6, and was also discussed in application to base expectancy analysis in chapter 4 (each chapter presents several examples). The simplest method is merely to classify potential clientele into groups by their rates of deviance in the past, for the best single predictor of future behavior is usually its rate in the past.

Lipsey (1984) calculates from Wolfgang et al. (1972), and from other studies, that the probability of delinquency in the future is related to past delinquency for metropolitan boys, as measured by police contacts or arrests, as follows:

a. for those with no record of prior police contact, the probability of an arrest or police contact for juvenile delinquency is 0.15;
b. for California boys with one recorded prior arrest, as estimated in a separate study of costs by Higgins (1977), the probability of a second arrest prior to age 18 is 0.5;
c. for those with two recorded prior arrests, one can calculate from Higgins' data that the probability of a subsequent arrest prior to age 18 is 0.72;
d. for those with three prior arrests, the probability of a fourth arrest is also 0.72.

These probabilities would be modified, of course, if additional factors were considered as control variables, particularly age. But the age variable is significant only for those with no police record for delinquency. For such presumed innocents, Lipsey calculates from data in Wolfgang et al. (1972) that the probability of a first police contact or arrest for delinquency before age eighteen, for boys, is .349 when they reach age seven, but it declines with increasing age thereafter until it is only .035 at their seventeenth birthday. In other words, the longer they have no record of such deviance, the less is the probability that they will have it in the future. Of course, setting an upper-age limit for this future—here eighteen—also reduces for older boys the duration of time at risk until this age limit is reached.

Analogous series of figures doubtless apply to most other types of deviance, such as excessive gambling, disabling use of alcohol, failure in school, or absenteeism on a job. For all of these and many other modes of misconduct, those with no prior record of the deviance are least likely to acquire a future record; those with some record are more likely to have a further record; and the more often they have been known to have such deviant conduct, the more likely they are to have more of it, at least until old age or other factors prevent it. Contrastingly, the older they get with no record of the deviance, the less likely they are ever to acquire such a record.

For a low-risk group, such as those for whom no deviance has ever been recorded, there is the least amount of potential deviance to prevent. Thus, for Lipsey's juveniles with no prior record of police contact, there was estimated to be only a 15 percent chance of delinquency, so that 85 percent would never have a delinquency record even if no prevention effort were made. On the other hand, for those with two recorded prior police contacts, a 72 percent chance further contact was estimated, so any effective prevention program could potentially change more of such clientele. It follows that it may be most cost effective to direct deviance prevention efforts to the highest risk group for whom efforts are likely to be successful; for low-risk groups, the cost of the effort may not be offset by the amount of deviance prevented. Also consider that different types of intervention seem to be needed for successful prevention efforts with different risk groups; indeed, for delinquency, Klein (1979) and others show that some prevention efforts with low-risk groups may increase the probability of deviance.

For boys referred to the Los Angeles Probation Department's prevention services without a police record, but on the basis of behavioral problems reported by school or social work agencies, Lipsey (1984) estimates that risk of future police contact is 0.30, and, as already indicated, the risk of a second arrest for those with one prior arrest is about 50 percent. These boys without prior police records are the lowest-risk groups handled by these programs, for whom his earlier (1981) experimental and quasi-experimental evaluations found a reduction of one or more subsequent police contacts for 15 to 20 percent of the clients.

Lipsey's estimation of C, the cost differential, required estimation of the per case costs for all clients of the prevention program, but the benefits per case only for those clients who would otherwise have had a subsequent police contact He estimated costs simply by taking the prevention program's total budget, including overhead and administration costs, and dividing by the total number of cases it handled per year, which came to $300 per case. As he notes, total costs might have included those paid by the boy and his family, such as transportation costs, and might have included what economists call *opportunity costs*, the value of the activities—such as school or work—that the clients missed because of their involvement in the prevention program. However, since only the agency's budget costs are likely to enter into its policy decisions, it is reasonable to include only these costs in cost-benefit assessment of an agency program.

To estimate benefits, Lipsey had a more complex task. First he compiled statistics on what happened to juveniles who were arrested, finding that for every thousand of them, 450 were released by the police and 550 referred to the Probation Department, which confined 192 of them in juvenile detention pending disposition of their cases. The 550 referrals to probation resulted in 135 being released by the probation staff and 78 placed by them on informal probation. But the staff petitioned 337 for hearings and action by the juvenile court, 30 of whom the court sent to the Probation Department's camps, and 18 of whom it committed to the custody of the California Youth Authority.

Lipsey then had to estimate the average cost per case of an arrest and of each of the above dispositions for the arrestees not released by the police. He did this by procuring the total amount spent per year for each service (arrest, detention, juvenile court processing, probation staff services, probation camps, and California Youth Authority operations) and dividing each of these totals by the number of cases received by each of these services per year.

Lipsey now estimated the total costs for all of the dispositions indicated above for a typical 1000 arrests. The estimated police cost of $153 per arrest would total $153,000. To this total he had to add the total of the following products for cases not released by the police: 550 probation referrals times $673, 192 juvenile detentions times $1,168, 337 complete juvenile court hearings times $944, 30 probation camp confinement terms times $6,704, and 18 California Youth Authority commitments times $27,064. The total, divided by a thousand, is $1,754, —which is the estimated average government cost per case of a juvenile arrest. Since the average arrestee in this system has 1.7 subsequent arrests, 1.7 can be multiplied by $1,754 to yield $2,982 as a minimum estimate of the benefit in juvenile justice system costs saved by preventing further arrests for one arrestee. Because those with a juvenile arrest record have a higher than average probability of committing crimes as adults, preventing juvenile arrests also yields benefits by saving potential costs to the criminal justice system. And in addition to saving the government costs due to future crimes, there are the savings for potential victims from property losses, personal injuries and psychological shock offenses by juveniles and adults.

Lipsey does not attempt to estimate all of these savings from the reduction of future arrests, but he does estimate from Higgins (1977) that, allowing for inflation to 1984, each juvenile offense causes damages that average a $756 cost to the victim. Multiplying this by 1.7 subsequent arrests presumed to be prevented, this adds $1,285 to the benefit of preventing further juvenile offenses. However, Lipsey conservatively estimates from victimization surveys that juveniles commit five offenses for every arrest that they incur, and thus estimates savings to victims from preventing subsequent juvenile arrests as 5 times $1,285, or $6,425.

Adding the $2,982 in savings to the police and juvenile justice system to the $6,425 savings to victims gives Lipsey an estimate of $9,407 as total benefits to society from the Los Angeles Probation Department's prevention services when they prevent subsequent juvenile arrests for an arrested boy. Since, as indicated above, he estimates the cost of these services as $300 per case, the cost differential is the ratio of these benefits to the cost, or 31.4.

Applying the R x S x C formula with the estimated value of C as 31.4 to boys with no previous record, if their risk of a police contact is estimated as .15 and the success rate of prevention efforts as .20, the efficiency is .94, or slightly less than unity. If you deal, as is more typical, with arrested boys for whom a future arrest risk of at least .5 is likely, a success rate of .20 yields an efficiency of 3.14, or a profit of $2.14 in benefits for every $1 invested in prevention efforts.

To summarize, applying Lipsey's (1984) model for estimating either cost-benefit ratios, which this book has called "efficiency," or cost-benefit differences, which this book has called "profit," requires estimation of:

R = the risk of deviance for various possible clientele;

S = the success rate of prevention efforts (which are likely to vary for different types of deviance, of risk groups, and of prevention modalities);

C = the cost-benefits differential for each successfully treated case actually at risk.

Such an analysis may be especially useful for guiding policy decisions when officials must choose among risk groups for the clientele of their prevention service, or when they must choose among prevention methods with different success rates and different costs. Efficiency can then be estimated separately by the above formula for each risk group that they can select and for each kind of treatment that they may employ.

Conclusion

Cost-effectiveness studies estimate expenditures per case for each unit of achievement of a particular goal in people-changing efforts. It is easiest to conduct such studies when evaluating supplemental programs, for which cost figures are needed only for added personnel and facilities. Assessing entire organizations requires more complex accounting, including estimates of annual capital costs per case. Cost effectiveness is also much easier to determine for intermediate goals, such as completion of a particular type of training or passing a specific test, than for remote goals, such as reducing recidivism.

Cost-benefit analysis evaluates the achievement of a people-changing goal in terms of money, then relates it to the cost to reach conclusions about whether it is profitable. This is most easily done with benefits that are normally expressed monetarily, such as increased client earnings. But a program's benefits may also include the reduction of crime, of government expenditures for police, courts, corrections, welfare, and other services, as well as a decline in public anxiety, all of which can be monetized, although with some difficulty and imprecision.

Increasingly, systematic and thorough cost-benefit analyses are most needed for large gains in the rational guidance of people-changing efforts. Because these evaluations are in terms of profit or loss to the taxpayers, they are especially convincing to today's fiscally strained governments. Yet endorsing a policy as efficient, profitable, socially protective, humane, or otherwise desirable and carrying it out in practice, are two different problems. There are many slips between the promulgation of policies and our next concern, their use in case and policy decisions.

The rational application of the best available scientific knowledge or expert judgment in the practical settings of agency administration is the problem addressed by the next two chapters. This problem's solution depends upon whether you want to make routine case decisions, for which much statistical data on past experience may be accumulated, the concern of chapter 6, or you must make nonroutine decisions, even with very limited information, which is the concern of chapter 7.

6

Maximizing Rationality in Routine
Case Decisions

Officials of people-changing organizations make innumerable decisions about separate clients. Acting alone or in committee, they decide, for example, how to treat a patient, where an inmate will be housed, how a probationer will be supervised, or in what other specific ways their agency will assist, control, or otherwise deal with a client. These decisions reflect the officials' anticipations of the consequences of alternative actions, based upon whatever information or impression they get on each case. Their knowledge of their clients may come from case records, test results, observations, interviews, or other sources. Decisions are made many times for each case to try to meet, with minimum risk, both the client's and the organization's multiple and often incompatible needs.

Such case decisions may be called *routine* if they are made frequently, for similar clients, and with the same choice of possible alternatives. The more routine these decisions become, the more readily they may be analyzed statistically to assess their consistency and their consequences. From such statistical analyses, actuarial prediction tables may be constructed, two of which were presented in chapter 4's discussion of base expectancy methods. These tables can guide routine case decisions to more rationality by showing how accurately they anticipate subsequent events, such as the clients' rates of relapse, rehospitalization, recidivism, or parole violation.

Unfortunately, statistics on the accuracy of predictions by decision makers seldom are compiled. Therefore, most people-changing organizations drift with much inconsistency and inefficiency in their routine case decisions. This drift prevails for three main reasons: no official sees the totality of decisions that are made on separate cases; no one sees the relationships between decisions and their consequences; and all human decisions are prone to several standard types of errors.

The Doctors' and People-Changing Officials' Dilemma

In the 1930s, when it was more customary than it is now to remove a child's tonsils if they were inflamed, the New York City Board of Health conducted an experiment in which physicians examined the tonsils of 1,000 school children. They found that 611 already had had their tonsils removed, but they selected 174 (45 percent) of the remainder for tonsillectomy. A second group of physicians then examined the 215 children with tonsils who, unkown to these doctors, had already been diagnosed as not needing tonsillectomy, and they prescribed this operation for 99 children (46 percent). A third group of physicians then examined the 116 children now twice diagnosed as not needing tonsillectomy, and they advised excision of tonsils for 51 (44 percent). All the diagnosticians recommended this surgery for about 45 percent of the children whom they examined, even for the children who—without the new physician knowing it—had been cleared in previous examination (American Child Health Association, 1934. This study first came to my attention in Scheff 1966:112, where it is erroneously credited to Bakwin 1945, a secondary account).

This medical experiment was conducted at a time when physicians thought that removal of tonsils prevented future throat infections, and they then knew of few of the benefits that they now recognize in retention of tonsils. Their pattern of decision making seems to prevail whenever three things coexist: greater prospects of future complaints or regrets if preventive action is not taken than if it is; vague and uncertain evidence of risks; some costs, risks, or customs that discourage taking preventive action in all cases. These same conditions prevail in the routine case decisions of courts, prisons, mental hospitals, and many other people-changing agencies. They also are found in other person-assessments and acts of precaution-by case-study methods, such as in screening applicants for employment, admission to college, insurance, or loans. Of course, the percentage separated out for precautionary action varies with the problem.

All of these types of decision makers have two opposing types of motivations. First, they want to avoid being blamed for not being cautious enough, which motivates them to take as much preventive action as possible. The physicians who thought that tonsillectomies prevent throat infections could minimize such ailments by operating on all children. The judges or parole board members who are asked why a probationer or parolee who commits a heinous crime was ever released could avoid this blame by locking up everyone for the maximum time permitted by law. Similarly, the psychiatrist who approves a paranoid schizophrenic's transfer from in-patient to out-patient status can be blamed if the releasee assaults someone.

These case decision makers have dilemmas, however, because there are also opposing motivations. Tonsillectomies (and other operations) impose pain, risk, and costs for patients, so physicians may defer operations for many (the experiment showed their tendency to defer tonsillectomies for the healthiest 55 percent whom they saw). If judges and parole boards release much less than the customary proportion of offenders, there are protests against such unusually harsh penalties, complaints about the crowding and costs of the penal institutions, and the probation and parole supervision staff become underworked. Analogous reactions follow sharp and sudden changes in mental hospital release rates or in college admissions. Norms develop in release, admission, and other types of routine case judgments that tend to stabilize the percentage of precautionary actions taken, although these norms vary in different organizations and for different types of decisions.

Evidence that the basic inclination of judges is to make the most cautious decisions is the observation that whenever jail or detention space is expanded, judges fill it with people who would otherwise be released (demonstrated in Pawlak 1977). When community supervision resources are expanded in hopes of thereby diverting some cases from confinement, judges or other decision makers often use these resources instead mainly for offenders who otherwise would have been warned and released without supervision (Klein 1979). Correctional administrators also tend to be conservative. Therefore, if a penal system has both maximum security prisons and minimum security camps, the percentage of capacity vacant is usually highest in the camps.

Humans as Predictors and Deciders

The compulsive precaution of case decision makers shown in the tonsillectomy experiment seems to be widespread. It probably reflects distinct features of human psychology that have been subjected to some research, as well as a sociological phenomenon, each of which merits separate attention.

Overconfidence in One's Judgments

Once people reply to a difficult question, they tend to become overconfident that their response was correct. It seems likely that such overconfidence prevails because it is positively reinforced by reduction of anxiety about the correctness of the answer, and because overconfidence eliminates the need to check on the answer's correctness. Leon Festinger (1964:4-5) asserts: "the greater the conflict before the decision, the greater the dissonance afterward. Hence the more difficulty the person had in making the decision, the greater would be his tendency to justify that decision (reduce the dissonance) afterward. The decision can be justified by increasing the attractiveness of the chosen alternative and decreasing the attractiveness of the rejected alternative, and one would expect a post-decision cognitive process to occur that accomplishes this spreading apart of the attractiveness of the alternatives" (1964:4-5). He then cites studies in which subjects are asked to rate the attractiveness of their alternatives before and after making a choice between them, and the findings conclusively confirm the above-quoted hypothesis.

In a British study of this phenomenon, university students in several countries were asked a series of forced-choice questions on which many people would be uncertain, such as What is the capital of Iraq, Damascus or Baghdad? and Which is longer, the Panama or the Suez Canal? After each answer they were asked to report their degree of certainty, expressed as a percentage of absolute certainty. Most students were overconfident in their answers, since their average percentage of certainty exceeded the percentage of their answers that were correct. It was especially interesting that overconfidence was greatest in students of the arts rather than the sciences, and that overconfidence was much more pronounced among students in Malaysia and Indonesia than among students in England. The researchers (Wright et al. 1978; Wright 1984:Ch.4) note that in these two technologically less-developed countries there is widespread reliance on astrology and other superstitions for making important decisions, even among educated people, whereas scientific and less mystical modes of thought are much more prevalent in Britain.

One implication that can be drawn from these research findings is that the remedy for overconfidence in judgments that are largely guessed is to educate decision makers in science, thereby fostering habits of reliance on evidence for answers rather than on hunches and on blind faith. Overconfidence produces *premature closure*, the tendency to reach decisions before carefully examining all available evidence. Premature closure results in a rigid adherence to initial judgments, regardless of contrary evidence that is encountered subsequently.

This source of misjudgment in case decisions is reinforced by additional psychological mechanisms.

Selective Perception

The persistence of error that is characteristic of many chronic failures in gambling, business, marriage, and crime, as well as of stubborn racial and ethnic prejudices often results from a tendency to note evidence confirming the wisdom of past judgments and to disregard, explain away too easily, or simply not recognize disconfirming evidence. One source of over-confidence in judgments could be such selective perception by which people delude themselves about their past rationality.

One form of selective perception is called the *illusion of control* (Langer 1975), conspicuous in chronic gamblers, but existing in most people. It is the tendency to attribute successful past decisions to superior personal qualities, such as intuition, but to ascribe failures to unusual chance events, unwarranted interference, or other factors that do not weaken faith in one's wisdom. Thus, gamblers recall past winnings with pride, but forget or dismiss their more numerous losses. An aspect of this illusion of control is the utterly unfounded notion that there is something called "luck" that some people have and that others lack, which explains their fortunes in purely chance events, such as the outcome of roulette or dice games. The delusion of luck leads people to overlook the fact that outcomes in purely chance matters are controlled and predictable not by any personal hunch but only by the laws of probability.

Another aspect of selective perception is the filling of gaps in information by imagining whatever your preconceptions lead you to expect. Thus eyewitnesses, without realizing it, tend to fill out their accounts of what they saw to make them more complete and coherent; they report details that did not occur, but that confirm their preconceptions of how a particular type of person would act, even reporting aspects of events that they could not possibly have seen (Loftus 1979).

The net results of much selective perception are sometimes called *priority effects*, whereby decision makers tend to persist in their prior viewpoints despite evidence that contradicts them. Conversely, however, when a spectacular failure in their past judgment of one or more past cases is traumatic enough to jolt them out of their past habits, as when someone they presumed was a safe risk for release commits a heinous crime, there are *recentness effects*; new decision rules then replace old ones, whether or not the new rules would be statistically supported by outcomes of typical cases. These, and many other psychological sources of misjudgment and research on them, are well summarized in Robin Hogarth's *Judgment and Choice.*

Subcultural Base Rates

The most distinctive feature of the compulsive proportioning of precaution, conspicuous in the New York tonsillectomy experiment described earlier in this chapter, is the tendency for all decision makers in a particular setting to make about the same proportions of each alternative type of judgment possible for them on a cross-section of cases. Because this is a collective phenomenon, it seems to require a sociological explanation. But it is also easy to infer a related psychological basis for it: any pattern of decision making is especially likely to evoke confidence if it appears to be the norm of one's occupational group in a particular work setting. This would explain the 45 percent tonsillectomy recommendations that physicians all unwittingly approximated in the New York study.

Wherever a number of officials routinely see approximately the same mixture of types of cases and react to one another's decisions on them, they tend to develop similar decision practices that might appropriately be called their occupational or workplace subculture. The subcultural norms create *base rates*, a statistics term that refers here to the percentages of a category of cases for which particular decisions are customarily made. Thus the physicians' base rate for tonsillectomy recommendations when examining elementary school children in the cited experiment was 45 percent.

The origin of subcultural base rates in the judicial system is indicated by David Sudnow's (1965) account of how, in a particular courthouse, the judges, prosecutors, and public defenders daily negotiate plea bargains. They develop shared conceptions of what constitutes a "normal" house burglary, street robbery, or other type of crime, as well as classifications of the types of moral character that differentiate offenders, and shared norms as to the appropriate penalty for each type of crime by each kind of person. As Littrell (1979) confirmed in a study of New Jersey courts, once such attorneys, who share the same workplace subculture, agree on the type of penalty that a defendant deserves, they adjust the charges to fit the penalty, rather than vice versa.

Norms as to the proportion of criminal cases settled by such plea bargaining rather than by trial, as well as norms on case dismissal rates, have been shown to vary greatly from one city to another, but to be relatively stable in each. Thus, James Eisenstein and Herbert Jacob (1977) found that in Detroit, 82 percent of convictions were by guilty plea, in Chicago 70 percent, and in Baltimore only 45 percent. But Baltimore and Detroit each dismissed 22 percent of the defendants, while Chicago dismissed only 12 percent. The authors ascribed this diversity to the fact that each city evolved different workplace relationships among court personnel, because each had pressures for particular patterns of court performance that reflected their somewhat contrasting histories of machine politics and of police department and prosecutor autonomy.

Martin Levin (1977) also found contrasts among courts of different cities, with only 28 percent of cases resolved by guilty plea in Pittsburgh, 56 percent in the District of Columbia, 85 percent in Minneapolis, but 62 percent in the Chicago courts that he studied. He also found divergence in rates of continuances, trial outcome, and almost all other parameters of court activities among these cities, yet much stability of each rate in each city for the several years that he traced them. He too ascribed these differences in base rates to the diversity of the political histories of these cities.

The clearest evidence of the stability of base rates in court dispositions of cases has been the failure of most efforts to alter these rates by mandatory sentencing legislation. Nelson Rockefeller, one of the most daring yet unsuccessful reform governors of a major state, spent a billion dollars in five years beginning in 1967 to cope with narcotic addiction in New York by coerced or rewarded treatment. When that did not work, he reversed the state's policy by getting the legislature to enact Draconian laws that prescribed mandatory long prison terms for even relatively minor narcotics offenses, prohibited plea bargains in these cases, and added judges to New York City courts to prevent their being clogged by the expected increase in trials. The effect was negligible, however, for plea bargaining and its base rates for disposition of such cases continued as always (Joint Committee 1977). Similarly, Loftin and associates (1983) show that a Michigan law to add two years to any felony sentence if a firearm was carried had no effect on sentences because plea bargaining produced traditional penalties.

Raymond Nimmer notes, in *The Nature of System Change* (1978), a review of other failed efforts to change the courts: "Prior judicial practice is not arbitrary, but reflects an accommodation of the interests of participants" (177). "Behavior norms in the judicial system," he adds, "define the reality with which practitioners have dealt and . . . in which the reform . . . is evaluated by the practitioner. . . . The success of the reform will depend on to what extent and how the reform fits into the system" (180).

Nimmer surmises at the close of his book that his conclusions probably apply to many types of organizations, in addition to the courts. In many people-changing agencies, as in the courts, there exists a wide distribution of discretion among interdependent personnel, with pursuit of one person's abstract goals or private interests likely to impede achievement of those of another. Therefore, innumerable trade-offs occur in case dispositions, so that each party's interests are usually achieved only in part. Their co-workers repeatedly caution new caseworkers to accept local norms, and as a consequence, caseworkers become cynical and disillusioned, as is well described by Neal Shover (1974).

While the stability of base rates suggests consistency, hence rationality in reaching decisions, the results of the tonsillectomy experiment are a reminder that too much stability may reflect a foolish consistency. Indeed, practitioners and observers of plea bargaining in the criminal courts frequently report that base rates are maintained partly by sequential exchanges of concessions between prosecution and defense; when the prosecution gets the sentences it seeks in a few cases, the defense claims that it is "owed" what it wants on few other cases. In many other organizations, decisions on a particular case do not depend only on its merits; classification and assignment of cases in mental health and correctional institutions, for example, frequently involves gratifying in turn the spokesperson for one unit who wants a particular type of resident, that of another unit who claims it already has its share of difficult persons, and still others of different units competing to confirm the adage that "the squeaky wheel gets the grease."

The norms of each of the various people-changing agencies set limits to the concessions that can be made to particular officials in the trade-offs described above, so that the disposition of cases usually is far from completely irrational. Nevertheless, in the mental health and criminal justice fields there have long been bitter complaints about the markedly disparate restraints imposed on ostensibly similar clients. Also, excessively cautious decisions are periodically exposed by studies which prove that little dangerous behavior follows when courts release, on legal technicalities, hundreds of people whom caseworkers had confined as dangerous (Steadman and Cocozza 1974; Thornberry and Jacoby 1979). Contrastingly, dramatic crimes by persons released as not dangerous, and public outrage at sentences or paroles that seem unusually lenient, have also sparked movements to make case decisions more consistent. Such pressures, as well as society's long-term trend toward an increase of what Max Weber (1922) called "formal rationality" in all organizations, have stimulated the development of a large variety of devices for enhancing the consistency of routine case decisions in many types of people-changing endeavors.

For more than thirty years, Herbert A. Simon, now a Nobel Laureate in economics, has been identified in the social sciences with the notion of *bounded rationality*. In successive editions of his *Administrative Behavior*, and in other writings, he drew on psychology and sociology to qualify the postulation in classical economics of a world of rational actors each making decisions that maximize goal attainment. Instead, he said, humans seek merely to "satisfice," to meet the level of goal achievement to which they customarily aspire. This level, that may not maximize but does satisfy in a particular workplace, is probably what is here called the subcultural base rate.

"The limits of rationality," Simon asserts, ". . . derive from the inability of the human mind to bring to bear upon a single decision all the aspects of value, knowledge and behavior that would be relevant. The pattern of human choice is often more nearly a stimulus-response pattern than a choice among alternatives" (1965a:108). Simon blames the incomplete knowledge, docility, poor memory, and force of habit of individuals, rather than group subcultures, for the limited goal achievement and imperfect rationality with which most decision makers are contented. Although he occasionally refers to group norms, he sees the group primarily as a formal organization that improves individual decision making by using authority to assign people to specialized roles and to coordinate their efforts. He points to the files of organizations as an improvement over individual memories, and he forecasts their still greater improvement by the computerization that can make routine case decisions more rational, but that would have less influence on nonroutine decisions (1965b). The examples presented in this chapter, and in the next, validate Simons' predictions.

Guidelines and Goals

Case decisions could readily be made more consistent if they conformed to a set of explicit rules. For example, if inmates were assigned to the separate units of a prison only on the basis of their age, number of prior prison terms, and years until parole eligibility, there should be few disagreements on their placement. If mental hospital patients were automatically released as soon as they completed, without new reports of clearly abnormal conduct, a specified period of confinement, decisions on their release would certainly seem to be more consistent than they now do. We currently rely on vague legal directives that they be released when they are not dangerous to themselves or to others, and that they are capable of self care or are assured of adequate care by others in the community.

To Ralph Waldo Emerson, "a foolish consistency is the hobgoblin of little minds." Would highly objective rules to keep officials from using personal discretion in case decisions produce only a foolish consistency? Or can case classification rules be devised that would make people-changing agencies more effective in achieving their goals? The answers to these questions depend on the particular decisions, rules, and goals involved and on how rigorously they are followed.

In the above examples of decisions on prison assignment or mental hospital release, a typical goal is to minimize risk that the client will subsequently be violent. Having this public safety concern, on which their job security greatly depends, officials typically reject proposals to make important case decisions purely by mechanical rules; they require personal assessments of each case by one or more experienced staff members with appropriate college degrees, who interview and test each client and study the case file and then make and justify decision recommendations. But such routine case analysts must make many difficult predictions from vague and uncertain evidence, hence they are prone to the many types of judgment errors detailed in the preceding section of this chapter and in John Monahan's *Predicting Violent Behavior.*

As leaders of people-changing organizations become concerned about the unreliability, inconsistency, or invalidity of the case study conclusions of their staffs, they usually develop some more or less definite case classification procedures or rules that will be referred to here as *decision guidelines.* These guidelines vary greatly in the decisions and goals that they address, in the research or assumptions from which they are derived, and in how mechanically they are applied. Nevertheless, all such guidelines help make explicit and consistent the contributions of specified types of case information to routine decisions. The crudest decision guidelines are simply forms that force staff to specify briefly all items that they take into account in reaching their decisions. Such forms, long used by many agencies, presumably enhance consistency in the types of deliberations that precede actions in separate cases. To assure that courts and parole boards are more rational in the use of information on such forms, Don Gottfredson and Leslie Wilkins have since about 1960 pioneered or inspired a tremendous amount of research on sentencing and parole decision guidelines (summarized in Gottfredson and Gottfredson 1980; Glaser, 1987). Their guidelines are directed at simultaneously maximizing achievement of two distinct goals: first, making penalties more consistent with what are presumed to be just deserts for each convict's crimes; and second, minimizing postrelease recidivism. This is illustrated by their most widely copied guideline, which is presented as table 6.1.

The offense-severity categories of the United States Parole Board's guidelines grade all federal crimes by what are presumed to be the just deserts that they warrant, but space permitted inclusion of only a few examples in table 6.1 The guidelines actually assign a severity level to every type of criminal lawbreaking. Thus the ratings for drug offenses include possession of less than ten pounds of marijuana as a *Low* severity crime, 10 to 49 pounds with intent to sell as *Low Moderate*, 50 to 199 pounds of marijuana or up to one gram of pure heroin or its equivalent opiate as *Moderate*, 200 to 1,999 pounds of marijuana or 5 to 99 grams of pure cocaine as *High*, a ton or more of marijuana as *Very High*, and more than a kilogram of pure cocaine or 50 grams of pure heroin as *Greatest I*. No drug crimes are *Greatest II*, but there are more drug offenses than those presented here in each of the other categories. These severity ratings were determined by statistical research to show the durations of confinement that the parole board had in the past imposed for each type of offense. Subsequently, however, the board at various times decided to reclassify some offenses from one category to another to express their changing views on what penalties constitute just deserts for some crimes.

TABLE 6.1
United States Parole Board's Guidelines for Deciding
Total ime of Confinement Before Release
(For adult male prisoners; per Hoffman & Adelberg 1980)

Offense severity (with examples of crimes in each category shown in parentheses below)	PAROLE PROGNOSIS (PER SALIENT FACTOR SCORES SHOWN IN PARENTHESES BELOW)			
	Very Good (9-11)	Good (6-8)	Fair (4-5)	Poor (0-3)
Low (property crimes such as theft or tax evasions of less than $2,000)	6 mos.	6-9 mos.	9-12 mos.	12-16 mos.
Low Moderate (property crimes such as interstate fraud of less than $2,000)	8 mos.	8-12 mos.	12-16 mos.	16-22 mos.
Moderate (property crimes such as interstate theft of $2,000-$19,999)	10-14 mos.	14-18 mos.	18-24 mos.	24-32 mos.
High (property crimes such as interstate theft or fraud of $20,000-$99,999)	14-20 mos.	20-26 mos.	26-34 mos.	34-44 mos.
Very High (property crimes such as interstate theft of $100,000-$500,000)	24-36 mos.	36-48 mos.	48-60 mos.	60-72 mos.
Greatest I (robbery, 3 or 4 instances; rape; voluntary manslaughter; arson)	40-52 mos.	52-64 mos.	64-78 mos.	78-100 mos.
Greatest II (murder; aircraft hijacking; kidnapping for ransom)	52 + mos.	64 + mos.	78 + mos.	100 + mos.

The "Parole Prognosis" columns in table 6.1 apply actuarial research for the board's goal of minimizing parole violations. Its prediction device is the salient factor score, which was presented in chapter 4 to indicate its possible application to base expectancy estimation, and will again be presented here. However, it may be well first to describe in more detail the research procedures by which such a predictive scoring system is developed.

For any outcome to be predicted (in the above example, success on parole, but it could be any goal sought in a routine case decision), a numerical scoring system is achieved by the following successive steps:

(1) For a research sample of past cases for each of whom the outcome is

known, compile statistics on the relationship to that outcome for all poten-tially predictive characterisics of these persons (henceforth called *variables* here) for which adequate and standardized data are available.

(2) Determine by statistical computation (multivariate regression) the set of variables that collectively is most predictive of that outcome.

(3) Assign points to each variable proportional to its contribution to this prediction (its beta weight).

(4) Divide each variable's points among its categories or ranges, from zero to the maximum points for that variable, in proporton to their predictive value for the outcome to be predicted. (In the salient factor score, each of the variables has a maximum score, and each category of that variable has a fraction of that score, from zero to the maximum, proportional to its value for predicting parole success.)

(5) Apply this scoring system to all cases in the research sample, so that each case gets a total predictive score.

(6) Compute for the cases with each score the percentage that has the outcome that is predicted (such as success on parole or aftercare, con-formity to institution rules, or any other outcome that is the concern of the routine decisions to be improved).

(7) Repeat this research on one or more other samples to gain confidence in the stability of the predictive scoring system.

Usually this last step, of validation and fine tuning, leads to a grouping of scores, such as "2 to 5" and "6 to 9", so that a prediction is made for the score group that is more stable in predictive accuracy than would be a prediction for each separate score.

Only seven predictors were used in arriving at the salient factor score because statistical research has demonstrated that after a prediction is de-rived by stepwise regression analysis from the relatively few items that separately are most correlated with outcome and least correlated with each other, more items add little to the accuracy of prediction. This occurs because each additional predictor is usually correlated with those already used, hence each is likely to add less to the table's total predictive accuracy than any that precedes it, but to add as much measurement error as any other predictor.

As is evident in its somewhat different presentation in chapter 4, the salient factor scoring to predict success of federal male parolees gives greatest predictive weight to the prisoner's:

(1) prior criminal offense convictions or confessions, juvenile or adult (3 if none, 2 if only one, 1 if two or three, and 0 if four or more);
Next greatest weightings go to three other aspects of the criminal record:

(2) number of prior institutional commitments (2 if none, 1 if one or two, 3 if three or more);

(3) age at the behavior that led to the first institutional confinement (2 if he was 26 or older, 1 if 18 through 25, 0 if under 18);

(4) he was never declared a violator or committed for a new offense while on parole or probation (1 point).
Thus, up to 8 of the 11 possible points on the salient factor score come from four indices of prior criminality. These findings on the optimum scoring factors, especially their penal confinement components, can be interpreted as support for a differential social learning explanation for criminality. One additional point is assigned to each prisoner if:

(5) the offense that resulted in the current prison commitment was not auto theft, check forgery, or check theft;

(6) the offender has no history of opiate dependence;

(7) the offender had verified employment or full-time school attendance for 6 months or more in total during his last two years in the community (the guidelines were only developed for males, who are well over 90 percent of all prisoners).

It is interesting that information in excess of an optimum not only fails to improve statistical predictions, but also fails to improve clinical predictions. In one experiment, seven experienced psychologists in the student counseling office of the University of Maryland were asked to predict the grade point score of forty randomly selected students with only four items of commonly used prognostic information on each, and then to make this prediction on the same students with eighteen additional items on each. Each psychologist separately (and collectively, with especially great statistical significance) was more accurate with four than with twenty-two types of information on each student (Bartlett and Green 1966).

The recommended periods of confinement are given in the body of table 6.1 for each combination of offense severity and parole prognosis. These time-range entries were initially derived from statistics showing the confinement terms imposed by the board in the past for offenders with the offense and personal characteristics indicated. On various occasions the recommended time ranges are altered by the board to express changes in the views of its members as to the appropriate duration of confinement. Of course, the differences in confinement terms from the top to the bottom of the columns, especially the first column for the "Very Good" risks, also reflect the statutory differences in length of confinement permitted for different types of crime; for petty theft of low severity there are upper limits to the sentences that may be imposed, and for each of the crimes of greatest severity, such as murder and aircraft hijacking, the laws establish a minimum penalty and sometimes no maximum.

Many people object to the idea that someone's fate may be determined mechanically by referring to a statistical table, instead of by considering all the unique human factors in each case. Yet the sentences recommended in Table 6.1 are not absolutely specific for any but the shortest terms; they usually show a range of discretion for each combination of offense severity and parole prognosis, so that parole board members may consider unique factors when fixing penalties. Indeed, even the range of confinement shown is only advisory; the board members need not conform to this advice, but usually choose to do so. If they impose a term of confinement that is outside the range prescribed, however, they are asked to record their reasons for the deviation in that case.

As mentioned in chapter 4's discussion of base expectancy tables, it has long been established that actuarial tables based on statistics that identify the correlates of outcomes in prior experience have almost always proven to have higher accuracy in predicting these outcomes than do clinical case study predictions. (The classic demonstrations are Meehl 1954 and Sawyer 1966; the most thorough rejoinder is Holt 1978, but it especially fails to challenge successfully the advantages of actuarial prediction for routine case decisions. See also: Glaser 1985).

A very useful aspect of the application of guidelines is the routine statistical monitoring of decisions made with them. At regular intervals, the U.S. Board of Parole receives from its research staff a tabulation of the actual confinement periods it has imposed on all cases that fit by offense severity and salient factor score each square in the grid of Table 6.1, as well as a list of the cases for each square in which the time imposed was outside the prescribed range, and the reasons that members gave for such deviations. The broad meets to discuss these data on its past actions, and when its deviations from the guidelines seem justified to most of the members, they may change a penalty range in the guidelines or the severity classification of an offense.

The model of the federal parole guidelines shown in table 6.1 has been adopted, although often with some alterations, by most state parole boards. Also, under the leadership of Don Gottfredson and Leslie Wilkins, analogous guidelines for judges' decisions in sentencing were developed for several state and city courts. Sentencing guidelines are usually somewhat different from parole guidelines because parole boards only consider people already sentenced to confinement, but in sentencing, judges may also impose nonconfinement penalties, such as probation and fines. An example of a sentencing guideline is provided in table 6.2. In this Denver application, separate guideline tables were prepared for each of the five levels of felony and three levels of misdemeanor in the Colorado Penal Code.

The main contributions of guidelines to rationality have been the following: to make explicit the basis for judicial or parole decisions; to keep most penalties for similar types of cases within a specified range; to reveal not only the frequency of deviations from the guidelines' range, but especially, the reasons for such deviations. This third contribution permits the decision makers promptly to be aware of shifts or of disagreements in their policies, and thus to consider and perhaps test atypical views more objectively and promptly than would be likely without the routine recording and compilation of deviant decisions and opinions.

When the reasons for penalties outside the guidelines' range is the belief that certain features of some offenders make them better or worse recidivism risks than their salient factor scores indicate, statistics can be compiled to determine the recidivism rates for such cases. In the unlikely event that these impressionistic prognoses prove more accurate than the

TABLE 6.2
Sentencing Guidelines for Type Four Felonies
in the Denver District Court
(Adapted from Wilkins et al., 1978)

Offense severity score	OFFENDER SCORE				
	− 7 to − 1	0 to 2	3 to 8	9 to 12	13 +
1-2	Out	Out	Out	Out	3-4 yrs.
3-5	Out	Out	Out	4-5 yrs.	4-5 yrs.
6-7	Out	Out	3-4 yrs.	6-8 yrs.	8-10 yrs.
8-9	Out	3-5 mos.*	3-4 yrs.	8-10 yrs.	8-10 yrs.
10-12	4-5 yrs.	8-10 yrs.	8-10 yrs.	8-10 yrs.	8-10 yrs.

*Refers to time in a work project, rather than in confinement.
Note: Type four felonies include manslaughter, robbery, and second-degree burglary. The term "out" refers to nonconfinement dispositions, such as probation, fine, deferred judgment, and deferred prosecution. All durations are for the maximum sentence; the minimum is always indeterminate, to be fixed by the parole board.

actuarial predictions, new actuarial tables can be computed with prognoses weighted to allow for the features taken into account by the superior case-study predictions. Thus, as Jack Sawyer (1966) stressed, clinical and statistical prediction should be thought of as complementary, each potentially improving the other.

Limits to rationality in sentencing and parole guidelines include vague and perhaps irrational goals for the decisions that they guide. Determination of just desert for a particular kind of offense is necessarily arbitrary; it cannot be proved valid by empirical research. Although surveys may indicate what judges, parole boards, or the public designate as just penalties for each kind of crime, they do not establish that the most frequently approved penalty is the most just. A just penalty is based on an arbitrary value judgment as to the evil inherent in an offense or in an arbitrary rule, such as making the offender suffer at least as much as the victim.

In contrast to the just-desert assessments, the offender scores at the top of tables 6.1 and 6.2 are testable as predictors of parole violation rates. Indeed, this salient factor system has been shown to provide highly dependable predictions (Hoffman and Stone-Meierhoefer 1979), and some statisticians claim that it can be made even more dependable (Wainer and Morgan 1982). Yet even if there were perfect predictions by these scores (instead of only an improvement on caseworker predictions for these subjects), the wisdom of the recommended penalties in these guideline tables would remain highly arbitrary for two reasons: first, there is little consensus on the goals sought in sentencing particular types of lawbreakers, as polls of judges, prosecutors and others show (e.g., Forst and Rhodes 1982). Second, there has not yet been adequate research on the effectiveness of alternative methods of pursuing those goals for which attainment is testable.

Goals in sentencing and parole that are officially proclaimed include the following: incapacitating dangerous offenders; deterring each separate offender from recidivating (special deterrence); deterring nonoffenders from becoming lawbreakers (general deterrence); rehabilitating offenders; imposing just deserts; its corollary, not imposing penalties that are excessive for the crimes committed.

Judges, parole board members, legislators, and others disagree on the relative importance to be given these goals in the abstract, and have further differences in their application to specific cases. Incapacitation and general deterrence tend to be stressed for murder, for example, but special deterrence and rehabilitation for petty theft; just deserts are sought for both of these crimes, but only petty theft evokes concern with avoiding excessive penalties. While all of these goals are manifest, a latent goal is economy— to achieve the manifest goals as cost-effectiely as possible. I have argued that pursuing crime prevention efficiently may be highly incompatible with the current emphasis on just deserts (Glaser 1984). The goal mixtures and the limitations of knowledge about what treatment of specific kinds of offenders best achieves the goals sought in sentencing them makes it unavoidable at present that the recommended penalties in guidelines such as tables 6.1 and 6.2 strongly reflect the collective judgments of past and current officials. This is evidenced in the statistics on their sentencing practices. More rigorously scientific guideline development requires both clear and definite decision goals and further evaluation research on the cost-effectiveness of alternative penalties and programs for achieving these goals with specified types of offenders.

Custodial Classification of Prisoners or Patients

Demonstrably effective formal devices for improving routine case decisions are most readily developed when focused on a single goal, the attainment of which is directly and quickly measurable. In most jails and prisons, and in many mental hospitals, prevention of violence or escape is the first consideration when deciding where a particular individual should be housed. Assignments to work, school, or other programs often cannot be made until custody level is determined. In this process, usually called *classification*, judgments on appropriate custody precautions traditionally stem from the study of case reports submitted by several staff specialists, such as psychologists, social workers, custodial officers, chaplains, and physicians. In many institutions these specialists meet as a classification committee to reach a collective decision on each case; in others the decisions are made by a senior official who receives the case-study reports.

Whenever inmate violence or escape rates increase, the classification procedures are likely to be revised. Forms frequently are developed to standardize the style in which salient considerations are summarized. Various decision rules may be promulgated that place custodial restrictions on persons with certain attributes, such as no outside work for persons with more than six months left before their expected release date. Increasingly, however, statistical guidelines are being developed for custodial classification at institutions that confine people.

In the California Department of Corrections, new male prisoners are received from the courts at two reception centers, one for the northern and one or the southern part of the state. At these places the new arrivals are interviewed, investigated, examined, and tested for about a month to determine to which prison they should be sent. On arriving at their next institution, all prisoners are interviewed by the casework staff to determine what housing and job assignments they should have, and periodically this process is repeated there to determine if the assignment should be changed or even if some inmate's transfer to another prison should be requested of state authorities. Transfer is usually sought for the most intractable inmates, but not for the others.

An analysis in the early 1970s showed that despite preparation of elaborate classification reports at the reception centers, and despite directives as to which type of inmate should be sent to each kind of institution, actual assignments were based mainly on where beds were empty in adequately secure facilities or where inmates with particular work skills were requested by an institution (Klempner 1976). An unpublished analysis in 1979 by the Department's researcher Norman Holt showed that this process had continued, but that in the interim the separate institution wardens had gained autonomy in keeping inmates. The net result, Holt found, was an almost random distribution of prisoners, except for the placement of each inmate gang into a separate institution in a vain effort to reduce violence. All the very secure institutions were overcrowded, and violence occurred in them at a high rate, but the prison camps and other less secure facilities were underfilled, despite their having their capacity defined at unreasonably low levels.

A long-term followup was made by Holland and Holt (1980) on caseworkers' classifications in 1968-72 of 293 prisoners received at the Southern Reception Center in the Chino prison. The caseworkers had rated each inmate on two ten-point scales, one for likelihood of being a serious disciplinary problem and the other on escape risk. There proved to be no significant correlation between the rating and the subsequent disciplinary record; there was only a marginally significant prediction of escapes. The researchers showed that both types of forecasting could be done more adequately from objective data on the inmate's age and prison confinement.

A multivariate correlation analysis by—Holt and associates (1981) identified and weighted the case record data that best predicted disciplinary problems during imprisonment. From this analysis of many variables, the following classification score system was developed:

Unfavorable Points:
1. Definite sentence length in years, minus one year, times 4 = (points)
2. Stability:
a. Under 26 years old at reception in prison (2 points)
b. Never married, legally or by common law, or marriage not intact (2 points)
c. Neither high school graduate nor high school equivalency diploma (GED) (2 points)
d. Not more than 6 months with one employer (2 points)
e. Never in military or not honorably discharged (2 points)

3. Prior escapes:
a. Number of walkaways or escapes, times 4 = (points)
b. Number of times breached perimeter or escaped in committing a crime other than escape, times 8 = (points)
c. Number of escapes with force, times 16 = (points)
4. Holds and Detainers (by criminal justice agencies requesting custody of inmate at his release from prison): Number in which a new prison sentence or deportation is likely, times 6 = (points)
5. Prior Sentences Served:
a. Number of jail or county juvenile detention terms of 31 or more days (not more than 3 counted), times 2 = (points)
b. Number of state level juvenile correction terms (not more than 3 counted), times 2 = (points)
c. Adult state or federal prison or civil addiction terms (not more than 3 counted), times 4 = (points)
6. Unfavorable behavior while incarcerated:
a. Number of serious or major disciplinary report in last incarcerated year, times 4 = (points)
b. Escape in last incarceration, times 8 = (points)
c. Number of physical assaults on staff, times 8 = (points)
d. Number of physical assaults on inmates, times 4 = (points)
e. Number of reports for smuggling or trafficking drugs, times 4 = (points)
f. Number of possession of deadly weapons reports, times 4 = (points)
g. Number of times reported for inciting disturbance, times 4 = (points)
h. Number of times reported to have caused serious injury or made a serious attempt to do so, times 16 = (points)
Favorable Points (to be deducted from Unfavorable Points)
1. Successfully completed last four months in any minimum custody setting or successful dormitory living in last incarceration (4 points) or, successfully completed minimum custody in last year of incarceration (8 points)
2. No serious or major disciplinary reports in last year of incarceration (4 points)
3. Full time work, school or vocational training of above average program in last incarcerated year (4 points)

When the unfavorable points are totaled and the favorable points are subtracted from them, the resulting net score determines classification into one of four custodial risk categories long used in California. These range from Level I, or minimum custody for those with less than 20 points who are to be housed in camps or in the unwalled prison at Chino, to those of Level IV or maximum custody, with 50 or more points, who are supposed to be in the San Quentin or Folsom prisons. Actually, when this system was initiated, inmates who scored at every security level were found in every facility that holds more than a hundred prisoners. As shown in table 6.3, a pretest of the scoring system on a sample of inmates classified by these points at reception, and followed up in their first year of confinement, revealed significant predictive power even in this brief testing period.

When the point system was applied in a weeklong dry run in 1980, the reception center caseworkers deviated from the scoring directives on prisoner placement in about half the cases, generally designating an institution of a higher security than the score indicated. This rate of deviation declined when they were required to document and justify to the research division any decision other than that which the score supported, with the research division later auditing the case and with a monthly check on the rate of exceptions. The fact that inmates now know of the objective basis for their custody level classification has greatly reduced their objections to their placements, and when they do appeal about the level at which they are classified, it is usually on an objective item of scoring that can be checked, rather than a challenge to the caseworker's subjective impressions of them.

Most noteworthy, there was a sharp drop in the overall escape rate, down to 0.47 per hundred, the lowest in two decades. Inmate assaults and homicides in prison also declined (Holt and Glaser 1985:359). The forestry

TABLE 6.3
A Preliminary Test of California Department of Correction
Classification Scores at Reception
as Predictors of Disciplinary Problems
(from Norman Holt, unpublished)

Custody level (and scores) Correlations	Average no. of disciplinary reports	Average no. of serious disciplinary reports	Most serious disciplinary points, average	Average days in lock-up	Average days of sentence credit lost	No. of cases
Level I (0-19)	1.0	0.5	0.4	2.9	1.4	126
Level II (20-29)	1.4	0.7	0.5	2.9	1.3	102
Level III (30-49)	2.5	1.3	1.1	13.5	2.7	111
Level IV (50 +)	2.6	1.8	3.5	64.5	7.4	17
Correlation of classification scores with disciplinary problems	.28	.33	.35	.31		
Correlation of custody level with disciplinary problems	.23	.23	.26	.26		

(All correlations are significant at the .001 level)

camps recorded the lowest escape rate in twenty years despite their simultaneously undergoing major expansion. The Prisoners Union, an ex-inmate and inmate organization with headquarters in San Francisco, tried to get a court order to block adoption of the point system, alleging that the scoring placed inmates arbitrarily and did not consider the fact that they want to be near their home communities. The court upheld the system for—as inmates seem generally to agree—it is less arbitrary than a caseworker's subjective judgment, and it still permits placement in one of the several facilities at each custody level that is nearest the inmate's home (actually, most prisons are not very close to large population centers). There is a routine, semiannual reclassification based on favorable and unfavorable points for prison behavior, and possibly on new holds and detainers or changes in the sentence. From the inmate's standpoint, the system's greatest deficiency is the relatively few favorable points that can be gained during confinement to offset unfavorable points assigned at admission.

California's classification procedure resembles the scoring systems adopted in recent years by the federal prisons and by the Oregon penal facilities, but each has unique features. Systems used less mechanically have provided less dramatic benefits than the California point system. One interesting variation in actuarial classification is the Assaultive Risk Screening System, initiated by the Michigan Department of Corrections in 1978, which is oriented primarily to the more remote objective of improving postrelease conduct rather than to California's focus on behavior while confined. Michigan's long-run perspective, which is more in the public interest, reflects the fact that its parole board consists of civil servants who are part of the same department that runs the institutions (as also occurs in Wisconsin and in most state youth corrections agencies, but not in other state or federal penal systems for adults in the United States).

The Michigan classification system's principal device is a configuration table that divides prisoners into assaultive risk categories, as shown in figure 6.1. This type of nonscore prediction table is discussed in chapter 4 (where its Massachusetts application to base expectancy analysis is described). The Michigan table, based on a three-year followup of released prisoners, was developed by analysis of the predictive value of over 400 items of information in the files on these prisoners. These were reduced to about 350 by eliminating some for redundancy and some because they were not reliably documented in the case files. Those used included both data on conduct in prison during the last confinement and prior background items.

After dissatisfaction with the results of a multivariate regresson analysis to predict parole violations classifed on a five-point scale of seriousness, the

FIGURE 6.1
Michigan Configuration Table for Assaultive Risk Screening
(per Michigan Department of Correction 1978)

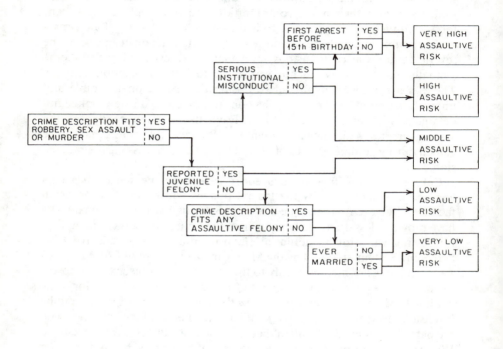

Michigan researchers used the Automatic Interaction Detector (AID) computer program (Sonquist 1970) to search for the sequence of dichotomies of cases on different variables that best predicted whether an assaultive felony was committed during the followup period. Such a felony was a difficult criterion to predict because of the low base rate of only 10.5 known to have committed these offenses in the time period covered. As table 6.4 shows, this procedure isolated the approximately 5 percent of the releasees of highest assaultive crime risk with which the department was most concerned, as well as the next most risky seven percent and the least risky 20 percent. Such tables are useful for making decisions because they isolate the high risk groups that cause the most concern, as well as the lowest risk cases for whom less security is needed.

TABLE 6.4
Michigan Assaultive Risk Screening Categories
(per Murphy 1980)

Risk Group	1971 Releasee Construction Sample		1974 Releasee Validation Sample	
	Failure rate (%)	Percent of sample	Failure rate (%)	Percent of sample
Very high risk: instant offense of rape, robbery, or homicide and serious misconduct or security segregation, and first arrest before age 15	40.4	4.9	32.0	4.2
High risk: instant offense rape, robbery or homicide and serious misconduct, and age over 15 at first arrest.	20.0	7.1	27.9	7.3
Middle risk: instant offense rape, robbery or homicide and no serious misconduct, or offense not rape, robbery or homicide and reported felony while juvenile.	11.3	46.8	17.4	50.7
Low risk: instant offense not rape, robbery or homicide (may be other assaultive crime), no reported felony while juvenile, and never been married at time of instant offense.	6.7	21.3	11.1	20.6
Very low risk: instant offense not rape, robbery or homicide, no reported felony while juvenile, and not serving on other assaultive crime, and has been married.	2.0	19.9	8.9	17.2
Total sample	10.5	100.0 (n = 2,033)	16.0	100.0 (n = 11.182)

A validation study (Murphy 1980) that followed up 1974 releasees for three years tested the predictive accuracy of various combinations of variables, but the AID search for an optimum sequence of dichotomies still produced the configuration shown in figure 6.1. In the 1971-74 interval, however, the three-year postrelease assaultive felony rate for Michigan prisoners rose from 10.5 to 16.0 percent, and the violation rate of all categories rose by about the same amount except for that of the very high risks, which regressed toward the mean violation rate. The small size of this group made it likely that chance variation influenced its rate more than the rates for the other categories. The 1974 study also showed that the contribution of marital history to isolating the very low risk group diminished, perhaps reflecting the smaller number of intact marriages in society. The percentage of the 1974 sample in the very low risk category would increase from 17.2 to 33.2 if marital status were excluded; its violation rate would then drop from 8.9 to 8.7 percent. This would leave only 4.7 percent of the cases in the formerly low risk category, giving it an only slightly higher violation rate than the middle risk group, so that the two could be merged.

The Michigan Assaultive Risk categories are used to determine the eligibility of prisoners for transfer to a halfway house, for release on furlough or on a pass to work or study in the community, and for other reductions in custody. It is also considered by the parole board in determining the release date. Prisoners classified as "very high" or "high" risks are notified that they are in this category within 30 days of their being so designated, and they have the right to appeal this label. Reclassification can occur if an error is shown in the information on which the risk rating is based. Even those in these high-risk categories are eventually eligible for furloughs and other temporary release, but only when they are very close to their parole or discharge dates and have a good conduct record during incarceration.

In addition, Michigan has a Property Crime Risk classification developed on the 1971 sample and replicated with the 1974 group used for the three-year followup study on assaultive risks. For the property crime risk study, however, all cases in these samples who had committed a violent crime in this postrelease period were eliminated before further analysis began. Property crimes are more frequent than assaultive offenses, and thus have a higher base rate. As table 6.5 shows, the AID program found early lawbreaking (arrest before fifteenth birthday) to be one of the best predictors of property as well as of assaultive crime, and it found that evidence of a drug problem is especially predictive of the property offenses. The property crime configurations divide cases into larger groups than does the violent crime configuration, and the property offense risk categories are more stable in replication.

Being in the high risk category for property crimes reduces an inmate's

TABLE 6.5
Michigan Property Crime Risk Categories
(per Murphy 1980)

Risk group	1971 Releasee Construction Sample		1974 Releasee Validation Sample	
	Failure rate (%)	Percent of sample	Failure rate (%)	Percent of sample
High risk: reported felony while juvenile, and major misconduct or reported felony while juvenile, no major misconduct, and age under 15 at first arrest	37.9	28.2	34.0	29.0
Middle risk: reported felony while juvenile, no major misconduct, and first arrest after age 15 or no reported felony while juvenile, and drug problem at time of instant offense	26.9	28.4	29.8	28.7
Low risk: no reported felony while juvenile, and no drug problem at time of instant offense	15.1	43.4	17.4	42.3
Total sample	24.9	100.0 (n = 1,820)	25.8	100.0 (n = 993)

release eligibility, but not as much as does the Very High assaultive risk classification. Thus, for eligibility for the Work Pass program (called "work release" or "work furlough" in most other states), prisoners may not have a very high assaultive risk designation or fit both the high assaultive and high property risk definitions. For family escort furloughs, eligibility requirements include no more than three years until release date for very low assaultive or low or middle property crime risks, no more than two years until release for low assaultive risk cases not serving currently for a violent crime, and for all others not serving currently for a violent crime, no more than one year until the release date.

Configuration tables, such as those used in Michigan (and those in Massachusetts presented in chapter 4), indicate the sources of risk assessments by the words that designate the particular combinations of variables involved, rather than by numerical scores alone, such as those of the federal and California guidelines. An official making a decision on an individual with the guidance of a configuration table can see at a glance which variables determined the table's predictions, and thus can judge how well that combination of variables fits each particular case. With a numerical score, however, the variables yielding the score are not immediately indicated, and may be a different combination for each of several cases that are in the same score group. Thus, the configuration table makes it easier to take into account for each case the distinctive features of those variables that are generally predictive. For example, if two individuals are placed in a high risk category largely because they both had an arrest and an incarceration at an early age, the decision maker who knows that this is a major factor in the risk determination can look into the grounds for arrests as well as the subsequent conduct of the two arrestees, on which the two cases may differ greatly.

Incidentally, all the California and Michigan objective classification procedures apply only to male prisoners. This gender differentiation occurs simply because only 3 to 5 percent of prisoners are female, and the women are more tractable than the men. Research on the records of women similar to that done for men would be necessary for development of guidelines to stabilize and rationalize classification of females in prisons and in other people-changing agencies.

Optimizing Community Caseload Assignments

Most clients of correctional and mental health agencies are not in institutions; they are supervised in the community on probation, parole, aftercare, or outpatient status. Most have been released conditionally, and can be institutionalized if their conduct seriously violates the rules imposed as conditions of their release.

Community caseworkers such as probation officers, parole agents and aftercare supervisors are supposed to assist these releasees and also to monitor them to determine as well as possible that they conform to the rules. Both the rules and the monitoring are imposed because of the presumed risk that some of the clients will endanger others or themselves.

Rational supervision in the community requires some classification of the clients by the relative risk of their serious misconduct. Those deemed most dangerous may then be monitored more closely than those deemed less dangerous. In addition, clients may be differentiated by the extent and nature of their needs, since some may be self-sufficient and require no help from staff, while others may need much aid.

Classification by risk and need permits a more rational allocation of cases to staff. For example, in determining workloads for probation, parole, or aftercare officers, releasees who need much surveillance or assistance should not be counted in an officer's caseload as equivalent to releasees who are low risks and self-sufficient, hence require little staff attention. Also, staff may be specialized in their skills or interests, with some particularly suited for monitoring high-risk cases, and others most competent for clients needing special types of assistance, such as vocational or family counseling.

Traditionally, the classification of probation, parole, or aftercare clients into risk and need categories has only been done impressionistically and informally by their supervisors, without precise rules. Such classification implies an assessment of risks, but as has been pointed out, research shows repeatedly that actuarial risk tables based on statistical analysis of past experience almost always have higher accuracy in forecasting rates of behavior for groups of offenders than do individual case-study judgments. The Division of Corrections of the Wisconsin Department of Health and Social Services has pioneered in statistical prediction research for probation and parole supervision, and its research products have been copied in several other jurisdictions.

To assure staff acceptance of its case classification tables, the Wisconsin officials involved their supervision agents (who have both probation and parole cases) in planning and conducting necessary research. The tables themselves were kept simple, and with an easily understood rationale. Especially important here, as in the prison classification systems, the forms for case classification were made to replace—rather than to supplement—other staff paperwork. Indeed, the concise and objective client classification forms for applying statistical risk tables to individuals usually are less work to complete than traditional case summary forms, and they are handier for later looking up facts on an individual. Finally, the Wisconsin officials deemed it important to plan that offenders under field supervision be reclassified every six months, with the initial assessment modified appreciably by staff's observation and investigation of the client's postrelease conduct. This keeps the agent's role in classification active, as it continually requires sophisticated field work and judgment to obtain new information rather than copying data from the files to fill out a new form.

Classification of Wisconsin probationers and parolees begins with an Assessment of Client Risk form. All but the last of the risk score factors on this form were derived by stepwise, multilinear regression analysis of past experience in the state, and these factors explain statistically 58 percent of the variance in criminal behavior of clients under supervision. The last item adds 15 points to the risk score of anyone with a record of conviction or juvenile adjudication for an assaultive offense in the preceding five years, thus expressing the state's outrage at violence. The form assigns risk-assessment points to each client as follows (with the references to address changes, employment, alcoholism or other past conduct, when applied to parolees, being for only the period prior to their last incarceration):

Number of address changes in last 12 months:
0 if none; 2 if one; 3 if two or more.
Percentage of time employed in last 12 months: 0 if 60% or more, or if not applicable (e.g., due to student status); 1 if 40 to 59%; 2 if under 40%.
Alcohol usage problems: 0 if not interfering with functioning; 2 if occasionally abused, or some disruption of functioning; 4 if frequently abused with serious disruption or need for treatment.
Other drug usage problems: 0 if not interfering with functioning; 1 if occasionally abused, or some disruption of functioning; 2 if frequently abused, with serious disruption or need for treatment.
Attitude: 0 if motivated to change, receptive to assistance; 3 if dependent or unwilling to accept responsibility; 5 if rationalizes behavior, negative, not motivated to change.
Age at first conviction or juvenile adjudication: 0 if 24 or older; 2 if 20 through 23; 4 if 19 or younger.
Number of prior periods of probation/parole supervision (adult or juvenile): 0 if none; 4 if one or more.
Number of prior probation/parole revocations: 0 if none; 4 if one or more.
Number of prior felony convictions (or juvenile adjudications): 0 if none; 4 if one or more.
Convictions or juvenile adjudications for any of the following crimes (including current offense, but total score not to exceed 5): 2 for burglary, theft, auto theft, or robbery; 3 for worthless checks or forgery.
Convictions or juvenile adjudications for assaultive offenses within last five years (an offense that involves the use of a weapon, physical force, or the threat of force): 15 if yes; 0 if none.

Table 6.6, based on the first two years of experience with this system of risk assessment, shows that these point assignments (excluding the 15 points for an assaultive offense) proved to be excellent predictors of probation or parole revocation. The assaultive offense points, however, added no predictive power to the score. Application of the Wisconsin Risk Assessment scores to 260 county probationers in Los Angeles also showed these scores to be highly predictive of outcome. Only 26 percent of those scored 15 or higher (not counting the aggression score) had a favorable supervision outcome, compared to 56 percent for those scored 8 through 14, and 87 percent for those scored still lower (Los Angeles County Probation Department 1982). For New York City probationers it predicted less well (Wright et al. 1984).

A form called Reassessment of Client Risk is completed when a client has been under supervision for six months and every six months thereafter

TABLE 6.6
Revocation Rate by Initial Risk Assessment Scores
for Wisconsin Probationers and Parolees, 1977-79
(based on Baird et al. 197 9: Table 1)

Initial risk score*	Number of cases	Percent revoked
0-3	543	0.9
4-7	1,124	2.5
8-9	492	5.7
10-11	387	9.8
12-24	432	12.5
15-19	498	15.7
20-24	362	26.0
25-29	252	37.3
30 and over	141	42.6
Total Sample	4,231	11.3

* Scores are aggregated here to the point where an additional increment in risk scores was accompanied by a significant increase in the revocation percentage, but the 15 points for a prior assaultive offense are not counted here.

during the total period of supervision. This form retains only five factors from the initial Assessment of Risk form, and it changes the weighting for four of these, but it adds seven others based entirely on the period since the last assessment. The five retained factors are:

1) Number of address changes in last 12 months:
weighting unchanged.
2) Age at first conviction or juvenile adjudication:
0 if 24 or older; 1 if 20 through 23; 2 if 19 or younger.
3) Number of probation/parole revocations;
0 if none; 2 if one or more.
4) Number of prior felony convictions or juvenile adjudications:
0 if none; 1 if one; 3 if two or more.
5) Convictions or juvenile adjudications for any of the following crimes (including current offense, and added for a total score):
1 for burglary; 1 for theft; 1 for auto theft; 1 for robbery; 2 for worthless checks; 2 for forgery.

The factors that are scored only on the period since the last assessment that are used in the Reassessment of Client Risk are as follows:

1) Percentage of time employed:
0 if 60% or more or not applicable (e.g., a student); 1 if 40% through 59%; 2 if under 40%.

2) Alcohol usage problems:
0 if no apparent problems; 2 if moderate problems; 5 if serious problems.
3) Other drug usage problems:
0 if no apparent problems; 2 if moderate problems; 5 if serious problems.
4) Problems of interpersonal relationships in the current living situation:
0 if none; 1 if few; 3 if moderate; 5 if severe.
5) Social identification:
0 if mainly with positive individuals; 3 if mainly with delinquent individuals.
6) Response to court- or bureau-imposed conditions:
0 if no problems of consequence; 3 if moderate compliance problems; 5 if has been unwilling to comply.
7) Use of community resources:
0 if not needed or if productively utilized; 2 if needed but not available; 3 if utilized but not beneficial; 4 if available but rejected.

The reassessment of risk scale differs from the initial assessment of client risk scale in that it is based more on opinions of probation or parole officers as to what factors should be considered, and on how they should be weighted, than on research evidence of its predictive validity. Regardless of its worth as a predictor, it at least fosters consistency in what factors agents deem important, and in their weighting of these factors, as contrasted to the traditional reassessment of risk by diverse and subjective case impressions of many officers.

The third case-classification device, introduced by Wisconsin Division of Corrections, is a needs scale, designed "to standardize the manner in which agents assess the problems and deficit areas of their clients" (Baird et al. 1979:11). It was developed by extensive consultation between researchers and experienced agents, and it was tested for eight months on incoming clients before a longer list of need categories was reduced to eleven, with scoring as follows:

Academic/vocational skills:

-1 if high school level or above; 0 if adequate for everyday requirements; 2 if low, causing minor adjustment problems; 4 if minimal, causing serious adjustment problems.
Employment:
-1 if satisfactory employment for one year or longer; 0 if secure employment, no difficulties reported, or homemaker, student or retired; 3 if unsatisfactory employment or unemployed but with adequate skills if unemployed and virtually unemployable, needs training.
Financial management:
-1 if long-standing pattern of self-sufficiency (such as good credit rating); 0

if no current difficulties; 3 if situational or minor difficulties; 5 if severe difficulties, which may include garnishment, bad checks, or bankruptcy. Marital/family relationships: -1 if relationships and support are exceptionally strong; 0 if relatively stable relationships; 3 if some disorganization or stress but potential for improvement; 5 if major disorganization or stress.

Companions: -1 if good support and influence; 0 if no adverse relationships; 2 if associations with occasional negative results; 4 if associations almost completely negative.

Emotional stability:
-2 if exceptionally well adjusted, accepts responsibility for actions; 0 if no symptoms of emotional instability or inappropriate emotional responses; 4 if symptoms limit but do not prevent adequate functioning (such as excessive anxiety); 7 if symptoms prohibit adequate functioning (such as lashes out or retreats into self).

Alcohol usage:
0 if no interference with functioning; 3 if occasional abuse, serious disruption, needs treatment.

Other drug usage:
scored the same as alcohol abuse, but 5 for most severe category.

Mental ability:
0 if able to function independently; 3 if some need for assistance, potential for adequate adjustment, mild retardation; 6 if deficiencies severely limit independent functioning, moderate retardation.

Health:
0 if sound physical health, seldom ill; 1 if handicap or illness interferes with functioning on a recurring basis; 2 if serious handicap or chronic illness, needs frequent medical care.

Sexual behavior:
0 if no apparent dysfunction; 3 if real or perceived situational or minor problems; 5 if real or perceived chronic or severe problems.

Agent's impression of client's needs:
-1 if minimum; 0 if low; 3 if medium; 5 if maximum.

An Assessment of Client Needs form is filled out whenever a risk assessment form is completed, that is, every six months. In addition to having a space for entering the points assigned to the client next to each of the eleven categories of need, there is a square at each category to be checked if the client should be given a referral for special assistance on that particular need. Finally, a Termination from Adult Field Caseload: Assessment of Needs form, without the recommendation of referral spaces, is completed when supervision of a client ends.

This regular assessment of needs permits a charting of changes in needs over the course of the supervision period. During the first six months on probation or parole there was an average decline of 9.2 points in the needs assessment score of those who initially scored 30 or higher; a drop of 6.6 points for those initially scoring 25 through 29; 4.4 points decline for those 20-24 points at first; 3.0 decline for those 15-19; and less than a point change for those initially scoring 14 and less. This suggests that there was considerable success in meeting the most serious needs.

A time study of the agents' supervision activities for individual cases indicated that average time varied closely with the needs scores, from 48 minutes per month for those scoring 9 or less to 186 minutes for those with scores of 30 or more. These data roughly validate the need scoring system. Although time allocations might have varied because of the agents' awareness of each client's total score, it seems more likely that the time devoted to a case is inspired by each officer's separate reaction to the perceived needs, rather than to the score.

Reliability of assessment scales ideally would be measured by separate investigation of the same cases by two or more officers and by their independently completing the forms. This, however, would be an imposition on the persons contacted for this purpose (such as employers, the clients themselves, and their families). Alternatively, groups of officers could conduct the investigations together but complete the forms independently. The Wisconsin researchers instead had some supervision officers tape-record their initial interviews with clients, then had other officers complete the Assessment of Needs forms after listening to these forty-five- to sixty-minute tapes. Nine tapes were presumed to cover a fairly representative sample of cases and were given to more than fifty officers, representing all areas of the state, who completed 449 forms. They averaged 87 percent agreement in their weighted average scores on the eleven separate categories, with over 90 percent agreement on scoring employment, financial management, alcohol usage, and drug usage. They had a low of 79 percent agreement in ratings of emotional stability and of mental ability. Apparently the need to supplement impressions from interviews was greatest on these lowest reliability items, but of course, in an actual assessment some supplementary information from the files and other sources would be available or would be sought.

The primary application of these risk and needs assessments is to a differential case management system. The assessment forms are to be completed by the supervising agents within thirty days of receiving a client on probation or parole. Each client is to be assigned the highest of three levels of supervision that is indicated by either scale. Thus, maximum supervision is given to those whose needs are assessed 30 or higher or whose risk is scored 15 or above. This means that all people with a record of assaultive offenses in the previous five years automatically receive maximum supervision for their first six months, since they initially are scored 15 on risk for this record alone. Medium supervision is prescribed for those with an 8 to

14 risk score and a 15 to 29 needs score or with one of these scores lower than this range, and minimum supervision is for all those with both scores below these medium figures.

Maximum supervision cases are supposed to receive at least one face-to-face contact by a representative of the agency every fourteen days, submit a monthly report, and have employment and residence checked at least monthly. They also receive home visits and other appropriate supervision. For medium supervision, the required frequency of direct contacts is once in thirty days, and for minimum supervision ninety days, with some minimum cases having the alternative of a mailed-in monthly report. Collateral inquiries or home visits are advised for any client whenever deemed appropriate.

To test the utility of this differential supervision system, the Wisconsin authorities initiated it as a quasi–experiment with a delayed treatment group as the control. Of the six supervision regions into which they divide their state for administrative purposes, the southern and eastern regions are very similar in demographic and criminological statistics. Therefore, this system was first introduced in the southern region, but the assessment scales were also applied to eastern region cases in the offices of the Bureau of Community Corrections without informing the eastern region agents of this classification system. These eastern region agents categorized their cases by a prior system with the same three levels of supervision, but with traditional case study impression rather than the objective score methods of determining the category to which a client was assigned. The researchers then matched each client from one region with a client from the other region on the basis of multiple criteria: age (within two years); sex; race; probation or parole status; supervision level; total risk score (within 3 points, but not across cutoff points for the supervision levels); total needs score (within 5 points, but not across cutoff points); risk score categories on age of first conviction, prior periods of supervision, and convictions for specific offenses; needs score categories on employment, alcohol usage, and drug usage.

As table 6.7 shows, Wisconsin's new system of classifying clients into three levels of supervision imposed rules on staff contact with clients that differed from their traditional requirements, in addition to using the objective scores for classification decisions. Traditionally the required minimum number of face-to-face contacts was one per month for all clients, regardless of how their supervision was classified. The increase under the new system to two contacts per month for maximum supervision cases was counterbalanced by a decrease to one contact every three months for minimum supervision cases, thus it did not greatly affect the total required number of contacts for most caseloads.

The table 6.7 figures show that this increased contact and/or the objec-

TABLE 6.7
Reported Criminal Activity of Matched Wisconsin Probationers and
Parolees with Guideline and Traditional Grading of Supervision
(Based on Baird et al. 1979: Tables 8, 9 and 10)

Level of Supervision:	Maximum		Medium		Minimum	
Method of grading:	Guidelines	Traditional	Guidelines	Traditional	Guidelines	Traditional
Minimum monthly contacts with client:	Two	One	One	One	One in Three Months	One
Percent with indicated misconduct reported (in 2-year followup):						
Any new offense:	17.7**	37.2	12.7	18.3	3.4	10.3
Felony (the most serious new offense):	10.6	16.8	5.6	2.8	0.0	0.0
Misdemeanor (the most serious new offense):	7.1**	20.4	7.0	15.5	3.4	10.3
Any arrests:	17.7**	39.8	14.1	18.3	3.4	10.3
Abscondence:	8.8	11.5	5.6	1.4	3.4	3.4
Any rule violations other than abscondence:	27.4*	40.7	21.3	14.1	1.7	3.4
Revocation of probation or parole:	10.6*	20.4	5.6	4.2	6.9	5.2
Number of cases:	113	113	71	71	58	58

**Difference significant at .01 level.
*Difference significant at .05 level.

tive case classification system significantly reduced the reported crime and other misconduct rates of maximum-level cases. The loosening of supervision for minimum-level cases apparently did not alter their misconduct rates and thus was cost-effective. It should be pointed out that more frequent contacts increase the probability that rule violations will be caught by staff; it seems that such possible fuller reporting from more contact with maximum level cases was more than offset by the crime reduction effect of more frequent opportunities for staff to assist or warn these clients in ways that reduced infractions. Possibly, however, the contrast in outcomes is partly a selection effect from the different bases for classifying cases as maximum level.

After the objective classification system was adopted throughout the state, approximately 250 agents kept detailed records for two months on the time that they spent on a randomly selected ten cases each. This study showed slightly more time per case in rural than in urban regions, but an average of about three hours per month for maximum-level cases, one hour for medium, and a half hour for minimum-level cases. These times spent were then made the basis for standards establishing normal workload, except that about 20 percent more time was authorized for medium- and minimum-level cases, plus nine hours for a presentence investigation, eight hours for probation social investigations, eight hours for admission investigations, and five hours for all partial investigations. Therefore, an agent with many maximum-level cases to supervise or many presentence investigations to conduct would be given fewer total cases than another agent with mostly minimum-level supervision and few investigations. Of course, the workload budgets also take into account other time demands, such as those for administrative tasks and professional development.

The main points to be learned from the Wisconsin experience are that a more rational system of routine classification of community supervision cases not only leads to more consistency in staff practice, but apparently reduces recidivism rates for the maximum-level cases, and even contributes to a more equitable distribution of staff workloads. However, as Clear and Gallagher (1983) conclude from their survey of its application in other jurisdictions, optimal use of this classification system requires a complex analysis of both the different distribution of risks and needs of clients in various communities and the diversity of staff concerns in these locations.

Conclusions

Routine case decisions in people-changing organizations are prone to a variety of errors, including excess conservatism and selective perception, as well as both priority and recentness effects. Nevertheless, case decision makers are likely to be overconfident in their judgments as they compulsively conform to established base rates for proportions of alternative decisions. These base rates become part of their workplace subcultures and reflect a not easily changed balance among pressures for various types of actions there.

Decision guidelines make explicit the contribution of different types of information to routine case decisions. Those developed for parole and sentencing in the United States specify a range of discretion for officials in most cases, and also permit some decisions outside this range, but require a statement of the reasons for any such deviant rulings. It is important that actual decision patterns be tabulated statistically at regular intervals so that officials can promptly be aware of their drifts and disagreements.

Actuarially derived guideline tables that are applied quite mechanically, permitting officials little discretion to deviate from the recommended decisions in the tables, can make routine case actions more effective in achieving a single measureable goal. This has been demonstrated in classifying prisoners for assignment to different custodial security conditions to reduce escapes and disorder, which can produce safer use of all placement resources, including more use of minimum-security facilities without sacrificing safety. A less mechanical system also fosters more effective case supervision on probation or parole.

Routine decision making based on actuarial rather than case-study predictions is likely to expand in the future for the following reasons: the purposes of routine decisions are being made more explicit; more and more, these purposes are likely to become the goals for which attainment is measurable, such as maximizing benefit-cost ratios; and computerized record keeping is making easier and more accurate the development of actuarial prediction tables that show goal attainment rates with alternative decision possiblities. A national survey of the use of formal classification systems in all types of criminal justice decisions concluded in its 1979 report that their use "has increased substantially over the past two decades" (Bohnstedt and Geiser 1979:Vol.5,p.26). Gettinger's 1982 article, called "'Objective' Classification: Catalyst for Change," reports the spread from one state to another of point systems for custodial classification of prisoners, often without research being done on their applicability to the new settings. Yet, he asserts that reliance on these devices increased several fold the number of prisoners placed in minimum custody without increasing the escape rates. It seems highly probable that the application of actuarial guidelines for routine decisions in a large variety of people-changing organizations could be cost-beneficial, but such applications should be based on careful research to develop the optimum statistical guidance for each type of decision in each setting.

For nonroutine decisions, such as choice among long run agency objectives or selection of a site for a new institution, there is not enough experience with the same type of decision in the past to permit development of actuarial tables. Nevertheless, as will be shown in the next chapter, formal procedures are available for more rational solutions to such problems.

7

Multiattribute Utility Evaluation: Combining Values, Knowledge, and Subjective Inferences in Nonroutine Decisions

Both personal and organizational decisions generally involve multiple goals, with disagreements as to their relative importance and different degrees of certainty about achieving each. Further impeding rationality is much uncertainty about some relevant facts. In difficult decisions there are almost always some questions for which the only feasible answers depend to some extent on guesswork. Therefore, strident debate often occurs when an agency must choose among alternative possible actions or policies in a complex, changing, and uncertain world.

Multiattribute utility evaluation is a procedure developed primarily by Professor Ward Edwards (a psychologist at the University of Southern California) and his associates to facilitate a group's reaching consensus in complex decisions, or minimally, to clarify the basis for disagreement or uncertainty (Edwards et al., 1975). It is a method of systematically specifying: the various goals that a decision is most likely to affect; their relative importance; and the estimated probability of achieving them by each of the alternative possible decisions. The version of this procedure to be presented here most closely resembles that given the acronym SMART, for Simple Multiple Attribute Rating Technique (Gardiner and Edwards 1975), but it is reformulated somewhat here, adapting some features of what is called MAUT—Multiattribute Utility Technology (in Edwards and Newman 1982, and in von Winterfeldt and Edwards, 1986). Therefore, the procedures to be presented here will be called SMARTS—Simple Multiattribute Rating Technique Supplemented.

Buying a Car

The ten steps involved in SMARTS will first be presented in an extra simple form for a decision made in everyday life, choosing which brand of automobile to buy. This will provide a quick overview of the formal procedures before their application to more complex decisions of people-changing agencies. The steps are:

1. Identify the Issue on Which a Decision Must be Reached.

In this case it is simply to buy an automobile. We shall assume that it has already been decided that this should be a four-door sedan of small-medium size.

2. Identify the Most Concerned Stakeholders in the Decision and Recruit Their Cooperation.

Usually all the prospective drivers of a car have a stake in the choice; sometimes it is only one individual, but sometimes there are several drivers in a family business that is making the purchase. In addition to involving those most affected by the decision, it may be useful to recruit some expert advisors on the factual questions that arise in assigning utilities. Thus, in the automobile choice, it may be useful to hire a consultant, such as a mechanic not connected with any automobile dealer (however, some scientific purchasers may prefer to consult research reports, such as those of Consumers Union, suspecting that so-called experts are biased by personal prejudices).

3. Identify the Decision Alternatives.

To simplify this example, let us presume that we live in a small town with only three automobile dealers, and we have decided to limit our choice to three lower-priced, medium-sized, American-made automobiles: the Chevrolet Celebrity, the Ford Tempo, and the Dodge Aries.

4. Determine the Values by Which the Alternatives Should be Assessed.

Values can be thought of as the goals to which a decision is directed. The stakeholders are important here, since they are each asked to write out separately all the values that they think should be considered in making this decision, and then to discuss their lists collectively to produce a single list of what they agree are the most important values. In this example we shall say that they agree on Style, Economy of Operation, Comfort, and Dependability. Of course, such other values as low initial price may also be mentioned by some people, but in this case that factor can be neglected because it will be assumed that the initial prices for these three cars are about the same, and that there is no trade-in car for which dealers might offer different amounts.

5. Rank the Values.

Let us assume that the stakeholders in this particular decision ranked dependability first, comfort second, economy of operation third and style fourth.

6. Assign Relative Importance Weights to Each Value, But Make the Sum of the Weights Equal 1.0.

We shall assume that the stakeholders decide to weight dependability 0.4, comfort 0.3, economy of operation 0.2, and style 0.1. Of course, individual stakeholders may rank and weight the values differently. If there is only one person involved in this car purchase, that is no problem, but if there are several, a feud may develop. It is important to settle any differences by some sort of compromise or vote before proceeding from one step to the next, but stakeholders should make note of the nature of the disagreements since it may be possible to reconsider and resolve some of them later.

7. Estimate the Utility of Each Decision Alternative for Attaining Each Value.

Here the stakeholders are called upon to rate the three cars on how well they are likely to provide the four values—comfort, dependability, economy of operation, and style. Usually this is done by picking a specific range, such as 10, assigning the maximum to the alternative that has the greatest utility for attaining that value, and zero to the lowest, and assigning a figure for each of the others indicating its relative utility compared to those highest and lowest in utility scores. Thus, after consulting the manufacturer's specifications, Consumers Union, and other reports, as well as developing personal impressions, the stakeholders may talk it over and reach a consensus or compromise on the utilities indicated in table 7.1. Of course, on style, the utilities they assign are a matter of taste, whereas on economy of operation, they may rely on official gasoline mileage data, and on dependability, they may consult the repair records for past models of each car as reported by Consumers Union from its annual membership experience poll.

TABLE 7.1
Calculation of Decision Weights in the Automobile
Purchase Example
(I = Importance weight; U = Utility; W = IxU)

Model of automobile	VALUES AND THEIR IMPORTANCE WEIGHTS				Total decision weight (W)
	Depend- ability	Comfort	Economy of operation	Style	
	I = 0.4	I = 0.3	I = 0.2	I = 0.1	
Chevrolet Celebrity	U = 0;W = 0	U = 10;W = 3	U = 0;W = 0	U = 5; W = 0.5	3.5
Dodge Aries	U = 8;W = 3.2	U = 8;W = 2.4	U = 8;W = 1.6	U = 0; W = 0	7.2
Ford Tempo	U = 10;W = 4	U = 0;W = 0	U = 10;W = 2	U = 10; W = 1	7.0

8. Calculate Decision Weights (Products of the Importance Weight of Each Value by the Utility Assigned Each Decision Alternative on That Value).

These weights, shown in table 7.1, integrate the information and judgments reached by the decision stakeholders.

9. Total the Decision Weights for Each Alternative and Consider Their Implications for the Final Decision.

Presumably the alternative with the highest total decision weight is the one to choose. However, if two or more of the choices are very close, you may want to review the decision. Indeed, review is always desirable to assure accuracy, even if the alternatives at first seem to have very different total decision weights.

10. Review the Determination of Weights and Utilities, as Well as the Total Decision Process, to Consider Possible Modification of the Conclusion Suggested by Total Decision Weights.

Now is the time to consider whether the margin of error is probably greater than the differences in final weights, whether more complete or accurate information might alter the utilities assigned, or whether in the light of the close final weights some of the earlier disagreements in subjective judgments on some values or utilities should be reconsidered. For example, since figure 7.1 shows that the Dodge and the Ford are very close in final decision weights, the husband might decide to be gallant and make a concession to his wife's wish to give greater importance to style and hence buy a Ford.

Multiattribute utility analysis may be applied to almost any type of decision, for example, to buying a computer, hiring a new superintendent, creating a new office, closing a mental hospital or abolishing parole. It may help to monitor a program, such as a staff-training program, by helping stakeholders to choose among alternative ways of assessing how adequately it is achieving a set of goals. This method of evaluation may also aid in selecting, continuing, altering or abandoning a program ("program" is used here very broadly to refer to any endeavors, practices or policies to be assessed). It can be applied to evaluating past decisions, current activities, or future plans. Of course, it is only worth the effort if the decision is important and difficult, but as will be evident, it can be done on a large or a small scale, depending on how much time and effort seem feasible for the problem. Even small-scale applications will usually improve upon less systematically analyzed decisions.

The use of multiattribute analysis has already been reported for a tremendous diversity of problems, for example: judging the quality of drinking water; assessing the combat readiness of Marine battalions; choosing among alternative urban development plans; selecting methods of controlling the budworm pest in East Canadian forests; picking one of the several possible trajectories for the Mariner satellite's fly-by of Jupiter and Saturn; deciding on policies for management of salmon in the Skeena River; and choosing sites for nuclear power plants. However, none of the completed applications resolve decision-making problems of the criminal justice or mental health systems, although a few have made some exploratory steps in this direction (Edwards 1980; Edwards and Newman 1982).

Two hypothetical problems in correctional administration, one a matter of broad policy, and the other a simpler operational choice will now be analyzed.

Expanding Prisons or Expanding Halfway Houses

Let us proceed again through the steps delineated in the example of buying an automobile but apply them to a broad policy issue confronting a people-changing organization. This will make some of these steps seem more complicated than they were in the previous example.

1. Identify the Issue on Which a Decision Must be Reached.

Most of our states and the federal government have the problem of coping with extreme crowdedness in their prisons. They have little ability to alter the increasing proportion of lawbreakers on whom the courts impose imprisonment or the longer duration of penal sentences. For purposes of our analysis, this issue can first be simplified by reducing it to two alternatives for any government:

a. Only expand the capacity of its prisons.

b. Only expand the capacity of its halfway houses.

These houses are generally in large cities, and are either old hotels, rooming houses, or structures converted to resemble rooming houses. Prisoners are transferred to them in the last few months before parole or discharge from confinement. They leave these abodes daily to work, seek work, or attend schools, and they are given passes for evening and weekend recreation or family visiting at an increasing rate as their date of parole discharge approaches. For misconduct, however, they can be denied passes or even returned to prison. When employed, they pay the state for room and board. Let us assume that in this correctional system, only 3 percent of the prisoners are in halfway houses at any time, but because they stay there no longer than the last three months before parole, about 10 percent are released through these houses rather than directly from prison. To avoid building more prisons, about 90 percent of the prisoners could be released through halfway houses by having about 10 percent spend the last eight months to a year of their confinement time there, about 40 percent the last four to six months, and 40 percent the last one to three months.

2. Identify the Most Concerned Stakeholders in the Decision and Recruit Their Cooperation.

SMARTS is useful whether a decision is made by one person or many. It is simpler to carry it out with only a few persons, such as a board of directors or a special committee. If they are paying a researcher, it may be appropriate for them to work with him or her. However, it is often unwise to make a decision without the views of all who have much stake in it, especially if their support and cooperation is valued. For decisions having broad policy implications that may concern many organizations, it is wise to have a large range of stakeholders; for internal decisions within an organization, a few key people may suffice.

When there are too many people who could help greatly in making the decision for all to be recruited, a representative should be sought for each influential group likely to have a distinct viewpoint on the issue. These stakeholders should be familiar with the issue and respected in the groups for which they speak. It is not so crucial that participants be representative of the total population of stakeholders as that they represent all the people who will be much affected and all the highly influential points of view.

Thus, to decide whether to expand prisons or halfway houses, it would be well to seek inputs from judges, prosecutors, police agencies, defense counsel, correctional officials, taxpayers, and possibly even ex-offender groups to identify and weigh the relevant values and utilities. If, in any of these groups, strong pro and con positions are evident, both viewpoints should be represented. Of course, the number of participants in any of the steps in SMARTS must vary because of limitations in time, in their availability, or in funds that may be required for their compensation. Yet confidence in a decision and public support for it is likely to be increased if it is perceived as the product of a broad range of competent contributors.

3. Identify the Decision Alternatives.

It is useful to identify all choices that may be seriously considered. However, for some problems, such as that analyzed here, there are so many possible gradations that it is best to formulate the issue first in terms of extremes, as was done in step 1. Of course, you may also begin with a problem for which no clear alternative solutions are formulated in advance. For example, what should the schools do about juvenile delinquency? With such a problem, it may be best to begin by gathering a group of concerned and informed stakeholders and possibly some consultants to discuss and revise statements on the distinct alternatives worth considering. Yet any list of alternatives should be limited at first to a few high-contrast ones, all of which are seriously considered. Analysis of the high-contrast proposals considered here for coping with prison crowdedness may provide a basis for deciding in step 10 on a politically more realistic possibility, such as much expansion of halfway houses and some expansion of prisons as well.

4. Determine the Values by Which the Alternatives Should be Assessed.

As demonstrated in the automobile example, a useful procedure is to ask the recruited stakeholders to identify all separate actors that would greatly concern them in deciding which of the alternatives is best. The values suggested initially are likely to overlap, and they will differ in degree of abstractness, with several concrete ones sometimes subsumable under one that is more abstract. There will be a mixture of language styles in the initial formulation of values by several people, but some of the items can be rewritten or deleted because they say the same thing as another but in different words. They should also be logically grouped by level of abstractness. After some editing, the factors you are likely to get in our policy problem may well include those grouped in the following logical clusters, which are also shown in figure 7.1. This is a *value tree* on its side; its "top" is the long line on the left. The more abstract values are placed and lettered so that they are over their more concrete components.

A. Public Protection
Aa. Incapacitation: Imprison felons so that they cannot commit new crimes in the community, but also place them in halfway houses during their first few months of freedom so that they will be under closer surveillance than they would be if released by parole or discharge.
Ab. Deterrence
Aba. General Deterrence: Impress nonoffenders that crime does not pay by imprisoning felons for all of their sentence (or for all less time off for good behavior in prison).
Abb. Special Deterrence: Impress each offender that if reimprisoned for new crimes, he/she will not serve the last part of the term in a pleasant halfway house.
Ac. Testing.
One can argue that the risk of paroling prisoners is not revealed nearly as well by their behavior in prison as by their conduct when in a halfway house, from which they depart into the community.
Ad. Crisis Aid
Halfway-house residents are less likely than prison releasees to feel desperate and forced back to crime as soon as they run out of money or out of companions. In the halfway house there are always shelter, food and companionship to fall back on, as well as a staff that can often sense when a resident feels desperate and then provide emergency control or assistance.
B. Rehabilitation
Ba. Crisis Aid.
Availability of aid in early crises increases a prisoner's prospect of learning how to cope with difficulties without resorting to crime. This example, in which Ad and Ba are identical, is given mainly to show that a more concrete value may sometimes fit under more than one abstract value.
Bb. Counseling
Advice by counseling specialists or other staff, and simply the presence of a readily available sounding board and legitimate role model, are likely to be more influential in a halfway house where the client is encountering real problems of life in the community than in a prison where he or she is only imagining them, often unrealistically.
Bc. Decriminalize Social Climate
In a prison the most aggressive and outspoken criminals tend to create a social climate that pressures all inmates to act tough and like a criminal to avoid being derided and victimized by the others. This climate can be changed considerably in a halfway house where there is preoccupation with success in legitimate pursuits, contact with the noncriminal world, and easy interaction with staff.

FIGURE 7.1
Value Tree for Factors in Decision on Expanding Prisons or
Expanding Halfway Houses

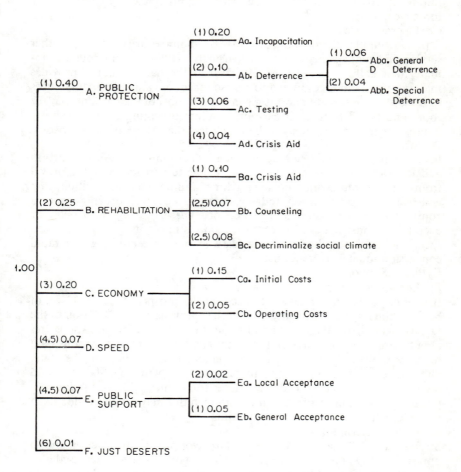

C. Economy

Ca. Initial Costs

Halfway houses cost much less to build, lease, or purchase than a maximum security prison, for the latter often require $50,000 to $90,000 per inmate capacity.

Cb. Operating Costs.

A prison's employees, including twenty-four-hour security force plus other service and management personnel, usually are more numerous per inmate than halfway house staff. However, if the halfway house provides many services and is compared to a prison farm or camp, these differences in personnel per inmate may disappear. Yet, if most of the residents pay for room and board from their earnings, the net operating costs of halfway houses per inmate are likely to be much less than those of most prisons.

D. Speed

Five to ten years usually elapse between a decision to build a new prison and its readiness to receive prisoners. Separate and sequential approval from the legislature must be sought for planning, land acquisition, and construction, with each step today generating prolonged hearings on area zoning and on environmental protection. These hearings may delay or even block construction. In contrast, administrators usually do not need special legislative authorization to lease or purchase buildings for rapid conversion to halfway house use.

E. Public Support

Ea. Local Acceptance

It is often important to take into account the prospect that neighbors of halfway houses and of prisons will mobilize protests against location of the facility near them. Politicians and community service organizations frequently are very influential in these matters. For this reason, prisons tend to be built in remote places and on land already owned by the state, although such locations reduce inmate contacts with their families and increase operating costs. Halfway houses sometimes minimize public opposition by locating in urban slums, although this may involve residents in crime, either as participants or as victims.

Eb. General Acceptance

Strong "law and order" advocates tend to favor prison construction and to oppose halfway houses, although they are also often against increased government spending and become appalled at the cost of prisons. There is also organized lobbying for a moratorium on prison construction.

F. Just Desert

An increasingly revived classical point of view in legal philosophy, is that punishment should be determined only by the wrong done by the offense, and not by the attributes of the offender. This perspective seeks to give each criminal the penalty that his or her crime deserves, without the utilitarian considerations of individual deterrence or rehabilitation (von Hirsch 1976; Singer 1979; for a criticism of this view, see Glaser 1984). Most spokespersons for such values seem to advocate definite prison terms, but they might accept halfway houses if inmates were assigned to them by offense alone, in accordance with an assessment of these houses as lesser penalties for less serious crimes.

It should be evident from these first four steps alone, that SMART can contribute much to decisions simply by fostering systematic thought about the values that should be considered. The logical relationships among these values can be represented by a *value tree*, such as that of figure 7.1.

The values in such a tree are traced down from the top: the most abstract values are in the top row, the next most abstract in the row below that, and so forth. The lines that move downward are called *branches*, their division points are *nodes*, and the last segment of each branch is a *twig*. The twigs identify the final value distinctions made in a particular tree. These may sometimes be abstract, such as speed and just desert, but include all those that are most concrete. In the discussion above, explanations are given only for the twigs, on the presumption that the more abstract values above some of them, such as deterrence over general and special deterrence, are adequately explained for our purposes here by the explanations for the twigs under them. In some problems the more abstract categories would require explanation, as would the more concrete ones under them.

5. Rank the Values

If there is more than one row in the value tree, all values in the top row are ranked first, then each cluster of values in the next row that are under a single value are ranked separaely, as shown in figure 7.1 by the numbers in parentheses. The stakeholders are asked to do this after they have finished identifying the distinct values in step 4. Sometimes domination of collective discussion by a few is reduced by asking the stakeholders to write their rankings separately on a sheet of paper containing the value tree. Then the average rankings assigned to each value are discussed, and perhaps are modified slightly. The value ranked as most important is, of course, assigned the rank of 1, and the others ranked in sequence, with a strong effort made to avoid ties in ranks. However, if there is near consensus that two or more values are equally important, each gets the average of the rankings they would get if ranked in sequence. Thus, if there is agreement that two values are tied for third rank, the sum of three and four divided by two, which is 3.5, is given to both of them; if three are considered tied for fifth rank, the sum of five, six, and seven divided by three, which is six, is given to all three of them, and none is ranked five or seven. Figure 7.1 shows, in parentheses, the rankings of a hypothetical group of stakeholders.

6. Assign Relative Importance Weights to Each Value, Making the Sum of Weights on the First Row Equal 1.0 and the Weights in any Set on Subsequent Rows Equal to the Weight of the More Abstract Value Above the Set.

The instruction for this step is now somewhat different than it was in the automobile example, to take into account here the possibility of a value tree with more than one row. Indeed, when there is only one row there may not be much benefit from drawing a value tree, which is why it was not done for the four values of the automobile purchase decision. The importance weights in figure 7.1 are those without parentheses, presumably assigned by our hypothetical stakeholders.

In assigning these importance weights, one procedure is to begin with the twigs, the final items, regardless of the row on which they are located, and decide which is least important, assigning it an arbitrary number, perhaps 10. The next least important is then assigned a number indicating the proportion of its importance to that of the lowest ranked one, perhaps 15 or 20. Then the third least important is assigned a number comparing its importance to those suggested by the numbers assigned to the ones below it, perhaps 40. This is continued until all of the twigs have numbers, but not the items above them. These numbers are now summed, and each s divided by their sum, which will yield a decimal figure less than 1.0, and the sum of these figures will be 1.0. When these decimal weights are given to each twig to replace the whole numbers, the decimal weight assigned to a more abstract value that is above a set of twigs is the sum of the weights of the twigs below it. The results of such a calculation process (called normalization in the cited works by Edwards) are shown in figure 7.1, rounded to eliminate decimals beyond two places. However, the weights could be assigned in decimals to begin with, provided you check continually that the weights for all of the twigs add up to 1.0, that the weights on the top row of the tree also add to 1.0, and that any set of twigs under a more abstract value has weights that add to those of the more abstract value.

If the ranking and importance weightings are done by a group of diverse stakeholders, there may be a lot of disagreement regarding the relative importance of different values, such as public protection versus rehabilitation. But this disagreement is often on the prospects of attaining the value with a particular alternative, such as rehabilitation in a prison. The value should be ranked according to the importance its attainment would have in the decision alternative where it is most likely to be attained. Thus, a person who thinks rehabilitation is wonderful but that it is unlikely in either a prison or a halfway house should rank and weight it as not a very important consideration or this particular decision. If this person regards it as more attainable in a halfway house than in prison, its weight should be based on the importance of its probable attainment in a halfway house.

If disagreements on values among stakeholders are great and are intensely felt, it is likely that there will be discontentment with the final decision that results from the procedures described here. Therefore, it is important to encourage open minds in the stakeholders, and continuous discussion, reorientations, consultations, and further discussion in an effort to reach consensus. If final weights are only attainable by averaging sharply contrasting recommendations of different stakeholders, it is desirable to keep a record of the divergent views to indicate who is likely to disagree with the recorded weights and why. Often these disagreements can be reduced in discussions at later stages in the procedure, especially in step 10.

Whenever the initial weighting is completed, but not before, it is usually wise to delete the values that have been given very low weights, since they are of trivial importance for the decision. Thus, in figure 7.1, "just deserts" with a weight of only .01 could certainly be deleted. Sometimes it is appropriate to designate a minimum weight worth retaining, such as .05, and to delete every twig with less than that weight.

Whenever twigs or branches are deleted from a value tree, it is necessary to distribute the importance weights of the deleted items among those that are retained. This redistribution need be neither equally among the remaining items nor in proportion to the weights of the remaining items; if a deleted item seems logically close to one that remains, the weights of the two can be combined, or the weight of the deleted value can be divided among several others that are logically close to it or seem undervalued. Figure 7.2 shows figure 7.1 revised to have a .05 cutoff point, with weights redistributed logically.

7. Estimate the Utility of Each Decision Alternative for Attaining Each Final Value (Twig).

Each decision alternative identified in step 3 must now be evaluated for its ability to achieve each of the values specified in step 4. For this purpose, you begin with a list of the final values (twigs) on the final revision of the value tree. Thus, prisons and halfway houses will have to be assessed for their relative contribution to achieving all the twig values in figure 7.2, from incapacitation and deterrence to speed and public support. In determining these utilities, it is often preferable to consult people who have special expertise on some of the issues, such as initial costs and operating costs, than to rely exclusively on the group of stakeholders recruited in step 2. For attaining some values, however, the utility of a program may only be

FIGURE 7.2
Value Tree for Factors in Decision on Expanding Prisons or Expanding
Halfway Houses
(This modifies figure 7.1, cutting off all twigs with importance
weights of less than .05, then redistributing the weights of the
deleted twigs among those that remain.)

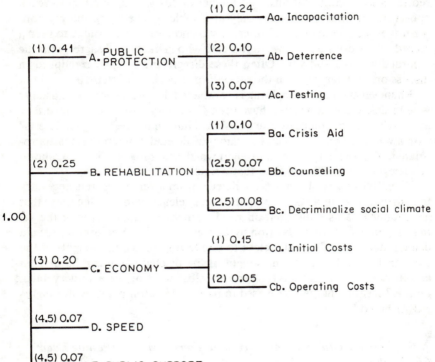

guessed by subjective impressions, for which the views of a variety of stakeholders may be preferable to those of any expert.

In the automobile example, a range of from 0 to 10 as used for estimating utilities. For a more complex problem it may be easier to work with a wider range, such as 0 to 100. For some problems, and the prison versus halfway house issue may be one of these, it may be best not to assign 0 and 100 to alternatives you are actually considering, but 0 to the worst and 100 to the best feasible decisions that you might consider, and then to assign utilities to the actual alternatives by comparison with these conceivable extreme possibilities.

It is also useful in step 7 to draw a graph for each value, such as those shown in figure 7.3, in which the vertical axis is utility and the horizontal one is the probable range of the value. This value should be expressed in appropriate figures, such as dollars for costs or years for time. But if it is a value such as public support for which there are no appropriate units and assessments are made subjectively, an arbitrary range such as 0 to 10 or to 100 may be best.

For most values, the utilty graph will be a straight line or close enough to it for a straight line to suffice, but for some values, a curvilinear relationship to utility prevails. Thus, if size is a value in buying an easy chair, most people would find the smallest and the largest less useful than an intermediate size. However, curvilinear utility graphs can often be converted to straight lines by reformulating the values, for example, by replacing "size" with "body fit" as a value in selecting an easy chair.

The graph for incapacitation in figure 7.3 assigns 0 for giving convicts complete freedom and 100 for their containment in an escape-proof prison (or for their execution, if capital punishment is a viable alternative). The utility of a typical maximum- or medium-security prison drops sharply in the minds of most of the public if its annual escapes (as a percentage of average daily inmate population) is even 1 percent (it usually is less than this, and most escapees are soon recaptured). Therefore, in this utility curve the typical medium- or maximum-security prison can be assessed as 99 for its utility in incapacitation, the value may drop to 90 or less for some prison camps and other minimum-security facilities, hence 95 may be a conservative utility estimation for all prisons.

Residents of a halfway house are not completely free, since if they flee they not only lose prospects of an early parole date and of time off for good behavior, but they can receive a new prison sentence of several years for the felony of escape from imprisonment. Also, residents must sign out when they leave for work or other legitimate activities outside the house, officials must know where they are going and for how long, and a warrant for their arrest is issued if they return too late. There are also telephone inquiries or

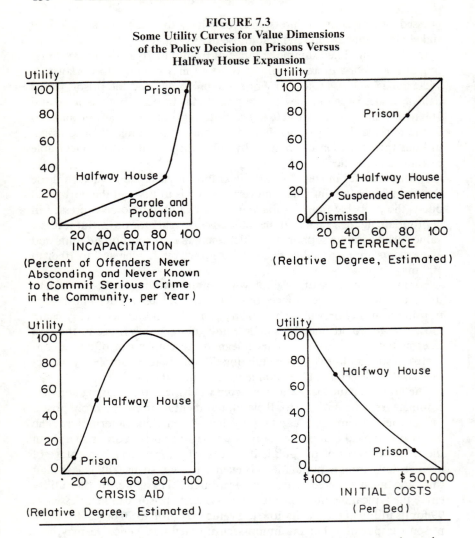

FIGURE 7.3
Some Utility Curves for Value Dimensions
of the Policy Decision on Prisons Versus
Halfway House Expansion

even personal checks by officials to determine if residents are where they are supposed to be when out of the house (such as at work or school, with further inquiries usually preceding issuance of a warrant). Thus, halfway houses are much more incapacitating than parole or probation, especially under current caseloads in these services, in which some conditional releasees are only asked to send in a monthly postcard, or at most are required to report to their supervisor weekly, biweekly or monthly.

The *deterrence* graph in figure 7.3 reflects both incapacitation and the total unpleasant consequences of the alternatives indicated, in which dismissal of charges is 0 and 100 is the worst probable prison term or even the death penalty. These estimations, of course, are subjective and may have appreciable error. Research indicates that both general and special deterrence, especially the latter, increase more with certainty than with severity of penalty (Tittle 1973), but that confinement is distinctly deterrent for young offenders with little prior experience of it (Murray and Cox 1979). Indeed, there is considerable evidence that the death penalty is no more deterrent for murderers than long imprisonment (Blumstein et al. 1978).

The value of Public Protection by *testing* of readiness for release is uncertain. In prison, the tests include observation of behavior while confined, as well as psychological tests. Chapter 6 showed how distinctively superior predictions of postrelease misconduct can be made by applying a few actuarial rules based primarily on information known before imprisonment, such as number of prior convictions and age at first arrest (Glaser 1985, 1987). Halfway houses provide a more adequate test, since the subject, although still somewhat constrained, is exposed to the temptations and opportunities for misconduct in the free community. Conceiving of its utility graph as a diagonal line like that for deterrence in figure 7.3, I have arbitrarily assigned values of 20 for public protection by testing in prison for readiness for release, and 50 for testing in a halfway house, with the prospect that the latter figure could be raised by longer terms or optimum staffing in halfway houses.

Crisis Aid is graphed as a curve in figure 7.3, because of the following assumptions: first, it has some utility for improving inmate adjustment and rehabilitation during any type of incarceration (for example, it may consist of facilitating communication to family members in an emergency at home); second, it is much more rehabilitative in the halfway house where problems are actually confronted in the community of future release and third, it can be antirehabilitative if it is so excessive that releasees maintain the dependence on others for help that develops in the prison. Thus, halfway house residents who develop toothaches are often startled when told to phone one of the dentists in the area for an appointment, instead of being sent to the dentist at a particular time by an official, as in prison. It is presumed that halfway houses vary in this type of rehabilitation service, but that most are below optimum, as shown in fiure 7.3.

Research suggests that *counseling* has little impact in prison, especially if it is group counseling, because it must compete with the antirehabilitative influence of most other interinmate conversation (Kassebaum et al. 1971; Lipton et al. 1975). Some contrary evidence exists that unadvanced young offenders may benefit from extensive individual counseling even in prison (Carney 1969), but that it can have a more definite contribution for them in the community (Glaser 1980). It is hypothesized that its utility increases with its volume, timeliness, and intimacy, but that these features vary greatly with qualities of the client and counselor. It is assigned arbitrary values here of 4 in prison and 30 in a typical halfway house, when compared to 0 for no counseling in prison and 100 for optimum counseling in the community.

Decriminalizing social climate is a major theme in the arguments of those who oppose further prison construction. The warehousing of convicts in prisons in recent years may be more criminalizing than it has ever been, because crowdedness has increased the use of congregate housing in which every inmate must adapt more to the most aggressive prisoners than they would if each had a separate cell. Massachusetts in 1972-74 dramatically pioneered the closing of all its juvenile correctional institutions, replacing them with a mixture of supervised youths allowed to live at home, foster home placement, forestry camps, group homes, boarding schools, secure homes, and temporary detention in local jails. Each of these alternatives involves smaller clusters, less regimentation, and more regular personal contact with staff and with the outside community than occurs in a traditional penal institution (Coates, et al. 1978). Conceiving of the worst prisons, dominated by rapacious inmate gangs, as having 0 utility for social climate, with a typical family home as having 100, prisons have been arbitrarily assigned a utility of 5 and halfway houses 60 for *decriminalizing social climate*.

For the value of Economy, *Initial Costs* are graphed in figure 7.3 as varying inversely in utility, from an initial cost of $100 per bed for the cheapest type of tent in a camp to $50,000 for a maximum security prison (which is often too low). A 1974 survey of halfway house costs converted the prices of purchased structures to annual rentals to make their figures comparable to those that were rented: the range was from $76 to $1,391 per bed per year, with a median of $335 and a mean of $404 (Thalheimer 1975). Very loose probation supervision may be as cheap as $100 in initial costs per client for setting up an office for caseloads per officer of 300; arbitrary intermediate costs are assigned here for the average halfway house and prison today.

Operating costs for state correctional facilities were given as about $10,000 per inmate in the 1975 census of these institutions (U.S. Departments of Justice and Commerce 1977), but were about twice that in California recently. Thalheimer (1975) estimated them as $7,000 in 1974, but inflation must have raised them since then. Annual operating costs of well over $20,000 are often reported for juvenile correctional institutions that are highly treatment oriented. It would be cheaper to send the inmates to Harvard! At any rate, utilities for economy have been arbitrarily set here as 10 for the average prison and 70 for halfway houses. In an actual government decision problem on which type of facility to expand, precise figures for their past experience would doubtless be procured from their accountants.

Speed, the next value tree category, is important to correctional administrators because a legislature tends to respond to prison overcrowding only when this problem reaches crisis proportions. As already indicated, prisons take much longer to develop from decision to occupancy than halfway houses do. It seemed reasonable here to give halfway houses an average speed of one year, since it takes some time to select one, arrange its financing, modify its construction, and furnish it. They were assigned a utility of 90 for achieving the value of speed, whereas prisons were assigned an average speed of seven and a half years and a utility of 10.

Public Support is a recurrent problem in efforts to expand both halfway houses and prisons. Polls regularly show that most of the public wants more prison terms imposed, although a majority of correctional administrators favor community over institutional programs (Gottfredson et al. 1978). Prison public support fluctuates, however, diminishing when its cost or its proximity to residential areas are publicized. Quite arbitrarily, a utility of 75 was assigned here to the average public support for prisons, and only 15 for halfway houses, which more regularly arouse intense local neighborhood resistance.

It should be evident that many types of research can contribute to the precision and validity of SMARTS, including impact evaluations, cost-benefit analysis, and public opinion polls. Whenever importance weightings or utility estimations are based upon assessments of empirical realities, more valid information should produce sounder decisions. Valuable contributions of SMARTS, therefore, include identifying the research priorities that can improve an important decision.

8. Calculate Decision Weights.

These multiplications of utilities by importance weights produce an index of the three main considerations in making a decision: the values pursued, the relative importance of the various values, and the relative utility of each choice for attaining each of the values. As shown in table 7.2, most of the decision weight for expanding prisons comes from the high utility of these establishments for incapacitation (95 of a possible 100), and the great importance ascribed by our hypothetical stakeholders to the value of incapacitation in this decision (.24 of a possible 1.0).

9. Total the Decision Weights for Each Alternative and Consider Their Implications for the Final Decision.

This step mechanically suggests a decision, in this case to expand halfway houses rather than prisons. The closeness of the totals, 43.9 and 46.4,

TABLE 7.2
Decision Weight Calculations on the Expand Prisons versus Expand Halfway Houses Issue

Final value dimension	Impor-tance weight	High contrast analysis				Minimum risk halfway House growth		Maximum rehabilitation Halfway house growth	
		Utilities		Decision weights		Utilities	Decision weights	Utilities	Decision weights
(Twig in figure 5.2)		Pri-sons	Half-way houses	Expand prisons only	Expand halfway houses only				
				(b x c)	(b x d)		(b x g)		(b x i)
a	b	c	d	e	f	g	h	i	j
Aa. Incapacitation	.24	95	30	22.8	7.2	20	4.8	40	9.6
Ab. Deterence	.10	80	30	8.0	3.0	35	3.5	20	2.0
Ac. Testing	.07	20	60	1.4	4.2	50	3.5	70	4.9
Ba. Crisis aid	.10	5	50	0.5	5.0	40	4.0	80	8.0
Bb. Counseling	.07	4	30	0.3	2.1	20	1.4	50	3.5
Bc. Decriminalize social climate	.08	5	40	0.4	3.2	80	6.4	30	2.4
Ca. Initial costs	.15	10	70	1.5	10.5	70	10.5	70	10.5
Cb. Operating costs	.05	40	70	2.0	3.5	80	4.0	60	3.0
D. Speed	.07	20	90	1.4	6.3	90	6.3	90	6.3
E. Public Support	.07	80	20	5.6	1.4	30	2.1	10	0.7
Totals	1.00	—	—	43.9	46.4	—	46.5	—	50.9

makes review especially appropriate here, not only to assess the possible margins of error in estimating importance weights and utilities, but to consider the persistence of disagreements on these estimations. When the decision problem requires an absolute choice, stakeholders may be content to act on the basis of a small margin of difference in the totals for various alternatives. In this problem, however, where a high-contrast pair of alternatives was considered, but you could actually pursue both alternatives to some extent—that is, expanding prisons somewhat while especially expanding halfway houses—a fine-tuning step is needed.

10. Review the Determination of Weights and Utilities, as Well as the Total Decision Process, to Consider Possible Justifications for Modifying the Conclusion Suggested by Total Decision Weights.

Divergent opinions among stakeholders in importance weighting the various values, and among experts in assigning utilities, are grounds for serious uncertainty about the conclusion reached in step 9, especially if the totals are close. The probabilities and implications of new events that would contradict the assumptions made in the preceding steps, and the highly divergent but reasonable opinions on approriate weights or utilities, can be reconsidered if good notes are kept on disagreements in prior discussions. Such a review of possible error in decision recommendations, as the final step in multiattribute utility evaluation, has been called *sensitivity analysis* (Edwards and Newman, 1982).

In high-contrast problems such as this one, pursuing more than one alternative to some extent may appear to have more total utility than complete adherence to a single alternative. Thus the need for more incapacitation resources for certain types of offenders may be stressed as justification for building a certain type of prison, even if halfway house expansion is accepted as the primary method of reducing crowdedness in the total penal system.

Affecting this particular decision is the fact that there are three contrasting approaches to assigning prisoners to halfway houses, as detailed in chapter 4. The most frequent approach can be called *minimize risk*. It can be pursued by sending white collar offenders and old or ill prisoners to halfway houses soon after they are sentenced to reduce the risk of residents committing violent and notorious offenses against them. Felons with high prospects of recidivism would not be sent to these facilities at all, or would be kept there for only a very brief period just before their parole or discharge. Risk-oriented officials tend to be more fearful of mistakes in assigning prisoners to reduced custody who then prove to be unsafe there (type 1 or false positive errors) than of the errors of keeping probably safe prisoners in secure custody (type 2 or false negative errors). Consequently, such administrators tend not to use all of the space available in halfway houses even when their secure facilities are severely crowded, persistently claiming that none of their prison inmates is suitable for a halfway house. As pointed out in chapter 6, actuarial guidelines for custodial decisions greatly alleviate this problem without increasing dangerous behavior.

A contrasting approach may be called *maximize rehabilitation*. It reflects the theory and research that suggests that the crisis aid, counseling, and decriminalized social climate of halfway houses, as compared to prisons, will especially reduce recidivism rates for intermittent offenders. These are the not very professional criminals who have tried both legitimate employment and lawbreaking with little success in either.

An early study of the first federal halfway houses indicated that the greatest reduction of recidivism was for those with a history of repeated auto thefts as juveniles. Their 47 percent postrelease failure rate was higher than that for other categories of halfway house residents, but the 25 percentage points between this figure and their 72 percent failure rate when released directly from the prisons was much greater than this difference for other types of prisoners. Indeed, the best-risk category had a slightly higher success rate if paroled directly from the prison to their homes instead of going first to a halfway house (Hall et al. 1966). Analogous findings have been reported in later studies (Beha 1977; Beck 1979). Thus, it is for some of the less stable and high-risk prisoners, but those who are not very professional at crime, that halfway houses may best protect the public.

Because halfway houses provide close surveillance on initial return to the community, a third approach of *maximize control* by releasing the most dangerous offenders only through halfway houses would be rational, but it is unlikely to have much public acceptance.

Table 7.2 suggests the directions in which utilities could be modified if expansion of halfway house use was based on a minimize risk or a maximize rehabilitation perspective.

Another Example

There is considerable difference between using SMARTS to address a broad policy issue, such as that just discussed, and using it for more concrete decisions on which more precise information is needed. For example, once a state decides to expand halfway houses, it must procure buildings for this purpose. SMARTS can aid in selecting the buildings.

In this application of SMARTS, *step 1—Identify the issue on which a decision must be reached*—is clear at the outset; you must decide which buildings are optimal for halfway houses in a particular metropolitan area, making the selection from those available.

For *step 2—Identify the most concerned stakeholders and recruit their cooperation*—officials of the Department of Corrections are likely to present themselves as the ones most concerned. Although using them alone may suffice, they could well be supplemented by criminal justice officials and representatives of prisoner aid organizations from the metropolitan area. It is especially important, however, that all the stakeholders who contribute to the analysis be familiar with common experiences in the establishment and operation of halfway houses. To educate or refresh them on these matters, they should visit and confer with staff and residents in a variety of halfway houses in diverse locations.

In *step 3—Identify the decision alternatives*—you are faced with a list of potentially available buildings, a list that might change from time to time. They may usefully be classified initially by some relevant features, such as:

A. Rental Space
(1) Whole structures
(2) Sections of larger structures
(a) YMCA hotels
(b) Other hotels or motels
B. Buildings to be purchased by the state
C. Buildings to be constructed by the state

Financial considerations, laws, and time pressures may exclude some of these categories; for example, rental may be mandatory or there may be only a choice of long-term lease or purchase on terms comparable to a lease, with new construction ruled out. As the decision analysis progresses, the participants may be able to alert those seeking buildings as to the types of structures to try to add to the list from which a selection will be made, and the types that can be ruled out before the analysis is concluded.

When working on *step 4—Determine the values by which the alternatives should be assessed*—the stakeholders might agree that selection of halfway house structures should be based on four main considerations:

1. Cost (per year per resident).

2. Building suitability. This may be further divided into three subordinate dimensions: Resident room comfort and privacy; Recreation and other activity space; Dining facilities. It is presumed that other essential space, such as offices and a conference room, would be suggested but can be

created from almost any other space in any building; thus, it would usually not be a great influence on choice among buildings.

3. Job market convenience (in terms of distance and public transportation to areas where the residents are likely to be employed).

4. Neighborhood suitability (prospects of residents being accepted by law-abiding neighbors and not criminalized by others).

Presumably, a list of buildings will be accumulated that has none that must be ruled out on any of these fourgrounds, but will differ considerably on each. Upper limits of cost will be specified, as well as the need to void neighborhoods that are either too likely to be highly resistant (such as upper-class residential areas) or too criminogenic and vice-ridden (such as skid row areas).

Probably in *step 5—Rank the values*—the stakeholders will agree on the ranks indicated in parentheses in the value tree of figure 7.4. There may be considerable disagreement on the ranks at first, however, with consensus only possible when agreement is reached on the acceptable range of each value.

In *step 6—Assign relative importance weights to the dimensions of the value tree*—it is conceivable that the stakeholders might start with only a tree consisting of the one row of four values from steps 4 and 5, but would expand the tree by adding the additional three twigs under the building suitability node in an effort to reduce their disagreements on weights for the first row.

If there is extreme and persistent disagreement in any of the ranking or weighting, each disputant's contentions should be recorded as an aid in the last step, the sensitivity analysis. Any disagreements by stakeholders or expert consultants in other stages of the analysis should also be recorded, especially *step 7—Estimate the utility of each decision alternative.*

In this step, the utility of 100 on each value dimension should be given to the potentially available building that would be most satisfactory on that dimension, and a utility of 0 to the worst that might be tolerated. The specific buildings from which a selection must be made are then assigned a particular utility on each dimension. It is possible that none will be as low as 0 or as high as 100, since these utility boundaries probably should be based on the best and the worst buildings observed that could be considered, and these may have been halfway houses that are visited or buildings considered but currently unavailable. The point is that a wide range of

FIGURE 7.4
Value Tree for Selection of Halfway House Buildings

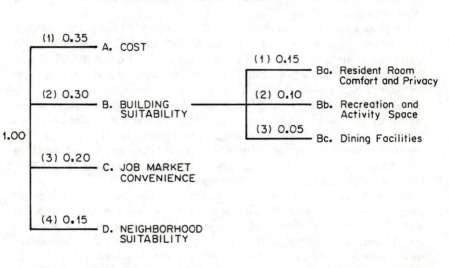

actual structures that might be considered should provide the standards for assessing those currently available, and not just those that are on the market.

Let us assume in this exercise that three sites must be selected from eight probably available facilities, as follows:

I. 35 scattered guest rooms and two small offices in the Downtown YMCA Hotel, a 350-room facility in an office area.

II. The two top floors, with 40 rooms, in the old four-story Harbor YMCA Hotel.

III. Two adjacent floors with 40 rooms each in the old 200-room Metro Hotel near the edge of the downtown business area, two blocks from the edge of skid row.

IV. Smith House, an old 14-room mansion in a former elite residential area now merged with the inner city and only two miles from downtown.

V. Brown House, an old 16-room mansion in the same area.

VI. Rest Haven, a 36-unit motel at the edge of an outlying small industrial area.

VII. Prairie Street, an old building with small stores and 3 apartments over them, in a large industrial suburb.

VIII. Regal School, formerly a small parochial school in a working class residential area.

These examples are based upon actual halfway houses in various cities. Let us consider how the stakeholders would assign utilities to them on the value dimensions of figure 7.4.

For Cost, the maximum utility would be assigned to the place of cheapest cost-per-resident-per year, and the minimum to the most expensive facility that can be considered. If some of the units—for example, I, II, and III—would have to be rented and the remainder purchased, then the cost per year of each purchased facility would have to be estimated by dividing initial costs by the life of the building and adding yearly costs, probably taking the duration of the longest mortgage procurable as the building's lifetime (it would probably have longer actual utility, but it is customary to presume that the mortgage duration depends on the structure's durability). The estimated cost of repairing and remodeling a building for halfway house use should be added to initial costs.

All utility graphs for the value dimensions used here can be straight lines. As shown in figure 7.5, the graph for cost has a negative slope, as would the graph for job market convenience (for which the base might be average minutes duration of travel to work). The other value dimensions have positive slopes. The final utility estimations are shown in table 7.3. In practice, many of these utilities, such as Cost, would not be expressed in

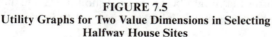

FIGURE 7.5
Utility Graphs for Two Value Dimensions in Selecting
Halfway House Sites

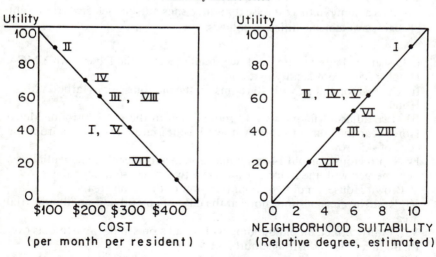

multiples of 10, and might even have decimals, but they have been simplified by rounding here (if all utilities were actually in multiples of 10 they
could be simplified by conversion to a range of 0 to 10 instead of 0 to 100).

In assessing resident room comfort and privacy, the larger rooms and
separate bathrooms of the hotel and motel buildings give them greater
utility than the other buildings, since the tiny YMCA rooms share
bathrooms, and the large sleeping rooms in the other buildings would have
several occupants for economy reasons, although this may be somewhat
criminogenic. The YMCAs are ideal for recreation because so much of
their space is equipped and staffed for this purpose, and residents would
become Y members eligible to participate in a wide range of organized
grouped activities with other members. Thus, there is a built–in neighborhood suitability in these resources. The motel has a pool, and the other
buildings vary in the space available for lounges and recreation. The
Downtown YMCA—but not the Harbor Y—operates a cafeteria; some of
the other buildings contain cooking facilities that the state could operate,
or they have adjacent or nearby restaurants for which residents could be
given or purchase meal tickets.

The downtown locations are best for job market convenience because of
all the employment opportunities in their area and because they are near
public transportation to other areas.

In *step 8—Calculate decision weights*—the utility of each location on
each value dimension is multiplied by the importance weight of the dimensions, as shown in table 7.3. This leads to *step 9—Total the decision weights
for each alternative and consider the implications of these totals for the final
decision*. The right-hand column of table 7.3 clearly assigns the highest
decision weights to the first three alternatives, the two YMCA hotels, and
Metro Hotel. If these three were the only ones selected for the entire metropolitan area, however, there would be the disadvantage that the Downtown
Y and the Metro Hotel are less than a mile apart. The next two most highly
weighted facilities, the Smith and Brown Houses, are not far from them.
This leads to:

*Step 10—Review the determination of weights and utilities as well as the
total decision process to consider possible modifications of the conclusions
suggested by the total decision weights.*

It is assumed that any prisoner with a prospective parole residence in the
state—such as the home of his or her spouse or parents—or a promise of
satisfactory employment will be placed in a halfway house near one of
these locations, if possible. With any new postrelease employment, administrators will want to reduce excessive time or cost of travel to work. Therefore, if three halfway houses are to be operated within a metropolitan area,
it is best to have them in scattered locations, each nearest to a different job

TABLE 7.3
Decision Weight Calculations for Selection of Halfway House Buildings

Utility (U) and decision weight (D) on each final value dimension; importance weight (I) in parenthesis; W = U x I

Decision alternatives	A. Cost (.35)		Ba. Resident room comfort & privacy (.10)		Bb. Recreation and activity space (.10)		Bc. Dining facilities (.05)		C. Job market convenience (.20)		D. Neighborhood suitability (.15)		Total Decision Weights (ΣW)
	U	W	U	W	U	W	U	W	U	W	U	W	
I Downtown Y	40	14.0	50	7.5	100	5.0	100	5.0	90	18.0	90	13.5	68.0
II Harbor Y	90	31.5	40	6.0	90	9.0	40	2.0	50	10.0	80	12.0	70.5
III Metro Hotel	60	21.0	80	12.0	40	4.0	80	4.0	90	18.0	40	6.0	65.0
IV Smith House	70	24.5	40	6.0	40	4.0	60	3.0	60	12.0	60	9.0	58.5

V Brown House	40	14.0	60	9.0	40	4.0	50	2.5	60	12.0	60	9.0	50.5
VI Rest Haven	10	3.5	90	13.5	50	5.0	40	2.0	10	12.0	50	7.5	33.5
VII Prairie Street	20	7.0	10	1.5	30	3.0	30	1.5	20	4.0	20	3.0	20.0
VIII Regal School	60	21.0	20	3.0	10	1.0	20	1.0	70	14.0	40	6.0	46.0

market. Thus, from the standpoint of job market convenience, selection of one site for a halfway house reduces the utility of the other sites near it. Accordingly, in our example, if the Downtown YMCA is chosen, the utility of Metro Hotel, Smith House, and Brown House diminish.

Furthermore, each estimate of utilities for halfway house sites is based on assumptions as to how much the state would expend on improving them. Stakeholders or consultants might argue that some larger expenditures than originally planned would raise the building suitability utility more than it would diminish the cost utility. Thus, subdividing resident rooms, putting in bathrooms, and improving dining and recreational facilities might be recommended for Regal School, raising its utilities to 70 for BA, 40 for BB, and 40 for BC, but dropping its cost utility only from 60 to 50. The low cost of Harbor Y releases the needed funds.

Finally, a review of neighborhood suitability ratings in terms of projected expansion of skid row and of other neighborhood deterioration might lead to reduction of the assessments of Metro Hotel and Smith and Brown Houses on this value dimension.

Table 7.4 shows the recalculation of decision weights for selection of a third halfway house from among Metro Hotel, Smith House, and Regal School, after the two YMCAs are selected. It reflects the reassessments of neighborhood suitability that were based on a longer-range prediction of city conditions and on a decision to invest more funds in improving Regal School. This revision after the sensitivity analysis in step 10 makes it evident that the three sites would be quite similar in decision weights, but that Regal School would have a slight advantage.

Conclusion

Multiattribute utility evaluation is a means of making nonroutine decisions by rationally combining both explicit and consensual formulation of the relevant values, weighted by importance, with the most valid and pertinent objective data and subjective judgments on how each alternative choice would achieve these values. For some decisions, such as purchasing equipment or buildings, there is usually much pertinent objective data available, particularly on costs, although some values are usually raised that require subjective judgments. For other decisions, such as whether to marry or remain single, the considerations may be mostly subjective, although objective considerations, such as monetary costs, may enter in. Difficult choices usually involve a mix of facts and values.

Ten steps were outlined for one variation of this method of policy guidance. Although the steps were applied to only two illustrative decision problems, there are innumerable others for which they would also be

TABLE 7.4
Revision of Decision Weights for Three Decision Alternatives on the Basis of Sensitivity Analysis

Utility (U) and decision weight (D) on each final value dimension; importance weight (I) in parenthesis; $D = U \times I$

Decision alternatives	A. Cost (.35)		Ba. Resident room comfort & privacy (.15)		Bb. Recreation and activity space (.10)		Bc. Dining facilities (.05)		C. Job market convenience (.20)		D. Neighborhood suitability (.15)		Total Decision Weights (ΣW)
	U	D	U	D	U	D	U	D	U	D	U	D	
III Metro Hotel	60	21.0	80	12.0	40	4.0	80	4.0	30	6.0	20	3.0	50.0
IV Smith House	70	24.5	40	6.0	40	4.0	50	2.5	40	8.0	30	4.5	49.5
VIII Regal School	50	17.5	70	10.5	40	4.0	40	2.0	70	14.0	40	6.0	54.0

useful. As other chapters show, evaluations of impact, process, and cost-benefit can make tremendous contributions to the improvement of policy and practice; nevertheless, the information that they yield is most rationally integrated with relevant value considerations if some systematic procedures are used for this purpose, such as those described in this chapter.

Conducting a multivariate utility evaluation for a particular decision problem may benefit the organization involved independently of the benefits resulting from this specific decision. Requiring stakeholders to communicate intensively with each other in order to try to reach consensus on values, or on the relative ranking and weighting of values, may raise the organization's morale and effectiveness, as well as the quality of its later decisions.

8

Ethical and Legal Issues
in Program Evaluation

Edna Erez

Background and Issues

Ethical and legal issues permeate the whole course of evaluation research, from the choice of research problem through data collection, analysis, and application, to its ultimate consequences. Concern with these issues in social science research is a recent development. As late as the 1970s, subjects of psychological experimentation were treated in a manner completely divorced from ethical practices that are now almost universally accepted and were already long established in medical experimentation. Deception, manipulation without consent, and even compulsory participation were commonplace (*New York Times Magazine* September 12, 1982).

In sociological field research, ethical concerns are now raised about long-used unobtrusive measures, secret observation of behavior or role playing by researchers, to assure that there is no potential harm to unknowing subjects. Long standard techniques, such as questionnaires or interviews, are closely examined for possible violations of subjects' rights or abuse of investigators' privileges. The trend toward scrutiny and supervision of research involving human subjects is closely tied to the civil rights movement and to social reforms showing new concerns for the rights of minorities (Barber 1973; Bloomberg and Wilkins 1977; Reynolds 1979).

In general, the dilemma confronted by evaluators is how to proceed in morally accepted ways with development of knowledge that may benefit mankind. Its solution requires balancing interests of the evaluator, the subject or respondent, program staff, the scholarly profession, and, above all, the state and the public. These interests are associated with values commonly held and cherished which, at times, conflict with each other. Ethical and legal issues emerge in the course of pursuing these conflicting values.

The evaluator is concerned with the pursuit of knowledge free from dictates of officials or program staff. The subjects of evaluation research have another set of values that they want to promote and protect: they want to regain privacy and self-determination, obtain benefits, avoid harm, and be assured of efficient and fair governmental or agency policy. Program managers are interested in dispensing successful and useful services. The state and public are interested in increasing knowledge and in achieving economy in programs, as well as in promoting dignity, liberty, and equality. The purpose of research ethics is to promote all these interests, while guarding against unnecessary or unjustified costs to program participants.

Participants in evaluation research may be affected in many ways in the course of research or by its consequences. Effects may be temporary or permanent, negative or positive, tangible or intangible, direct or indirect. Some effects are immediately visible, others materialize only after a prolonged period of time. Some effects become known, others go unnoticed. Negative effects for participants may consist of personal expenses, denial of facilities or privileges, time taken from other activities, resentment of treatment, harm from the new norms established or enhanced by the research, discrimination against the social category to which the participant belongs because of the research, or deprivation of assumed benefits and infringement of rights because the participant is in a control group. Benefits may consist of cash payments, use of facilities or privileges, psychological and social gratification from an interesting experience, and satisfaction from contributing to a worthy program.

The general concern of this chapter is in evaluation that involves risk of negative consequences. The problem addressed is how to minimize harmful effects and interference with participants' rights, in the course of pursuing knowledge.

Writings on ethical problems in research focus on:

1. *Coercion*: the exercise of undue pressure to induce subjects to participate in research.
2. *Deception*: misleading the subject about the nature of the research.
3. *Invasion of privacy*: intrusion into matters that the subjects would rather keep to themselves.
4. *Breach of confidentiality*: permitting information about individual subjects to be passed on to others.

5. *Stress*: psychological difficulties that participation in a study might cause.

6. *Collective risks*: harm that a study might cause to others beyond the individual subject himself (for elaboration on possible harms see Bower and de Gasparis 1979:Ch.3; Diener and Crandall 1978:Ch.2).

Some modes of research have acquired distinct sets of ethical problems. For instance, social experiments conducted by sociologists evoke concern about collective risks. Psychological research and experimentation raise issues of deception and stress. Qualitative research by sociologists, whether using unobtrusive measures or participant observation, involve invasion of privacy.

This chapter addresses issues and problems that may accompany most research methods used in program evaluation. These broad issues are the following: informed consent to be a subject of research; confidentiality of the information that the researcher collects; and manipulation of a research participant by random assignment to an experimental or control group.

The mechanism that guarantees protection of participants' rights and welfare and allows researchers to engage in responsible evaluation research, is restriction of the autonomy of researchers. Such restriction results from self-imposed rules, such as those appearing in various professional codes, in government guidelines for research conducted with its funding and in the application of legal rules and principles to situations where rights and interests are in conflict. The legal mechanisms to cope with conflict problems come from enactment of legislation, establishment of administrative guidelines and procedures, judicial decisions that involve interpretations of existing laws and, in the United States, the Constitution.

The large role government plays in evaluation research, both in funding programs and in their assessment, prompted federal action concerning the ethics of research. Following the passage of the National Research Act (1974), and the establishment of the National Commission on Protection of Human Subjects in Biomedical and Behavioral Research (NCPHSBBR), guidelines were issued by the Department of Health and Human Services (HHS), formerly Department of Health, Education and Welfare (DHEW), for any studies that it funds.

The current government control system was prompted by much publicity given to several dramatic examples of medical and social science research in which the treatment of participants was questionable on ethical grounds. These events fostered widespread suspicion among concerned academicians and government personnel that researchers could not always be trusted to make decisions affecting their subjects. Many of the issues were addressed in the professional literature, in litigation, and in the codes of ethics drawn by various professional associations.

Among professionals there is a fear of control by laws. Laws tend to be unresponsive to changing needs, and must apply to a wide variety of situations; thus, they cannot be sensitive to the specifics of particular cases. Since laws applying to scientific research are largely created by politicians, researchers fear that statutory ethical standards will be less enlightened than guidelines created within the scientific community. Self-control is preferable to control by others (Douglas 1979). For that purpose, most of the major professional associations engaged in research have created codes of ethics to help guide their members. These codes comprise wisdom gained from past research experience and consensus of values within the profession. In evaluation research by a staff identified with a particular profession, it is natural to apply that profession's set of standards or code of ethics. But even with all the existing mechanisms, the major regulatory force in the ethical aspects of research is the individual evaluator's self-control. Laws and codes serve only as adjuncts to personal conscience, the major form of ethical control. Neither approval by peers nor following ethical codes will relieve individuals in a court of law from their responsibilities toward research subjects.

In examining the selected ethical issues pertaining to evaluation research in people-changing organizations, these various sources will be used to provide directions for solutions or answers. Of course, most ethical issues raised in conducting research do not have a right or wrong answer (Federal Judicial Center 1981). A researcher's response to these issues depends heavily on his or her background and experience. Those who put more weight on the maintenance of civil rights will be less willing to allow violations than those who view scientific progress as the overriding objective (Rivlin and Timpane 1975:4). Also, there is still considerable ambiguity about the legal status of many social science research activities. This is partly because many of the issues have been raised only recently, and those who are affected by the social science research have only lately begun to seek redress through the courts or control through legislative action (Reynolds 1979:280).

Risk and Informed Consent

Risk pertains to the possibility of a negative effect resulting from involvement in research, whether it is physical, psychological, social, legal, medical, or other (Institute for Social Research 1976). In general, the probability of effects, positive and negative, depends upon the focus of the research: biomedical has the highest probability of effects, behavioral intervention has the lowest, and virtually no effects are associated with secondary analysis of administrative information or other products of prior inquiry.

According to government guideines, a subject is considered "at risk" if "the individual may be exposed to the possibility of injury, including physical, psychological or social injury, as a consequence of participation as a subject in any research or related activity which departs from the application of those established and accepted methods necessary to meet his needs, or which increases the ordinary risks of daily life, including the recognized risk inherent in a chosen occupation or field or service." (Title 45 CFR 46.103[b]). This definition excludes activities that are therapeutic in nature, and not "experimental." Any unnecessary or unacceptable hazards for participants that are introduced intentionally or unintentionally by evaluators for enhancing the quality of evaluation have to be guarded against.

The 1981 HHS guidelines for research fail to cover broad categories of research activity, specifically: experimental studies of educational innovation in educational settings (such as testing instructional strategies or the effectiveness of instructional or classroom management techniques); secondary analysis of existing data or records publicly available, if the information included does not facilitate identification of the subjects; routine surveys, interviews and field observations of public behavior that avoid the following three conditions: (1) responses are recorded in a manner that human subjects can be identified; (2) the subjects' responses, if they become known, place him or her at a risk of criminal or civil liability or may be damaging to his or her financial standing or employability; (3) the research deals with sensitive aspects of the subject's own behavior, such as illegal conduct, drug use, or sexual behavior.

Research involving risk to participants may be viewed as acceptable if there is a favorable costs-benefits ratio, that is, if risks to participants are outweighed by benefits to participants, scientific progress, society, or all three. Cost-benefits analysis of ethical issues may imply the moral suggestion that the end justifies the means (Diener and Crandall 1978:24). It is here that some disagreements about the ethics of research ensue, as differential weight is assigned to risks and benefits by various concerned parties.

Any research that has both risk of negative effects for participants and potential benefits to society require selection of individuals to bear the risk. The most widely accepted solution has been to allow potential participants to make their own decisions on involvement, that is, to express their informed consent to their participation in the research.

Consent, an independent ethical and legal criterion in human experimentation and social research, is primarily justified by the right to self-determination (Veatch 1975:32). Other justifications for the informed consent requirement include the following: promoting respect for participants as unique individuals; minimizing fraud, deceit, coercion, and duress; encouraging self-scrutiny by investigators; promoting responsible rational and legal decisions by participants; reducing possibility of criminal or civil liabilities for the investigator; allowing participants to have an interesting experience; promoting involvement of the public and public support and trust in research (Reynolds 1979:78-80). Informed consent is viewed as warranted even when the researcher has the professional (Parsons 1970) or anthropological model (Mead 1970) of the research endeavor, both of which view the participant as a collaborator rather than a mere subject. Other respected researchers suggest that participation in research be viewed as a civil duty of subjects (Levine 1975) or as a moral obligation for future generations (Reynolds 1979:331-32).

From a legal perspective, consent to participate in research and to forgo rights is binding; in fact, the right of self-determination implies that individuals should be able to forgo certain rights if they so choose. The legal action (one recognized by the courts) that transfers these rights is the giving of consent.

The first authoritative application of consent to research with human participants was formalized by the Nuremberg tribunal during the trial of Nazi medical researchers and it was prompted by the atrocious experiments carried out in concentration camps. It focused on informed consent and was interpreted as having four important characteristics (Annas et al.1977:6-7):

1. Legal competence to give consent.
2. Voluntary consent.
3. Sufficient knowledge of the subject to make an enlightened decision.
4. Comprehension of the elements of the subject matter, particularly the possible outcomes and risks associated with each.

The freedom from exposure to unnecessary risks as a basic human right, and the right to participate in research if social benefits outweigh risks, is dependent on the individual's being fully and correctly informed of the problem of risk, the potentiality of benefit, the implication of consent, and the issue of confidentiality. The degree to which participation is voluntary depends upon informed consent.

Informed Consent consists of procedures to solve conflicts between desirable societal objectives and the rights of the individual. It is a specification of conditions—competence to make a decision, complete information, comprehension of that information, and a setting devoid of coercion or undue influence—that provides assurance that an individual has made a voluntary decision to forgo personal rights or accept risks. It means that the subject has been provided with adequate information regarding the nature of the research, is fully aware of the possible outcome, and is free to choose alternative courses without the risk of added disabilities.

Underlying the concept of informed consent is the assumption that a decision made by a responsible, rational, and mature individual who is given the available information will be a correct decision (Reynolds 1979:90). Certain individuals cannot be considered competent and are therefore to be treated in special ways that have been identified. The criteria for determining lack of competence are inadequate mental capacities or situations where there is some doubt about the ability to exercise self-determination. Those considered not competent include fetuses, children, comotose medical patients, and mental patients. Other categories are less clear cut, such as mentally infirm, older children (teenagers), and prisoners. It is generally acceptable that parents or guardians will make decisions for incompetent individuals when the participants may receive direct benefits. If there is the possibility of no benefits and no risk, it is still acceptable for guardians to make such decisions; but if there is no possibility of benefits to the participant while there is some risk for one who is not considered competent, it has been suggested that the research be prohibited altogether (NCPHSBBR 1977).

Consent also has to be voluntary. Deterministic arguments about free will notwithstanding, it means that the person making a decision is able to exercise free choice without any elements of force, fraud, deceit, duress, coercion, or constraint (see Veatch 1975:32-5).

Voluntariness and Institutionalized Populations: Voluntariness depends on the number of realistic options available. Some of the theoretically feasible alternatives may be foreclosed because the subject's freedom to choose is reduced for financial, ethnic or other reasons. The moral dilemmas of freedom are accented in situations that involve substantial influence from a person in authority (a physician, a professor, a judge), or in institutional settings such as a prison, mental institution, class, or hospital. Particular populations susceptible to undue restrictive influences, such as prisoners, student, and patients, are the residents of these settings. Subtle forms of persuasion occur when prisoners are offered reduced sentences or better living conditions, students are offered chances for better grades, or the poor are offered medical aid for participating in medical studies.

The overrepresentation of underprivileged and disadvantaged groups in social policy and evaluation research poses both ethical and external validity problems: how well can we generalize from them to other populations? On the other hand, social policy research by its very nature is concerned with ways to increase the welfare of those who are least well off, undereducated, criminal, or sick. Voluntary consent will be extremely difficult to obtain in most social policy research if it means consent free from subtle forms of persuasion and psychological coercion (Veatch 1975). The plight of incarcerated inmates particularly stands out in this respect; because freedom is especially limited for such offenders, the meaning of informed consent to them may be largely diminished.

Some argue that the de facto environment of prisons renders informed consent without coercion an impossibility. They contend that informed consent made with competence, full knowledge, and voluntariness is constitutionally invalid in the context of prisons which inherently are coercive, secretive, and closed (Irwin 1976:5-7). The extensive use of indeterminate sentences, the existence of parole boards, and the barrenness of prison life are all coercive elements of imprisonment (National Academy of Sciences 1975:131-33). In the words of Geis (1967:69), "for a desperate man, hope of award is apt to undercut his freedom of choice and the requirement of voluntary participation necessary as an ethical stipulation for correctional research." The past experience in the use of prisoners for medical experimentation is instructive; it illuminates the low capacity of prisoners to resist trivial awards (such as cigarettes) and subject themselves—or "consent"—to most grave consequences (such as getting venereal disease) (Mitford 1973:Ch.7)

The feasibility of voluntary consent by prisoners to medical and pharmaceutical experimentation has become controversial in the last decade. Strong objections were raised by representatives of correctional authorities (American Correctional Association 1976:14) and were followed by various governmental acts designed to prevent such research. Prisoners who favored continuation of these experiments initiated a suit to defend one of their last remaining rights, the "right to volunteer" (Rosenfeld 1981).

Proponents of the use of prisoners in medical research emphasize the multitude of reasons that prisoners have to volunteer: for financial awards, to reduce boredom or a tedious existence, to prove that they can do something good, to gain respect or simply to satisfy curiosity (see Barber 1980:Ch.7). In evaluation research, assistance in verifying the effectiveness of programs is another important reason for participation in research, particularly for those who are genuinely interested in their own improvement or change.

Although not all aspects of prison life are boring, and not all research is fascinating, that the contrast between the two may affect many prisoners' decisions is something to be considered in allowing research within prison walls (Brodsky 1980). But allowing prisoners no choice may be the ultimate coercion.

The effect of compensation for participation in research on voluntariness is also controversial. It is argued that low-income groups are coerced into research by bribes of amounts of money that in relation to their normal income, are irresistible. It is also argued that captive subjects receive inadequate compensation (Veatch 1975:34).

In prison contexts, a special dilemma arises with respect to inmates' pay. On one hand, any payment above the very low prison wage will strongly motivate confined people and compromise their free choice. Ordinary outside world rates for participation in research would be an overwhelming incentive for prisoners (Brodsky 1980:81). On the other hand, standard prison wages for participation may be criticized as exploitation (Geis 1967). One solution to this dilemma, although not yet possible in U.S. prisons, is a full-wages prison, in which all services by prisoners are paid for at going market rates (Brodsky 1980:81). Some have suggested that prisoners be paid what is required to attract a free volunteer to the research project, and that any differences between that amount and current prisoners' wages be placed in general inmates' welfare funds (Mills and Morris 1974). The usually accepted rule is that if research participation provides rewards equivalent to the rewards for other forms of prison employment, it does not compromise free choice, and it is acceptable (Reynolds 1979:327).

Suggestions to Overcome Impediments to Voluntary Consent: To combat the problem of a substantial influence from a person in authority, it has been suggested that evaluators create an egalitarian relationship with the participant, providing a setting where both view the endeavor as a collaborative effort in exploring the unknown (Mead 1970; Parsons 1970). Others suggest having a neutral third party present during the informed consent procedure to minimize the coercive element implied in the situation of a person in authority requesting consent (Fletcher 1967:648). Some urge that participants be allowed to consult with others after a request has been made, and before their decision is reached (Veatch 1978:31; Lidz et al. 1984:331), or that the consent of participants should be obtained by a person who is not the investigator, and who is not directly involved in the research project (Veatch 19783:32). The latter suggestion has been criticized because such a delegation of responsibility may encourage evaluators to be less conscientious about the ethical issues of their research project than they would be otherwise (Reynolds 1979:94). It has also been suggested that institutions hire a person specifically to educate patients, and to provide them, over an extended period of time, with the information necessary to make an informed decision (Lidz et al. 1984:331). Prisoners should have an access to a counselor who can advise them without having a vested interest in the outcome, and they should have at least twenty-four hours to make a decision about their participation in research rather than having to respond at the time that the request is made (Annas et al. 1977:132-34).

With respect to particular situations in which individuals are placed that may reduce their ability to resist temptations, it has been suggested that the inducements be not exceptionally attractive but rather minor "luxuries." This is feasible only when the general living situation of those individuals provides them with necessities (Freeman 1975:36). Only in studies directly testing the effectiveness of alternate or improved living conditions are such improved conditions for research participants acceptable (Brodsky 1980:84).

Another ethical problem with respect to voluntary consent of institutionalized populations is unique to evaluation research. In such research, which has the intent or reasonable prospect of improving the health or well-being of institutionalized populations, such as prisoners or mental patients, these individuals "may be ethically required to cooperate in therapeutic or corrective programs oriented toward their own rehabilitation." By extension, this argument would hold that cooperation in research for the improvement of rehabilitation might also be required of them. A difficulty with this position is that it is too readily available as a rationalization for exploitation (American Psychological Association 1973:48-9).

While such an argument, that prisoners be required to participate in correctional program evaluations, may be used by evaluators of people-changing programs, it loses much of its force in programs with an explicit or avowed purpose of incapacitation or punishment (American Psychological Association 1973:49). However, the presence of a mixture of goals, of multiple rationales for the correctional system, may still constitute a reason for forced participation in evaluation of rehabilitation programs.

To guard against possible misuse of the treatment argument, it has been suggested recently that the due process model be applied to the delivery of treatment or mental health services in correctional settings, and that prisoners be afforded the same kinds of protections that due process affords them in court, such as assumption of non-dangerousness and psychological normality unless proven otherwise, opportunity to confront psychological information and accusers, appelate review, and right to remain silent or refuse treatment (Brodsky 1980:90-2).

Comprehension, Informed Consent, and its Elements: Fully informed consent is virtually impossible, as not all results are predictable or known to the researcher, and not all details of the study can be easily transmitted and comprehended by every subject. This "competence gap" (Parsons 1970) is particularly problematic in social experiments that include large numbers of low-income, less-educated participants (Brown) or when individuals are considered by the researchers to have limited intelligence or low psychological health Lidz et al. 1984).

If experimenters provide only points of information that are of practical importance or relevance to the subjects, they may usurp the subjects' decision-making power. On the other hand, if too much information is given, subjects may fail to perceive the central questions. It is agreed that researchers are not morally obligated to give subjects more information than the subjects need to act in their long-run best interests, particularly if there is a risk that they might respond differently if they only knew that they were being studied (as the Hawthorne effect, described in chapter 3, might suggest) (Gramlich and Orr 1975:107).

The ease with which participants may be overwhelmed with complex information led to suggestions about criteria for selecting the critical items to be given to participants. These suggestions include having a committee representative of potential participants who will make the decision (Veatch 1978:27), using a committee representative of both investigators and participants, or systematically interviewing surrogate subjects and allowing them to determine what is relevant (Fost 1975). With respect to psychiatric patients for whom research and treatment are intermingled, it has been argued that informed consent forms that provide minimal information are preferable to forms giving details of procedures. The former are less likely to be used as a substitute for discussions that the patients need for adequate comprehension of how and why they are to be treated. If consent forms with substantial written information are to be used, they should be subjected to review by parties other than those who have drafted them and be tested on "normal" and clinical populations to assure that they are reasonably comprehensible (Lidz et al. 1984:331). With respect to psychological research in prisons, a suggested ethical guideline is that the researcher be obliged to insure the prisoner/subject's understanding of its meaning (Brodsky 1980:83).

A representative list of the elements that might be divulged to the participants when obtaining their consent consists of: statement of overall purpose of the research; definition of the role of the participants in the project; explanation of the procedures involved (such as parties to interact with the participant, location of the research, time when the research is to be conducted, repetition of procedures, if any, and time required of the participant); description of possible discomforts and risks; description of possible benefits; alternative procedures to benefit participants, if any; an offer to answer any questions; and a review of what may not be disclosed to the individual (Levine 1978). Others (see Bower and de Gasparis 1978:36-7) suggest adding statements on data protection, auspices for the inquiry, publication of results, and the fact that the investigator cannot legally guarantee the identity or privacy of sources of information (as will be discussed later).

HHS guidelines define informed consent as "the knowing consent of an individual or his legally authorized representative, so situated as to be able to exercise free power of choice without undue inducement or any element of force, fraud, deceit, duress or other form of constraint or coercion." The following requirements, somewhat overlapping those listed above, are specified for informed consent in HHS-supported research: a fair explanation of the procedures to be followed and their purposes, including identification of any procedures that are experimental; a description of any attendant discomforts and risks reasonably to be expected; a description of any benefits reasonably to be expected; a disclosure of any appropriate alternative procedures that might be advantageous for the subject; an offer to answer any inquiries concerning the procedures; an instruction that the person is free to withdraw his or her consent and to discontinue participation in the project at any time without prejudice to the subject; and with respect to biomedical or behavioral research that may result in physical injury, an explanation as to whether compensation and medical treatment is available if physical injury occurs and, if so, what it consists of or where further information can be obtained.

An important aspect of the subject's rights and welfare pertaining to consent to participate has to do with freedom to withdraw from the study at any time. The American Psychological Association in Principle 5 of the "Ethical Principles in the Conduct of Research with Human Participants" (1973) states that ethical research practice requires the investigator to respect the individual's freedom to decline to participate or to discontinue participation at any time. The obligation to protect this freedom requires special vigilance when the investigator is in a position of power over the participant. Any decision to limit this freedom increases the investigator's responsibility to protect the participant's dignity and welfare. Similarly, the HHS guidelines require that subjects be notified of this right, which means that the researcher gives prior ethical commitment to the right to withdraw from research.

The right to withdraw, which is acceptable and reasonable in the context of medical research, may raise problems in social policy and evaluation research. Opposition to the right to withdraw may arise when research programs have made large investments in subjects. Moreover, sometimes this right is no longer available to the participants, as the research, particularly in large-scale social experiments, may have caused various irreversible social changes. In other cases, the unit of research is larger than an individual (such as a housing unit, class, hospital etc.); thus, the subject actually cannot withdraw (Veatch 197F536-7). With respect to subjects' withdrawal, it has been suggested (Capron 1975:140) that while subjects should not be forced to perform their contracts if they want to cancel them, it may be appropriate to include a provision for liquidated damages should they withdraw without adequate reasons spelled out in advance. (Other problematic issues specific to social experimentation will be discussed in a later section.)

Problems in Implementation of Informed Consent: In general, informed consent has to be implemented to prevent any violation of individual rights for self-determination and autonomy (for an example see Lidz et al. 1984:328). Under certain conditions, however, the procedure's utility and justification is questionable, and a more flexible application is warranted. This is particularly true in cases where the procedures of informed consent may interfere with the scientific objectives of the study. Certain elements in informed consent procedures (such as request for signature) may influence the decision of some individuals to participate in the research even though the experience may be relatively innocuous or benign (Singer 1979). What is more, in other cases, full disclosure of the purpose and the procedures of research may have substantial effects upon the phenomenon under study. "Experimental" or "expectancy effects" in overt experiments and need for social approval in surveys and observation techniques were found to affect the validity of responses (Rosenthal 1967, 1968).

Other difficulties concerning informed consent particularly important in the context of people-changing organizations pertain to its effect on the success of the treatment. Under certain conditions it may be defeating to convey to the subject the nature of the experiment or the type of treatment because the information may distort the outcome. In psychological testings the attitude of "being a guinea pig" may interfere with the reactions created by the experiment and preclude the ability to generalize to populations that do not have experimental attitudes (Campbell 1967: 304). Some experiments require deliberately concealing from the subjects what is being done to them, in order to arouse anxiety or fear so as to impel them toward what is believed to be more mature confrontation of their problems, rather than depending on their previously unsuccessful adaptations to these problems (Empey and Rabow 1961:679). In others yet, correct information about sponsorship of a study may result in "compliance bias," that is, the subjects trying to give responses that would please the treatment or research sponsor (Bower and de Gasparis 1978:38).

In some cases it is impractical to require consent because the costs of obtaining it from a large number of participants may be prohibitive, perhaps greater than the worth of the evaluation. For instance, regulations regarding access to records compiled by government agencies require the consent of the individual before information (such as on academic performance, measures of intellectual aptitude, delinquency, and crime) can be examined by researchers. These problems have raised questions concerning the utility of informed consent under certain conditions, where the research objectives are incompatible with the full implementation of consent procedures. It has been suggested that dogmatic insistence upon the procedure for all research, regardless of its impact upon the cost, selection of participants, phenomenon studied, or treatment provided, does not promote an optimal solution to the conflict between the pursuit of knowledge and subject rights and welfare. This is especially serious when the gain in confidence that rights are being protected is small, and the achievement of scientific objectives is substantially impaired (Reynolds 1979:110). Other more adaptive mechanisms might be used to demonstrate consideration for the rights and welfare of participants in such circumstances and are recognized by standard procedures. For instance, in research related to major policy issues, particularly in social experiments in natural settings, participants can be considered to have consented to such experiments by their general expectation that officials will try to improve the effectiveness and efficiency of government activity (Reynolds 1979:156).

HHS regulations specify that the informed consent procedure may be "modified" when three conditions are met (Title 45 CRF 46.110):

1. The risk to the subject is minimal.
2. Informed consent would interfere with the objective of the research.
3. Any alternative means for obtaining the research objectives would be "less advantageous to the subjects," that is, would provide for greater infringement upon their rights and welfare.

Other organizations funding research also emphasize interference with research objectives or invalidation of the responses as a reason for not requesting full disclosure when the research involves no or minimal risk (see Reynolds 1979:260). In short, as the purpose of informed consent is to ensure the ethical foundation of evaluation research, it may be desirable to substitute other guarantees for ethical conduct by the evaluators when implementation of informed consent procedures is incompatible with the research purpose or too costly. Therefore, evaluators must make judgments as to which strategy will best achieve their scientific objectives with negligible or no interference with subjects' right and welfare. In making their judgment, they inevitably may be criticized by some as paternalistic or be blamed by others for being autocratic. The ultimate responsibility for ethical conduct and the consequences of research lies, however, with the evaluators themselves, even where informed consent has been obtained. If sufficient guarantees for participants' rights have been provided through such mechanisms as government regulations and professional codes of ethics, most problems in evaluation research can be resolved to the satisfaction of all parties by relying on the evaluators' judgment and by attending to the rights and welfare of subjects. However, since many ambiguous situations and uncharted areas on the ethics of evaluation are still abundant, the final decisions on what is satisfactory practice by evaluators rests with the legal system, with the courts.

Confidentiality of Evaluative Data

Confidentiality and the Physical Protection of Evaluative Information. The need for evalation data, whether acquired through interviews, observation, records, or experimentation, frequently conflicts with the deeply held American value of personal privacy. Privacy, or the right "to be let alone," has been called by Louis D. Brandeis "the right most valued by civilized man" (Dissent in Olmstead v. U.S. 277 438, 48 S.Ct. 564 1928). Personal information is often considered to be an individual's property, to be used only for those purposes to which the individual agrees; it does not thereby become the collector's property to do with as he or she pleases.

Evaluation research in people-changing organizations poses a particular threat to individual privacy. It not only requires large-scale collection of information about individuals, but also collection of data for relatively long periods of time. The most important questions about the effectiveness of programs concern their effects over time, and the validity of their answers is enhanced by longitudinal research (Boruch and Cecil 1979:31-8). Therefore, prolonged protection of individual privacy is essential. But as Edsall (1975:22) notes, there are two sides to the confidentiality question: "the restrictions are necessary . . . not only to protect confidentiality, but also to get honest answers from the people studied." People will not cooperate in giving accurate information about themselves to researchers unless they are assured that what they reveal will never be used against them by bill or tax collectors or by law enforcement agencies, and that it will not become the subject of their neighbor's gossip. Assurance of confidentiality is necessary when information elicited is sensitive or when it could be used in threatening and nonresearch activities (Boruch and Cecil 1979:90).

The problems of confidentiality in governmental evaluation research were discussed elaborately, and specific solutions were offered, by the Committee on Federal Agency Evaluation Research (COFAER 1975), which was set up in 1971 by the National Academy of Sciences at the request of and funding from the U.S. Office of Economic Opportunity (OEO). The Committee was given a broad mandate to examine the government's activities in evaluation research and social policy experimentation, and to recommend ways of making these activities more effective and useful. In particular, it was asked to examine the confidentiality of data collected in these types of research, and to recommend ways of protecting the privacy of individuals who provide information to researchers.

The concern of the Office of Economic Opportunity with these issues arose from a particular incident during the New Jersey income maintenance project. This project was a major social experiment designed to measure the impact of various negative income tax plans on labor force behavior and other activites of low-income families (Kershaw and Small 1972). Participants in the experiment were asked to complete detailed questionnaires about their incomes, employment, and other activities, and were promised by the researchers that this information would be kept absolutely confidential. However, law enforcement officers saw in the experiment an opportunity to check on welfare cheating, and endeavored to get hold of confidential information. The researchers in charge of the experiment found themselves in a difficult position as they promised confidentiality but might not have been able to honor their pledge if the court saw fit to issue a subpoena.

This episode raised numerous issues that the committee addressed. Many are aspects of the physical protection of data or how to guard it against misuse. The committee recomendations discuss reduction of the number of people with access to identifiable records and reduction of the probability that individuals could be identified even after names and addresses or other identifiers (such as social security numbers) are removed (for instance, by merging files). The committee urged that administrative data collectors and evaluation researchers refrain from collecting sensitive personal data not directly relevant to research, and that identifying information not be collected at all.

To restrict the uses of data to those to which the individual agreed and had anticipated when providing information, the committee recommended that the forms used for data collection announce that the data would be used for statistical summaries in which the individual would not be identifiable. Restriction of secondary uses of data to statistical products in which individuals are unidentifiable may prevent any use of archived data for intelligence or investigatory purposes, that is, for actions or descriptions targeted on the individual. Identification of individuals is feasible when routine demographic data (such as age, sex, marital status, occupation, residence area) are maintained in the file and available with a comparable coding scheme in public records, when the participant has a unique set of demographic characteristics, or when significant resources are devoted to comparison of known data with the characteristic on the research file.

The HHS guidelines on confidentiality also require safeguards in the design of questionnaires, inventories, interview schedules, and other data-gathering instruments and procedures to limit the personal information collected to that absolutely essential to the project. The guide further recommends special coding, locked spaces for data, a ban or restrictions on "computer to computer" transmission of data (to be discussed later), provisions for destruction of edited, obsolete, or depleted data, and the eventual destruction of primary data.

Awareness of the possible identification of individuals has also led to a number of techniques for allowing access to research data to the scientific community but reducing the probability that identity of the respondents can be determined. It is an ethical concern in evaluation that research workers should not use the excuse of confidentiality to prevent their analyses from being checked by others (Bloomberg and Wilkins 1977:441). The techniques proposed include using the initial program research personnel to complete analysis for the outsiders (charging them the cost of the activity), restricting the public identifiers that are provided (such as birth data or Social Security numbers), providing a randomly selected subsample of the total sample for analysis, or using microaggregation (releasing average data on small subsets of participants) (Reynolds 1979:170-71).

Ways to maintain confidentiality can therefore be divided into two types: procedural methods and statistical strategies.

Procedural methods are designed to eliminate or to minimize the need to maintain direct links between respondents' identifications and other information that they provide to the evaluator about themselves (Boruch and Cecil 1979:93). Whenever feasible the most effective procedural technique to ensure confidentiality is to maintain participants' anonymity. And anonymity is best maintained if names or identifiers are not acquired or if identifiers are destroyed after the data are collected (for elaboration see Boruch and Cecil 1979, Ch.4).

When research requires repeated measures on the same individuals, a requirement common in evaluation or longitudinal research, identifying information must be retained for the course of the evaluation. Certain techniques have been developed to safeguard the anonymity of participants whose identity is retained (Reynolds 1979:171-72). A simple technique is to separate the list of participants from the data and keep them in separate locations with an identifying number providing correspondence between the two files. A more sophisticated technique is the link system, which requires maintaining three files: one with the identifying information and its own identification number, one with the data and a data-identifying number, and a third file indicating the correspondence between the two numbers (Astin and Boruch 1970). The third or linking file can be kept at a separate location to prevent breaches of security by project staff. The linking file could be stored in a foreign country, with an agreement that it not be released to anyone outside that country. This may aid in resisting disclosure of confidential data in legal proceedings (Blumstein 1967).

Statistical techniques for hiding individual identities include randomized response methods (Warner 1965; Boruch and Cecil 1979:Ch.5), the validity of which was found to be high in a criminal justice context (Fox and Tracy 1981). Another statistical technique is contamination. This rather drastic technique developed by the COFAER (Appendix B to COFAER report by Campbell et al. 1975), involves "innoculating" the data by adding a small "error" term to each variable, a random error with known distribution and an average value of zero. Such innoculation would not change the average values of variables used in the analysis and would increase the variance only slightly, but would have the advantage of precluding precise comparisons that would unambiguously identify respondents. For a large sample such modification would have little appreciable effect on the analysis and would almost guarantee anonymity for participants.

Another statistical method is the use of anonymous subsamples to estimate sensitive data for the larger sample that has identifying data (Boruch 1971).

Evaluators are also expected to ensure that the procedures used for acquiring information prevent their possible misuse. These procedures pertain to the security of data not only while they are collected, but also when stored or analyzed.

Special problems of security arise when data are processed—coded and key-punched—before they are entered into computer files for analysis. At this stage, a useful way to ensure anonymity is to destroy all identifying information or completely separate it from the research data. Further safeguards would include limiting access to data to authorized staff only and avoiding the duplication of records. Special problems occur when computers are used to process data. If data are stored and processed at a computer with diverse users, then it may be useful to have passwords to control access, cryptographic coding (scrambling), automatic monitoring of the use of files, or system verification of hardware-software integrity. Different users could be given access to different types or amounts of data, with no one user having access to the entire record on any individual (Reynolds 1979:170).

Use of data collected on the same individuals from several sources (for example, government agency and program data) may create additional problems. In most cases, data have to be merged efficiently from two or more sources, and additional information in each file is disclosed to personnel working on the other set of files. The following procedures will help to safeguard participants' anonymity: microaggregation (comparing average data on individuals aggregated into small homogeneous groups from two different sources); a synthetic linking by matching (merging data for pairs of individuals who have similar basic characteristics but are different persons) called "link-file brokerage"; cryptographic coding of information not required for merging, and provision of summary information on groups of participants (Reynolds 1979:172-3). These suggested techniques to maintain confidentiality are based on the assumption that the evaluative data are from a large sample size, and that the investigators have the financial and computer resources to implement them.

While data may be protected from misuse by technical procedures or statistical strategies, the possibility of a court ordering evaluators to divulge information has not yet been ruled out in legislation or case law.

Confidentiality and the Legal Protection of Data. As used by the law, confidentiality refers to the duty of certain people (typically professionals) not to reveal information that they receive in the course of their practice; they are liable to penalties for breach of their responsibility if they fail to protect these confidences. In evaluation research, these confidences are protected with a contract between evaluators and subjects, just as in written or unwritten contracts between physician and patient or attorney and client. Such contractual obligation in these established professions is either expressly agreed to or, more often, is required by the common law or by professional licensing statutes.

A contract solely between evaluator and subject cannot adequately preclude disclosure that is compelled by third parties, particularly the state. This presents an issue that is related to that of confidentiality: whether there is a legal privilege to resist forced disclosure of information conveyed under the promise of secrecy. In the attorney-client relationship, the concept of a testimonial privilege is very old. The privileges to withhold information gained by a physician or psychotherapist from a patient, accountant from a client, priest from a penitent, or journalist from source are conferred by legislature, and are immune to subpoena by courts of law.

Unlike such professionals, evaluators have little protection by law for the information that they acquire during the course of research. In fact, research conducted under government agencies could conceivably be brought under the Freedom of Information Act. The Code of Ethics of the American Sociological Association warns explicitly that research information is not protected as privileged communication under the law (Clapp

1974). The new threat that has arisen to the confidentiality of data collected by researchers in the course of evaluation is that a researcher will legally be compelled to reveal such information to a court or to Congress. In the New Jersey experiment already mentioned, both of these threats occurred. For the issue of confidentiality, this implies that researchers can no longer in good conscience promise that the information that they collect will be kept confidential (unless they will promptly destroy it or place it in a safe, foreign place). If they are being honest with their respondents, they must alert them to the danger that the information they give may be made available to courts or to Congress. Such warnings may decrease both the proportion of people willing to give information needed for evaluation and the honesty and validity of the responses.

Resolution of this dilemma involves a balancing of values. There is a strong public interest in enforcing the laws and making evidence available to courts, but these interests may conflict with other values, particularly with the protection of individual privacy. Current legal standards for confidentiality are based on the assumption that all citizens have a duty to provide information to assist the legal and legislative systems in executing their responsibilities; these standards apply to criminal trials, grand juries, legislative bodies, civil litigants, and administrative agencies. Only few and limited exceptions to this rule are acceptable. For instance, a constitutional amendment denies admissibility in court of the fruits of arbitrary search or seizure. Society is willing to take a risk that some criminal acts will be unpunished in order to guard against greater threats to the civil rights and liberties of all citizens. Similar reasoning led to the exclusion of certain "privileged communications," such as between a lawyer and client or a priest and penitent, from consideration as evidence in a court proceeding.

Some feel that the professional-client relationship of psychologists and patients is close enough to that of evaluators and respondents to justify extending the privilege of confidentiality to evaluators. Others view the analogy between newspapers and social science research as more convincing, since both seek knowledge that the public values (Hallowell 1985); in fact, much descriptive social science has been viewed as "slow journalism" (Reynolds 1979:308). The reasoning in both of these contentions is that society has an interest in fostering certain exchanges of information that would be jeopardized if their confidential nature could not be guaranteed, and that this interest outweighs the interest of producing additional evidence. There has been an attempt to apply this reasoning to communication between researchers and subjects (see COFAER 1975; also memorandum by Judge Renfrew in Richards of Rockford, Inc. v. Pacific Gas and Electric Co., U.S. District Court, Northern District of California No. C-74-0578-CBR May 20, 1976). It is argued that society has a profound interest in the research of its scholars, work that has the unique potential of facilitating change through knowledge. The public interest, the argument continues, would be served by making the information furnished in the course of evaluation research a class of privileged information.

Additional legal problems may arise in research pertaining to criminal justice issues. Researchers who acquire such sensitive data as self-reported criminality (crimes that have not become known to the police or in which the police did not relate the crime to the perpetrator) from known and identified subjects may stand in a posture of obstructing justice; they may be held in contempt of court if they do not submit the files for examination or impounding by a court order. It has been argued that not disclosing information that scientists acquire in the course of their research about crimes committed does not constitute obstruction of justice. Obstructing justice is generally construed in a narrow way, and usually requires interference with proceedings actually pending, with specific intent to do so. Researchers, the argument continues, are neutral and disinterested recipients of data collected for scientific purposes, who have no obligation to execute police or judicial duties (Wolfgang 1976, 1981). The present legal situation, however, does not ensure that such arguments will be sustained, and that the researcher's promise of confidentiality to respondents will be honored in court.

One way to prevent the use of such data in legal proceedings is to increase the generality of questions (for example, no precise date, place, or context about the criminal acts are collected). For illegal behavior, only precise information can be used for legal action. However, the trade-off for this technique is the reduced potential for analysis, as general information is usually less useful than precise data for understanding, theorizing, or evaluating (Bradburn et al. 1979).

Several suggestions for overcoming the problems of evaluators' confidentiality and legal protection of data have been made. All are premised to some extent on the state's placing greater weight on the benefits it will obtain from the evaluation than on its interest in seeing that laws are enforced when the latter would cause it to violate the confidences of evaluators and subjects. One solution is a statutory protection for information revealed to investigators as part of a social policy program, like the confidentiality given census data that is directly in the hands of the government itself (Capron 1975:141), or as are data collected by the Social Security Administration. More relevant in this case is the privileged status granted to approved projects related to alcohol and drug abuse according to the Drug Abuse Office and Treatment At of 1972, or to sponsorship by the Omnibus Crime Control and Safe Streets Act of 1976, or any type of research for which researchers have applied for and received a "confidentiality certificate" authorized by the secretary of DHHS (Title 42 CRF part 2a). This certificate authorizes researchers to protect the privacy of their research subjects; they may not be compelled in any proceedings to identify the subjects.

The second solution is the development of roots for privileges in the constitutional rights to freedom of expression, privacy, and fair trial. The communications of subjects to researchers could be recognized as privileged under such grounds (Nejelski and Lerman 1971). Courts, however, have in the past rejected this line of reasoning when it was asserted by journalists and scholars who fought for privileges against having to testify about their sources of information [for example, Branzburg v. Hayes, 408 U.S. 665(1972); Popkin v. United States, 460 F 328 (1st Gr.1972)].

Another possibility is to secure a promise from the prosecutor that nothing that respondents reveal to the researcher will be used against them in court (see Capron 1975:142).

The most direct route for developing a legal privilege for evaluators is through legislative efforts, as a common agreement prevails that such privileges will not come through case law (Reynolds 1979:309; see also Hallowell 1985). Two model statutes have been proposed. Boness and Cordes (1973:258-59) suggest that except in cases of murder, sabotage, espionage, or specific threat to life, researchers shall not be compelled in any proceedings to disclose the identity of the research subject, facts from which the identity of the research subject might be inferred or information furnished to the researcher by a research subject. The exclusion of serious offenses in this model statute, however, will still hinder collection of self-reported serious criminality.

The second and somewhat stronger model statute appears as an appendix to the COFAER report. Section 2 of the proposal (Nejelski and Peyser 1975:8-9) states that:

> No person shall be compelled pursuant to a subpoena or other legal process issued under the jurisdiction of the United States or any state during the course of any judicial, administrative, or legislative investigation or adjudicative proceeding to give testimony or to produce any information storage device, object, or thing that would (1) reveal any subject or impair any subject relationship by revealing the identity of the subject or the contents of information ... whether or not any explicit or implicit promise of confidentiality had been made ... or (2) reveal the contents of any information received, developed, or maintained by a researcher in the course of [analysis and publication].

As proposed, there are no exceptions to this privilege except when waived by both the researcher and the participant. This proposal would provide a much more general, unambiguous privilege than is now extended to any category of individuals in the United States (Reynolds 1979:309).

Another suggestion (Kershaw and Small 1972) is to grant immunity from subpoena process to types of projects designed to resolve policy or administrative issues, on the basis that such immunity is an executive privilege.

Arguments against extension of some form of privilege to researchers range from practical problems of the definition of bona fide research or researchers, as well as the possibility of impediments to prosecution of illegal activities, to broader considerations, such as society's current trend toward openness, and the tendencies of many legal experts to resist expanding the class of privileged communication (COFAER 1975:12). A major counterargument of scientists is that if such a privilege is denied them, it will deprive courts or Congress of substantial evidentiary sources provided by research, which could not elicit important information if confidentiality were not guaranteed. Furthermore, experimentation and evaluation research to improve public policies could be hindered if confidentiality privileges and immunity were not granted to evaluators.

It is, however, unusual for a social scientist to be confronted with a subpoena that requires disclosure of information. Similarly, the number of research projects that have actually terminated because of public disclosure is small, although there may be others that were not initiated over concern about lack of protection (Reynolds 1979:317). Aside from the special case of those doing research on crime and the criminal justice system, there is little evidence that a subpoena threat is a major problem for evaluation research. To evaluators in the criminal justice area, however, the issue of legal privilege is often a realistic matter (see for instance, Wolfgang 1976, 1981). The issue to most researchers undertaking program assessments may be only one of appreciating their worth; the subpoena threat is clear evidence that the value of their enterprise is not recognized by current legal standards. A legally sanctioned researcher's privilege or any other proposed procedure for providing immunity (such as by specific projects) will express the importance of evaluation research to the development of effective public programs and policies and will help to achieve them.

Program Experimentation, Random Assignment, Ethics, and Law

The research method most recommended in the evaluation literature is experimentation (Weiss 1972; Berk et al. 1985). As chapter 3 elaborated, classical experiments, with random assignment of subjects to experimental or control groups, have the potential of minimizing sources of internal invalidity in the research aprocess. As indicated in that chapter, controls by randomized subject selection permit experiments, if well designed and administered, to provide the most reliable comparison between results of existing programs and those of proposed innovations (see also, Federal Judicial Center 1981:2). Only when classical experiments are unfeasible for some practical reasons should the quasi–experiment be substituted and the random assignment of subjects be compromised with statistical or other types of control (Weiss 1972). Yet when program experimentation or conscious and systematic intervention "designed to yield results useful in the formulation of public policy . . . involves a sample of human population and sometimes a control group" (Brown 1975:79), it raises special ethical and legal problems. Several issues that pose problems in any context of program experimentation acquire more significance in the criminal justice area.

Respect for the Person. From an ethical viewpoint, social experiments epitomize the central dilemma posed by all experimentation involving human beings. They violate Kant's categorical imperative of "not treating mankind as an end, merely as means" (Kant 1938:97). The individual is "used" to achieve goals that do not give primary consideration to his or her own objectives, a violation of the principle of respect for the person. In experiments that use random assignment of subjects to treatments, people become means because the assignment disregards the needs and desires of individual subjects. People are also used as means when they are exposed to a novel program in a pilot study, because the purpose of the project is not exclusively to further the subjects' interests, but rather to produce information that may be used in future policy decisions.

The principle of respect for the person is not violated, however, when subjects consent to participate or when individuals incapable of exercising autonomy (such as children or mentally incompetent adults) receive adequate protection of their rights and interests in respect to their participation in an experimental program. Informed and voluntary consent obviates the potential for violating this ethical principle. It has therefore been suggested that in program experiments that are mandatory and cannot involve consent (such as those conducted in the context of law and criminal justice), special care should be taken to avoid unnecessary use of people to serve merely as means to the ends of experiments. Respect for the person requires that any mandatory requirement imposed for the purpose of experimentation should be justified. This problem, like other ethical problems that arise in the course of research, should be addressd by weighing the harms and benefits that the research may produce.

The cost-benefit analysis should consider who receives the benefit (the subjects or groups other than those harmed) and the ratio of benefits to harm. Because most often those harmed are likely to be the subjects, and those who are likely to benefit are future members of the class of the experimental subjects, the requirement that benefits clearly outweigh harms is a stringent standard for program evaluation (Federal Judicial Center 1981:27-8).

Due Process and Equal Protection or Treatment. From a legal perspective, programs sponsored by the government can be considered governmental activities, and they are thereby related to the rights of any citizens with regard to all government actions, specifically to rights of due process and equal treatment. These rights become an obvious issue because in government sponsored experiments, unlike medical or other experiments, the process of selection of individuals is highly visible and formal (Capron 1975). The concept of *due process* included in the Constitution (Fifth and Fourteenth Amendments) guarantees that fundamental rights, such as life, liberty, or property, will not be arbitrarily restricted by the government. Due process clauses have been interpreted to include both procedural and substantive review. *Procedural review* is limited in scope, and guarantees only that there is fair decision making before the government takes some action directly impairing a person's life, liberty, or property, before a determination that an interested party should suffer some burden.

. In *substantive review*, the court is concerned with the constitutionality of a rule rather than the fairness of the procedure. Its constitutionality is examined by questioning whether this type of lawmaking goes beyond the proper sphere of governmental activity. Two issues are examined: the relationship of the law (in our case, the protocol or directive for program experiments) to the goals or ends of legislation, and the means by which programs will help in achieving the goals.

In principle, the practice of experimentation, and the legitimate role of government in undertaking social and economic experiments, was recognized already in the 1930s when the Supreme Court was faced with challenges to attempts by state and federal authorities to restore economic and social order following the Great Depression. In his dissent in New State Ice Company v. Liebman [285 U.S. 262:31 (1932)], Justice Louis Brandeis stated, "There must be a power in the states and the nation to remould, through experimentation, our economic practices and institutions to meet challenging social and economic needs."

With respect to the relationship of program experiment to ends of legislation, the production of knowledge about the factors underlying legislative choices on what social policies to pursue was held to be an inherent part of the purpose of all social policy legislation (Aguayo v. Richardson 473 F. 2d 1090 2d Cir. 1973). If the contribution of an experimental program to legitimate public programs is clear and explicit (preferably in the original legislation), it appears that courts will assume that initiation of the project is appropriate (its actual design and implementation is a different matter). Further, once Congress permits experimentation, those charged with program administration have broad discretion in deciding when and how to conduct the experiment. Judicial officers are reluctant to rule on the wisdom or efficacy of such experiments (California Welfare Rights Organization v. Richardson 348 F. Sup. 491 N.D. Cal 1972). Nevertheless, it has been recommended that designers of social experiments adequately articulate ends which are reasonably related to legitimate goals of the state, that they demonstrate that the state has a legitimate interest in providing new knowledge about social interactions related to its policies, and that valid conclusions can be drawn concerning the relative effectiveness of various methods of distributing public services, benefits, and costs (Capron 1975:154).

With respect to means in relation to due process, the issue is whether the nature of the procedures or programs designed to achieve the goals of legitimate legislation interferes with or infringes upon fundamental rights. In *Aquayo v. Richardson* 473 f.2d 1090 (at p.1109), it was held that the state's legitimate desire to determine whether and how improvements can be made in a public program is suitably furthered by controlled experiments. Proof of the experiment's validity would therefore seem to be a minimum requirement if due process is to play any part in deciding about social policy experiments. Judges (as well as legislators and administrators) can be expected to require, however, that the burdens on the public treasury and on citizens' lives from research are justified by its being well-designed and properly executed (Capron 1975:153).

In sum, the conduct of social experiments is not likely to be challenged by the courts on the basis of failure to observe due process if they meet the following conditions: They are designed to achieve important state objectives (as expressed in legislation), the knowledge needed to improve either the goals or the programs designed to accomplish these goals is impossible to obtain in any other way, the state has a compelling interest in such knowledge, and the experiment has been designed to minimize its adverse impact upon its subjects' fundamental rights (Capron 1975:154).

The second related issue is equal protection of law (or equal treatment) which is more problematic from both legal and ethical viewpoints. Equal protection of law, which is mentioned in the Fourteenth Amendment, and incorporated through interpretation into the Fifth Amendment, is applied whenever legislation or governmental activity involves some classification. The equal protection clause requires that government treat similarly situated individuals in a similar manner. But the advantage of social experiments over other research methods is that they provide individuals with different experiences or "unequal treatments," so that the effect of such "inequality" or variations in treatment can be systematically measured.

Typically, an experiment involves differentiation at three stages: Selection of a problem for a study, and hence, of a target population, of a particular locale, and finally, of individuals for treatment or control groups (Capron 1975:156). With regards to selection of a problem, there appear to be no fundamental rights associated with establishing priorities of one problem over another. Legislators and administrators are not obliged to give equal treatment to all problems (Reynolds 1979:296)

In choosing places for the experiment, it is preferable for scientific, economy and efficiency reasons to select locations with manageable subsections of the population. The choice of groups may depend on matters related to their representativeness, the cooperation of local government, or simply proximity of the evaluator to the evaluation site. In Aquayo, which dealt specifically with equal treatment concerning the choice of locales for experimental programs, the court held that the equal protection clause does not require "that the state plunge into statewide action or do nothing." It is legitimate to introduce programs gradually, as long as such a gradual process is in line with the goals set by the legislature. Decisions reached by the legislature on the basis of factors related to economy, efficiency, or scientific demonstration would very likely be sustained by the courts. Such decisions made by the administrators of a social experiment without legislative guidance would be more vulnerable (Capron 1975:156).

The right of equal protection acquires special importance in the actual selection of individuals to participate in the research program. Three factors appear to be critical: The individual characteristics used as a basis for selection procedures, the nature of the selection procedure, and the types of effects the individuals would be expected to experience (Reynolds 1979:296; Federal Judicial Center 1981). With regards to individual characteristics, any selection procedure that uses variables related to race, sex, or religion ("suspect categories") as criteria for selecting research participants is likely to receive close scrutiny by the courts if fundamental rights are in question. Procedures such as stratified sampling in attempts to study group differences or variable effects of programs by demographic characteristics are a case in point. It is questionable whether a mere desire to produce knowledge for its own sake will be a compelling enough goal to justify the use of such procedures when fundamental rights are involved. It seems that the court will decide each case individually, weighing such factors as the importance of the knowledge for implementing legislative ends, the severity of problems created by the lack of knowledge, and the feasibility of substituting alternative research designs (Capron 1975:155; Federal Judicial Center 1981).

The Selection Procedure: Random Assignment. The final stage of selection in experimental settings is the selection of individuals or, more specifically, the assignment of individuals to different treatments.

In general, citizens have a right to expect that rational criteria will be used for assignment of treatment or receipt of its benefits. Random assignment to a treatment or control group may unfairly discriminate in controlled experiments. It has been argued that random assignment by definition is discriminatory: "some people receive the experimental treatment while others are excluded from it, and either the treatment or its withholding may involve the risk of harm" (Zeizel 1983:49). It has also been argued that if a decision concerning allocation of benefits (the treatment) is random, meaning it is made on the basis of chance, such a selection procedure is in violation of constitutional requirements for rational, rather than arbitrary, differentiation or classification of similar individuals (Geis 1967; Baunach 1980). This is particularly problematic in situations in which eligibility for the proposed treatment is presumed to be based on needs.

The response to such an argument is that as long as there is no confidence in the relevance of the presumed criteria, random assignment is the most rational way to distribute benefits and burdens. Furthermore, random assignment is the only way to verify the validity of these presumed criteria. Under such conditions, random assignment is not arbitrary, and it can be considered rational by constitutional criteria. Any other basis would involve personal judgment that would reduce confidence in the validity of conclusions from the evaluation of the proposed treatment. Random selection is arbitrary only in the sense that it depends on the operation of chance, but that is what makes it both valuable in experimentation and fair to all of those whom it gives an equal chance of being chosen to be a research subject.

Random selection is not arbitrary in the constitutional sense, namely, that it is dependent on the pleasure of a person making the selection who may impose burdens unfairly, arbitrarily or on impermissible grounds. Also, random selection in experimentation can be reviewed by statisticians who can determine whether the method used did generate a random result (Capron 1975:161-62). As it is agreed that random assignment is the most rational (or preferred) way of achieving the objectives of evaluatin (Zeizel 1983; Federal Judicial Center 1981), and as the acquisition of knowledge is a legitimate, perhaps compelling, governmental interest, this method is likely to stand legal challenges to its constitutionality (Capron 1975; Winick 1981).

To summarize, if proposed research is not otherwise constitutionally impermissible, random assignment of research subjects should not be considered a violation of equal protection or be regarded as discriminatory treatment (Winick 1981:359). Cases such as McGlohen v. Department of Motor Vehicles, 1977, and Healy v. Bristol, 1975 (experimental projects under which some individuals guilty of driving under the influence had their license suspended while similarly convicted persons were sent to alcoholism treatment programs without having their licenses suspended) support the principle that provision of benefits for some but not for others similarly situated, benefits for which there is no constitutional entitlement, will not offend equal protection as long as the selection criteria are rational (Winick 1981:361).

In situations where other methods seem more reasonable or our sense of justice demands individualized treatment (such as taxing or criminal sentencing), random assignment would be an inappropriate and arbitrary method of selection.

Type of Treatment and Expected Effects. Although random or other scientifically based assignment of subjects to treatment or control groups may withstand constitutional tests, ethical difficulties still arise when these selection procedures are not practiced. These difficulties pertain to subjects' expectations concerning the type of treatment they will be receiving and its effects.

In people-changing organizations, decisions about treatment accorded to individuals usually are based on some relevant criteria for differentiation, such as individuals' needs, qualifications, merits, or deserts. When differences in the qualifications of people can be identified, equal treatment often calls for differentiation based upon these attributes in order to achieve individualized treatment fairly, efficiently, and effectively.

Individualization of treatment by relevant criteria reflects the principle of respect for the person—by attending to needs, qualifications, merit and equal treatment—rather than treating unequal persons equally (Federal Judicial Center 1981). Random assignment to treatment, on the other hand, by definition is blind to differences among individuals, and when substituted for individualized treament, it can cause harm that has to be justified.

In the context of criminal justice, random assignment is particularly problematic because its hallmark is chance. This makes it seem especially incompatible with penological ideas of just deserts (von Hirsch 1976; Fogel 1978), which stress that the individual should receive the particular treatment or penalty that he or she deserves, rather than one selected randomly. However, an examination of the just deserts theory suggests that this concern is unwarranted.

The principle of just deserts means that penalties will be neither more nor less severe than the ones reserved, but within the same range or degree of severity the content of punishment can vary. For example, judges may send offenders to similarly severe but different prisons, and prison administrators or staff may assign equally severe but different cells, programs or treatments, but all may be in accordance with the principle of "desert." Norval Morris (1981:264) in another context has noted that:

> desert is not a *defining* principle, but is rather a *limiting* principle; [it means]

> that the concept of just desert properly limits the maximum and the mini-
> mum of the sentence that may be imposed, but does not give us any more fine
> tuning to the appropriate sentence than that.

In other words, the principle of just deserts dictates only the boundaries of severity. It does not require the application of identical sentencing disposi-tions or correctional treatments, nor does it rule out equivalent but equally severe dispositions.

A commonly raised argument in favor of random assignment in the context of criminal justice is the following: in comparison with the in-justices and disparity resulting from the individualized treatment model (see Cullen and Gilbert 1982:104-24), justice will better prevail by using randomization. Random assignment, it is suggested, is preferable to pur-poseful assignment (such as assignment by need) which has been shown to be subject to individual bias and misdirection. In the words of Geis (1967:34): "from the offender's viewpoint, the vagaries of random assign-ment for experimental purposes might seem preferable to the lottery of exposure to the considered judgment of a member of the judiciary."

This argument, however, is misplaced. Where methods other than ran-domization seem more reasonable under the circumstances or where our sense of justice requires individualized treatment, random assignment will be found arbitrary (Winick 1981:362). When random assignment is sub-stituted for individualized decisions, it carries a heavy burden of justifica-tion because it means there has been no bonafide attempt to tailor treat-ment to individuals' qualifications. The Federal Judicial Center (1981) has emphasized that the good faith attempt to individualize is itself valued, independent of the worth of its results. In other words, even if the actual results are believed to create such great disparities (in the dispositions of treatments) that they amount to randomness, that alone does not justify allocating treatment on an intentionally random basis. The Judicial Cen-ter's report suggests, however, that it is possible to suspend individualized judgments when the status quo is believed to produce harmful results, and when the proposed experiment is likely to produce important improve-ments in the results of future individualized judgments.

While randomization and disparate treatment practices may not violate legal criteria for deserved dispositions, they still raise some ethical dilem-mas about the disposition given to the control groups. The accepted ethical rule concerning participation in research is that participation is justified if it is advantageous to the experimental subjects, and if no added restraints are placed on participants for experimental purposes. As straightforward and as logical as this principle is, it still neglects the problem of relative deprivation falling upon those unfortunate enough to be included in the control group (Morris 1966).

The principle pertaining to the effects that research participants can expect to experience has been that the use of a control group is justified if subjects receive the disposition that they would have received anyway, if the experiment did not take place. Such subjects suffer no consequences that ordinarily would not have come their way. They should have anticipated receiving the traditional treatment now used for the purpose of contrast with the innovative one. "That their confreres drawn by random lot are being released much earlier is not their ill fortune but rather that other's good fortune" (Geis 1967:39). Only burdens that might be greater than would ordinarily be expected, such as longer imprisonment, can cause substantial objection (Morris 1966).

Nonetheless, an argument of harm and unfairness resulting from unequal treatment may still be raised by those who are assigned to the control groups if they are deprived of what they suspect to be experimental benefits or a more favorable treatment accorded to others with the same qualifications or of the same "desert" (Morris 1966).

The use of control groups in the context of correction raises another ethical dilemma concerning a presumed (rather than relative) deprivation of benefits for the control cases. An experimental design that tests a new treatment implies that some offenders (the controls) will be deprived of the presumed benefits of the innovation. If a proposed program, which is grounded in a potentially viable theory, is expected to bear fruits of success, then it would be unethical to bar some offenders from participation, from sharing the expected benefits.

Some scholars have argued that this concern is misplaced and unwarranted, because in the absence of definite information about the benefits, if any, from the program, control group offenders are not knowingly deprived of any benefits. As Boruch (1976:187) put it "there can be no benefit if the program is useless, and often we cannot know if it is useful without an experiment." The validity of this response, however, may be somewhat attenuated by the claim that doubt and uncertainty characterizes all social science results that are based on probabilities and statistical inferences. Such evidence is avowably tentative and suggestive rather than conclusive and firm. Furthermore, it has been argued that we do not institute policies or programs that we think are inferior, but rather those that we have strong reasons to assume are superior, that have the potential to improve the offenders' condition (Capron 1975).

With regard to the presumed superiority and benefits of proposed programs, recent empirical evidence from the area of medicine indicates that when trials of expected benefit are carried out, the preferable treatments (those presumed to be beneficial) are not known in advance. Although the common expectation in a trial study is that the innovation will be a clear winner, the outcome is often one of grave doubt (Gilbert et al. 1983:77-8). Empirical evidence from nonmedical fields also suggests that educated guesses, even by experienced and intelligent adults, are far off about half the time, which is reason for discounting pretrial expectations or hunches of investigators about the superiority of proposed programs (Gilbert et al. 1983:79). A study that examined the effectiveness or the presumed benefits of numerous correctional programs has also seriously questioned any beneficial results of numerous programs that were expected to have positive effects (Martinson 1974). Although the exact scope of these findings have been challenged (Palmer 1978; Gendreau and Ross 1979; Wilson 1980), there is still much agreement that a great number of programs did not produce the expected results or the anticipated desirable effects.

Several solutions have been proposed for some of the ethical problems posed by evaluation research that uses random assignment. First, the pursuit of knowledge concerning the improvements of human conditions has to be recognized as an ethically desirable activity as long as the benefits outweigh the risks to the participants (Reynolds 1979; Zeisel 1983). Because evaluation research that uses random assignment provides the least ambiguous results concerning the effectiveness of a program or treatment, it is in itself ethically superior to any other design. Rutstein (1969:384) asserts:

> It may be accepted as a maxim that a poorly or improperly designed study involving human subjects . . . is by definition unethical. Moreover, when a study is in itself scientifically invalid, all other ethical considerations become irrelevant.

Because experimentation nonetheless presents unavoidable ethical difficulties, it has been suggested that program evaluations: should only be considered when the following threshold conditions are met:

> First, the status quo warrants substantial improvements or is of doubtful effectiveness. Second, there must be significant uncertainty about the value or effectiveness of the innovation. Third, information needed to clarify the uncertainty must be feasibly obtainable by program experimentation, but not readily obtainable by other means. And fourth, the information sought must pertain directly to the decision whether or not to adopt the proposed innovation on a general nonexperimental basis. (Federal Judicial Center 1981:7)

Fortunately, these threshold conditions are likely to be met in almost any situation in which a reasonable and theoretically grounded program is proposed.

Some scholars have argued that ethical concerns about relative or presumed deprivations can be transformed into a scientific advantage, and randomization can thereby be justified if the reality and constraints of treatment resources are taken into consideration: random assignment is a fair and equitable procedure for allocating benefits where there is an over-supply of eligible recipients for scarce resources (Boruch et al.1979:38; Winick 1981:361; Zeisel 1983:50). Furthermore, it has been suggested that randomized experiments are most likely to be carried out successfully when the benefit (real or imagined) is short in supply, and the demand for the benefit is high. This rationale dovetails neatly with normal managerial constraints: "new programs cannot be emplaced all at once but must often be introduced gradually. Experiments can then be designed to capitalize on the staged introduction" (Boruch et al. 1979:38). Thus participation of the control group at a later date can be scheduled or other programmatic options can be provided for them. These arrangements can be justified when there are not enough vacancies to include all eligible subjects, and they may answer the criticism of depriving the control group of benefits.

Provision of other programmatic options for a control group means that rather than comparing a novel program against no program or against the traditional dispositions, the design may compare program variations against one another. Such comparisons, it has been argued, may also provide valuable insights into variations of the program that are appropri-ate or effective with certain types of offenders (Baunach 1980:438). However, such a solution may result in the traditional treatment programs never being persuasively challenged or empirically tested for their pre-sumed ineffective results or their relative effectiveness compared to the innovative programs.

Another way to overcome deprivation claims is to find groups that are identical but do not have expectations of identical treatment (for instance, due to their geographical distance) (Federal Judicial Center 1981).

Conclusion

This chapter has presented some of the legal problems and ethical dilem-mas that evaluators face in the development of knowledge about the merits of proposed innovative programs. It should be evident that the role and importance of ethics and law in evaluation research is only beginning to unfold. There are still many ambiguous situations and uncharted areas in which the ethics of evaluation may be a concern.

In solving these unanticipated or unforseen problems, the judgment and integrity of evaluators are crucial. Their awareness of the various demands and conflicting interests involved in any successful program evaluation, and their attention to these matters, will determine if science develops in a manner acceptable to ethics and morality and with a legitimacy recognized in the courts of law.

9

Institutionalizing More Rational Policymaking

Each of the preceding chapters discusses a different aspect of evaluation research and decision guidance. All are concerned with increasing the effectiveness of people-changing efforts by providing valid information on how well alternative types of practices and policies achieve their goals. But how can decision makers be assured of continual feedback on the impact of their activities? How can the knowledge thus gained become cumulative as guiding principles, be regularly applied in making decisions, yet always be amenable to further testing and to justifiable revision? How can what is learned be profound, practical, and politically acceptable?

These questions have multiple answers. There are alternative ways of organizing evaluation research, of using it to guide decision makers, of deciding what studies are to be done, how, and by whom. Each way of doing any of these things usually has both advantages and disadvantages compared to the others. Probably, a balanced mixture is optimal. But what are the alternative sources, sponsors, functions, and methods of evaluation research and decision guidance in people-changing efforts?

The Three Fountains of Knowledge

Traditionally, there have been three major sources of scientific direction for people-changing activities: universities, independent research organizations, and in-house research offices in government agencies, such as departments of mental health or correction, and boards or departments of education. Each of these three sources has had a different role and history in evaluation research and decision guidance, each has both special potentialities and limitations, and all vary greatly in the volume and quality of their work.

Universities often have advantages of expertise, independence, detach-

201

ment, and continuity over other organizations in research, but none of these advantages is guaranteed. Professors, especially in graduate schools, are expected to be familiar with the frontiers of knowledge in their fields, but these fields are often narrow and separate disciplines. There are also competing specialties and approaches within each discipline, and little certainty as to which is best. Furthermore, although university research is presumed to be sophisticated, much of it is carried out by graduate students employed as research assistants who are prone to error because they are novices or are unfamiliar with the settings of their studies.

Because professors are independent, especially when tenured, they are free to shift their focus of inquiry away from the concerns of people-changing agencies. In addition, the academic objective is publication. While the audiences addressed are diverse, the respect of other academicians is an uppermost concern, hence the topics and style of professorial writings often seem strange and useless to practitioners. Finally, of course, the first claim on a professor's time is teaching: research, publication, and public speaking strongly compete with teaching in major universities, but do not have the regular schedule and persistence of instructional activities. Overall, universities stimulate, review, and sometimes administer evaluative research on people-changing efforts, but often cannot assure continuity of service to a particular government agency. Professors best serve government or other large organization evaluation efforts as consultants, trainers, innovators in theory and methodolgy, and directors of research projects in which their independence from the agencies studied is especially important.

Partly because of the unavailability of universities as sources of hired research when and where it is wanted, and partly as a free-enterprise response to the possibility of profits from government-funded evaluations, a large variety of independent research organizations study people-changing efforts. Some are old, such as the Brookings institution, but many are new, evoked by the burgeoning of research grant and contract money in recent decades. Some are clearly for profit and others are nonprofit, but all attempt to maintain a dependable income from research. They are extremely diverse in size and quality.

A major advantage of these organizations is that they have research staff for full-time assignment to a project, whereas professors and graduate students have other commitments. However, major universities now have autonomous research centers or institutes with full-time professional staff, and many academicians can obtain leaves of absence to direct research, especially when they secure grants that pay their salaries. Thus, schools, non-profit firms, and purely profit-seeking companies compete for research funds from government agencies, foundations, and other sources.

The universities prefer grants to study new problems, to test abstract ideas, or to experiment with innovations, while the firms more often seek government contracts for impact evaluations on specific laws or programs; but neither concentrates exclusively on one or the other type of research. Indeed, all tend to shift their interests considerably when changes occur in the types of research for which funds are available.

A major advantage of the most experienced research organizations (Rand, Abt, Inslaw, and others) is their development of teams of researchers from diverse educational backgrounds (law, psychology, sociology, mathematics, systems engineering, and other fields) who have completed numerous large research projects in a variety of local, state, and federal agencies. They thus develop distinctive procedures and expertise for doing research efficiently in new settings. They also have exceptionally good communication techniques, both for oral and written presentations, and to diverse types of audiences, for which they give their staffs special training. Their emphasis on learning by comparison of different practices makes them particularly effective in large studies that cover several city, county, or state jurisdictions. They have developed well-tested team organizations and management principles (detailed in St.Pierre 1982).

One disadvantage of many firms and of some university research centers or institutes is the insecurity of their earnings, hence their high staff turnover. Dependence on "soft money" from a few grants or contracts makes their income fluctuate greatly with their success or failure in competing for these awards. There probably are a larger proportion of grossly inferior research groups among firms than among universities, but these are concentrated mainly among firms organized for profit which expanded rapidly when government crash programs poured unusually large sums temporarily into certain categories of study that were then receiving much political attention (mental health in the 1960s and crime in the 1970s, for example). In analyzing 236 evaluations financed by government grants or contracts, Bernstein and Freeman (1975) developed a research quality scoring system that stressed experimental design, random sampling, multivariate statistics, and good measurements. By their system, academic researchers had an average rating of 5.9 and entrepreneurial researchers an average of 2.9.

The growth and impact of knowledge in large people-changing organizations (primarily government agencies) probably depends most upon the quality and stability of their own in-house research personnel. How well evelution research is institutionalized, and how it affects policy, is also influenced tremendously by the relationships between staff researchers and government policy makers. In some times and places the research unit is coopted by the agency directors who suppress findings that are critical of agency policies; contrastingly, in some organizations the in-house researchers are asked to evaluate specific policies, to report whatever they find, and to discuss fully and fairly its implications for policy. In such settings, the researchers often take the initiative in proposing to test various practices or trying to resolve issues that they find are of concern to administrators.

When university and independent research organizations undertake special projects sponsored by government, it is usually in studies for which in-house researchers are thought to lack time or other resources, or independence. However, outsiders often have problems due to their unfamiliarity with the research setting, their inadequate rapport with the persons studied, and their constraints from having to travel a considerable distance to the research sites. This may be why Conner's (1977) study of twelve evaluations of reform programs found that planned randomization was achieved in six of eight studies by in-house researchers, but in none of four studies by outsiders. Collaboration of in-house and outside researchers is often essential for good studies by outsiders.

Whether in-house researchers are purely data collectors or are also interpreters of studies by themselves or others, but most of all, whether they are independent and constructive critics of the organization or are sycophantic toadies, largely determines their impact on policy. In these respects, the performance of agency researchers has varied greatly. Therefore, much can be learned from even a minimal exploration of their history and variation.

The Evolution of In-House Research

All people-changing agencies have to compile statistics to justify their budget requests. These figures are presented in an agency's annual or other reports. Minimally, the statistics summarize population movements (clients recieved and released) for various units of the organization, as well as the administrative basis for entry or departure, such as new commitment, transfer, or discharge. At best, they also count many demographic and other attributes of the clientele: sex, age, race, offense, diagnosis, sentence, prior criminal record, security classifications, county from which committed, and so forth. There may also be statistics on employees. The growth of computerized record keeping has made such compilations easier than ever to compile with much detail and speed. Often their raw data comes from precoded record forms filled in by casework or administrative staff with copies retained by them for their purposes. Indeed, increasingly the entries are made directly on a computer rather than on a paper form, they are stored electronically, and they are retrievable at various computer terminals in the agency. As pointed out in chapter 1, all this activity is part of what is often called the MIS, or management information system. In recent years, organizations that have developed scientific decision guidance that relies on routine compilation and analysis of standardized record data refer to these operations as their "decision support system" (O'Sullivan 1985).

MIS statistics measure a people-changing organization's achivement of its immediate goals—what it does, for whom, and to some extent, how. They are needed by administrators for rationality in seeking appropriations and in planning. But in-house research has a better chance of influencing policy when it expands its concern from measuring the achievement of immediate goals to cover activities more pertinent to long-run goals (such as providing trade or academic courses). It is a major advance when an organization assesses attainment of intermediate goals (such a gains in vocational or academic ability, rather than merely exposure to instruction). Its optimum contribution occurs, however, when it also assesses achievement of ultimate objectives (such as reduction of recidivism or relapse).

The in-house evaluation of ultimate goal attainment that now exists in long-established people-changing organizations developed after crude types of MIS were already long established. While there were sporadic followup studies by mental health, correctional, and other types of agencies earlier, efforts to institutionalize such activities by in-house research units had their first period of rapid growth in the late 1950s and early 1960s. Their beginnings in correctional systems occurred at about the same time in several parts of the English-speaking world, and were always initiated by people outside the organization.

In Britain, the Criminal Justice Act of 1948 called for government-sponsored evaluations of correctional programs, which led in the 1950s to establishment of the Home Office Research (now "Research and Planning") Unit. It achieved an international influence in 1955 by publishing Mannheim and Wilkins' *Prediction Methods in Relation to Borstal Training*.

In 1957 the Budget Committee of the California legislature, faced with demands for tens of millions of dollars for rehabilitative treatment in California's rapidly growing correctional facilities, accepted a recommendation of its legislative analyst that it create research divisions in the departments of Correction and Youth Authority. These departments were to use about 1 percent of their appropriations to determine how well the 99 percent used for other enterprises "cured" those who were "treated." For the next decade, California probably had more full-time personnel in long-term-oriented evaluation research (rather than in MIS) than all other American correctional agencies combined.

In the U.S. Bureau of Prisons, a Research and Statistics Office long existed as an MIS for federal prisons. Dr. Francis Sayre, a retired Assistant Secretary of State whose distinguished career had included a stint on leave from Harvard Law School's faculty to direct Massachusetts' prisons in a period of crisis, urged Federal Bureau of Prisons Director James Bennett in 1957 to secure funds for a scientific assessment of whether the Bureau's rehabilitation programs were effective. Deciding that a university would provide independent outside research specialists, they sought a professor who had worked in prisons. I was fortunate to be selected, and the study, done while I was at the University of Illinois, was published in 1964 as The Effectiveness of a Prison and Parole System. Meanwhile, the Bureau started its own evaluation research unit around 1960.

Simultaneously, a number of state correctional systems added outcome evaluation to the work of their MIS units, with Massachusetts, Wisconsin, and Washington especially prominent. Many state agencies also collaborated in research with interested departments of state universities, and conducted a variety of abstract criminological studies in addition to program evaluation. In the 1970, aided by the U.S. Department of Justice and other federal and state government financial grants, there was much improvement in MIS capacities, and additional states began evaluative research. In many correctional agencies, however, nothing more than an MIS unit has ever existed as in-house research.

In education, mental health, addiction treatment, and other people-changing fields, where federal or state" offices increasingly demanded evaluations of the programs that they funded, in-house outcome evaluation research grew in the same decades.

What features distinguish the in-house research units that have been most stable and influential in their efforts to enhance the rationality of people-changing efforts? Until Mary Kennedy's (1983) study of in-house evaluations in education, no systematic study addressed this question. From her inquiries in sixteen very diverse school districts in fourteen states, and from my numerous observations over several decades in some of the most successful and a few abortive efforts to institutionalize evaluation research in national, state, and local correctional and drug-treatment agencies, several tentative generalizations emerge.

The Shaky Supports of In-House Research

As might be expected, the most important source of security and autonomy of in-house evaluation research is the stability of leadership in the larger organization of which it is a part. This has been dramatically evident in California corrections in the following two examples: there has been over a quarter century of stability in the research office of the Youth Authority, directed by Keith Griffiths from its inception in 1958 to his retirement in 1983, but a number of turnovers of leadership and drastic reorganizations in the Department of Corrections research staff, although they began in the same year. The Youth Authority had five directors in this period, each of whom worked amicably in a central post with his or her predecessor. Contrastingly, the Department of Corrections had a larger number of changes, several of them sweeping and acrimonious; its research leadership and staff changed drastically numerous times, undergoing shifts largely because the evaluators and managers failed to develop a mutual understanding of how each could best help the other.

One additional factor that has greatly influenced the impact of evaluation researchers on policy makers in several organizations has been the extent to which evaluators control the MIS. The ability to make efficient assessments of programs depends upon ready access to MIS data on the organization's clients, as well as on use of the data-processing equipment and personnel who are in an MIS unit before evaluation research directed at intermediate or ultimate goals is attempted. MIS units are there first, have routinized operations, and are customarily called upon for quick tabulations whenever top officials want separate counts of available data on the organization's current or recent operation. Because they can answer questions from organization directors more quickly and confidently than other types of researchers, MIS units are often valued most by these directors and kept autonomous. The MIS personnel also have frequently resisted the addition of other types of researchers, as well as evaluations by outsiders, and many give low priority to data-processing that they are asked to do for the newer researchers. One feature of the most stable and influential in-house evaluation research units, such as those of the California Youth Authority and the Massachusetts Department of Correction, is that they operate the MIS in addition to performing other types of evaluation research. One research director supervises all statistical and other studies, and all of their personnel are regarded as part of one collaborative unit.

Ideally, an in-house evaluation research unit in a people-changing organization should be more stable than the policy-making leadership, as are accounting and bookkeeping units in a business. Like these fiscal assessment personnel, evaluation researchers should be respected as autonomous professionals who present objective and accurate figures that speak for themselves to a large extent. Financial statements that accountants produce usually are accepted and valued even when they deliver bad news. MIS has achieved this status, but more long-term-oriented outcome evaluations of people-changing efforts are not sufficiently standardized and well-established for such acceptance. Too many policy makers are unaccustomed to scientific assessment of their effectiveness, and they do not routinely seek it when reviewing their policies. Too often, when they call on evaluation research, they expect it to serve their career interests and fund-seeking efforts by confirming the wisdom of their past decisions. Therefore, many state and county in-house evaluators avoid testing their agency's well-established policies, or test them but have unfavorable reports suppressed by their superiors.

Resistance to disconfirming research results is understandable and has occurred even in agencies with well-accepted and secure evaluators, such as the California Youth Authority. For example, correctional administrators early in the 1960s had an inordinate faith in "talk" methods of treating prisoners, equating psychotherapy and counseling with all rehabilitation (as many people still do). Officials wanted to employ psychiatrists in such prisoner treatment activity, but usually could not afford them full-time, so they used the more available clinical psychologists, psychiatric social workers, and most often, specially trained line correctional staff. The Youth Authority, anxious to get funding for more individual psychotherapy for confined wards deemed emotionally disturbed, authorized controlled experiments in 1959-60 at both the Preston School of Industry and the Nelles School for Boys. After random selection of experimental and control cases at each institution, the experimentals received about one hour of psychotherapy twice a week, a few with a part-time psychiatrist and the rest with clinical psychologists or psychiatric social workers whom the psychiatrist supervised. The control groups were in the regular programs without this extra service. Results were different in the two schools: the subsequent parole records were slightly better for the experimentals than for the controls at Nelles (which had the least criminal youth), but there were distinctly higher parole violation rates for the experimentals than for controls at Preston (which had more chronic offenders) (Guttman 1963).

This contrast between findings and expectations was a bitter pill for the senior policy makers to swallow. They argued that the results may have reflected the qualities of the individual psychiatrists or the brevity of treatment. However, publication of results in the Youth Authority's regular series of research reports, as well as the earlier announcement of the experiment's inception, alerted the state's Finance Department; they squelched efforts of the Youth Authority to proceed with plans for adding psychotherapy teams headed by psychiatrists to the staffs of all of its institutions. The Department of Correction's unsuccessful efforts to justify group counseling on the basis of their research, part of which was described in chapter 4's discussion of the quasi-experiment by Kassebaum, Ward, and Wilner (1971), also ended financial support for its even more clearly ineffective talk programs.

A quite different consequence of resistance to research results emerged from the Fricot Ranch Experiment of the Youth Authority, designed to test the impact of the size of a residential dormitory on prisoner behavior. The experiment, continued for five years, randomly assigned the agency's youngest wards (aged eight to fourteen) to a twenty-person or a fifty-person dormitory at this remote, low-security correctional facility in the state's northern mountains. At the end of a year on parole, those from the smaller unit had 37 percent violations and those from the larger one a 52 percent violation rate (Jesness 1965). These differences continued in longer followups, and they seemed to be explained by a process evaluation which showed that the personal contacts between inmates and staff were five times more frequent in the smaller than in the larger residences. Later, a survey of social climate in sixteen different-sized dormitories at several institutions confirmed Jesness' impression of more personal relationships in smaller units (Knight 1971). Nevertheless, the state's architects did not shift from their long-established standard of 50-person dormitories which, because of their isolation from evaluation research, they mistakenly thought were economical.

Still later, when new construction was not occurring, a federally funded quasi–experiment at Preston School of Industry compared the consequences of placing an average of thirty-eight or an average of forty-seven youths in the standard dormitories designed for fifty. It also compared for each of these housing conditions the use of five with the use of six staff per unit (not all on duty simultaneously, but as the total personnel assigned to cover the unit for twenty-four hours, seven days a week). The findings were that fewer youths per unit, but not variations in staffing, resulted in fewer violent incidents and escapes; better youth-staff relationships; more youth concern with postrelease problems; earlier release of the boys by the parole board, which was unaware of a boy's housing crowdedness, but reacted to the better behavior records of those in the less crowded dormitories. Cost-effectiveness analysis showed that because of the briefer confinement of youths in the less-crowded units, the state had a net savings of $68,923 per year by not filling a fifty-person dormitory to capacity (Duxbury et al. 1980).

It is unfortunate that cost-effectiveness data were not estimated for the Fricot Ranch findings, and, conversely, that the Preston study did not have a behavioral or an economic analysis of the postrelease records of the youths in the two conditions of housing density. If the Preston postrelease findings on parole violation rates proved consistently to favor the less-crowded units, as did those at Fricot, the cost-savings would be still greater for it. In any event, correctional architects and administrators in the United States, unlike those in the Netherlands and Sweden, have been slow to learn from such research that they can save the state money in the long run by more investment in the compartmentalization of correctional institutions. A reduction in resistance to guidance by research requires better communication between researchers and the higher officials in government, and also of researchers with legislators and the mass media.

Although in-house researchers are located administratively within the departments of the executive branch of government that are concerned with people-changing efforts (such as education, corrections, or mental health departments), their impact and stability depend not only on attitudes of these division heads, but also on how well their capabilities as researchers are known to those who assist the governor (or mayor or other executive) in budget making, and to key staff in legislative (or council) budget committees. It has been said by the best-informed sources that in California, among the most influential supporters of Youth Authority researchers have been the offices of the Legislative Analyst and the Finance Department. The fact that the proposal for such an in-house evaluation unit was initiated by these offices doubtless sparked their interest, but subsequent communication of research results contributed to their persistent support of the Authority despite their failure to appreciate the significance of the findings on architecture.

Crucial to widespread support for an evaluation research unit are its research record and its dissemination of findings. To best survive political struggles and turnovers in government, the heads of research agencies should be tenured civil servants with records of nonpartisan employment, competence, honesty, enthusiasm, and dependability. To establish such a reputation, the research for which they have been responsible should be routinely published and distributed to a wide range of interested parties in the government, as well as to universities and to other research organizations. These reports should always include a clear, nontechnical summary in front. Popular summations should be disseminated even more widely as oral presentations at many meetings and as press releases. There should also be publication, at least annually, of a summary of research in progress and of past completed studies, topically arranged to show the accumulation of knowledge on each issue that they address. These practices build widespread confidence that the research unit always makes a full disclosure of results, whether popular or not.

An important factor in the need for institutionalization of evaluation research is that the effectiveness of programs changes over time. These changes may be partly due to shifts in the characteristics of an agency's clients, societal trends, and other developments independent of the agency's programs. They also often reflect changes in the agency. As Malcolm Feeley observed in trying to explain the limited impact of once much-heralded court reforms:

> Ultimately the success of an innovaton must be judged by how it performs under . . . routine rather than . . . initial conditions. . . . What worked when supported by ample federal funds often fails when supported by fewer local tax dollars. . . . What worked for a charismatic leader and zealous followers may bog down with an ordinary staff. (1983, p.37)

Who determines what an in-house research unit studies? Should the researchers passively await requests for evaluation of particular practices and policies, or should they take the initiative in deciding what to assess? The quoted observations by Feeley suggest the desirability of continuous monitoring of the achievement of goals, especially when computerized records make this feasible and inexpensive. Ideally, decisions on what to evaluate, when, and in what manner, should be collaborative, with inputs from many parties, but not at the cost of sacrificing researcher objectivity in assessing the validity of findings. Frequently an independent assessment of the quality of in-house evaluations is desirable, serving functions similar to those of an audit of an agency's accounting staff by an outside CPA. Such an audit may well be done by university or independent agency researchers.

The security of an in-house evaluation research unit depends largely on widespread confidence in its ability to provide useful solutions to management problems in the pursuit of generally accepted organizational goals. Some clues as to how this may be achieved are available.

Convergence of Research and Management on Intermediate Goals

The various types of experts on the needs of people-changing agencies are like the legendary blind men and the elephant. Each focuses on a different part or aspect of the whole, so that every expert reacts correctly to a portion of the problems, but is unaware of what others discern.

Management is especially preoccupied with pressing problems in maintaining order, providing essential services, securing or developing competent staff, avoiding scandals, keeping expenses within budgetary limits, and maintaining good relationships with the powerful people in government or elsewhere whose support is most crucial to managerial careers. These are primarily problems of meeting immediate goals in daily activities, although some, especially staff development and keeping good will, are directed to more distant objectives that can be called intermediate. This is not to assert that managers are never interested in ultimate goals, such as recidivism reduction, but the ultimate is not nearly as salient for them, as urgently pressing for action, as the other objectives listed above.

Academic experts, on the other hand, are most likely to focus on more remote goals, such as reduction of crime, mental illness, or addiction. These, of course, are also the people-changing objectives that are of greatest interest to the general public. Some academicians, however, also attend to more intermediate goals, such as, increasing clients' knowledge or skill, giving them psychological insight, or understanding their social relationships and subcultures. A few may even have considerable interest in management but may conceive of its problems more abstractly than the actual managers are likely to do in the course of their pressing everyday operations.

When researchers come directly from the academic world to government agencies, the rapport, mutual aid, and understanding between them and agency managers are limited if each persists only in prior orientations. Sensing this, agency directors often recruit in-house researchers from their operations staff, particularly clinical psychologists or social workers. These clinicians combine training in research methods with a better understanding of agency perspectives and settings than do people coming directly from the universities. Some of the clinicians have become outstanding evaluation researchers, but many prove rather narrow in their concerns, focusing on illustrative cases rather than on statistical demonstration to check ideas, or relying excessively on test and questionnaire data rather than on the behavior records of their research subjects.

New heights of rapport between researchers and administrators became evident in many people-changing agencies during the 1970s and 1980s. The contraction of jobs in academe simultaneously with increased federal and state support for evaluation research shifted the career orientations of many Ph.D.'s to applied rather than abstract science. Policy makers became more familiar with research for the following three reasons: there was wide dissemination of evaluation research findings by the federal government and the news media; federal funds were allocated to agencies for duplication of what research indicated were exemplary projects; many new professional journals and organizations in people-changing fields brought policy makers and researchers together. Perhaps most important, however, has been a shift in evaluation research from focus on ultimate goals to greater concern with intermediate goals, and thus, a convergence with management interests.

In the criminal justice field, the shift in concerns of evaluators was much affected by the popular conclusion from the Lipton, Martinson, and Wilks (1975) survey that, as Martinson (1974) put it, "nothing works." Officials grasped at this release from pressure to demonstrate that they could change criminals. They drew support from some law professors and others who asserted that just desert and humane treatment rather than recidivism reduction should be correctional goals; some also implied that such an approach might both increase justice and reduce crime (Morris 1974; Fogel 1978; Singer 1979).

Actually, several publications showed that the conclusion that nothing works in efforts to reform lawbreakers is achieved only by analyzing evaluations without guidance from well-grounded theory (Gendreau and Ross 1979; Andrews 1980; Glaser 1980). These publications, as well as this volume, present much evidence that a large variety of soundly conceived and targeted efforts can reduce recidivism. Yet the National Institute of Justice (1981) emphasized achievement of intermediate goals in touting its "Exemplary Projects." For example, in corrections, it endorsed Montgomery County's Work Release/Prerelease Center in Maryland as a source of employment and training for offenders, and only added later that this was shown to reduce recidivism; it praised the California Youth Authority's Ward Grievance Procedure as resolving disputes and gaining acceptance from inmates and staff, with no mention that youthful offenders often need to learn peaceful dispute resolution skills to reduce their difficulties in dealing with employers and others; it extolled the Columbus, Ohio Parole Officer Aide Program as expanding the job opportunities of ex-offenders, with no reference to its crime-reduction potential. Similar focus on intermediate more than on ultimate goal accomplishment is typical of other recent publicity for criminal justice innovations.

Any immediate goal, such as providing academic instruction for prisoners, is directed at reaching intermediate goals, such as improving reading, writing, and arithmetic skills. The intermediate objectives, in turn, are presumably means of achieving ultimate goals, such as recidivism reduction. Impact evaluation is easiest for researchers and most attractive to officials if measurement is undertaken one goal at a time. This may also prove to be the most successful way to identify the most effective means of achieving ultimate goals.

Failure to separate types of goal achievement issues was the glaring deficiency of most of the evaluations of correctional education and vocational training reviewed by Lipton and associates (1975:184-207). These reviewers only probed whether the exposure of prisoners to instruction reduced recidivism rates, rather than whether the prisoners learned anything. Most inmates assigned to prison schools have previously had much difficulty in their schools in the outside community. They found the classroom experience humiliating, but often were passed to higher grades when they had not learned enough to meet the higher standards in their new grade. This makes schooling even more frustrating. Therefore, in evaluating correctional education it is especially important to obtain valid data on the learning gains of the pupils during their incarceration. These learning gains are the intermediate goals, sometimes achieved with impressive success in prison settings, especially with teaching machines and rewards for demonstrable progress. Only when there is information on such gains is it appropriate to evaluate the impact of correctional education programs on postrelease criminality; this is done by relating these gains rather than school attendance to recidivism rates.

Giving priority to evaluating intermediate goal attainment can muster stable support for in-house evaluation. It is in assessing the achievement of middle-range goals that researchers assist management most promptly and definitely, because the research provides data on what their programs accomplished. Indeed, budget offices and legislators increasingly demand evaluation report. Sometimes such reports are mandated in the funding or enabling legislation, such as the statute in California that provides state funds to counties to establish and operate youth service bureaus and delegates to the Youth Authority the task of monitoring these bureaus (see California Youth Authority, 1985).

In large people-changing organizations that rely on hundreds of disconnected individual case-study judgments by officials but do not check them for consistency or consequences, there are opportuities for in-house researchers to take the initiative in determining the patterns in routine case decisions, and their relationship to attainment of intermediate objectives. This kind of research can then produce prediction tables and decision guidelines for attaining not only more consistent decisions, but also both intermediate and ultimate case objectives. Such guidelines were demonstrated in chapter 6 for parole, court, prison and probation or parole supervision decisions that were oriented to a variety of goals. Similar gains could come from the development of guidelines for routine case decisions in education, mental health, personnel administration, and many other settings.

Roles and Relationships of In-House Evaluators in People-Changing Organizations

It is always well to remember, as Kennedy (1983) points out, that "in-house evaluators are hired to fulfill specific organizational needs, and their budgets . . . are determined by the [management's] . . . estimate of what is required to meet their needs. Evaluators compete for funds with the very programs they evaluate. Under these circumstances, the organization necessarily influences at least some aspects of the evaluator's activities"

(1938:522). Her observations are based on an intensive study of in-house evaluators in sixteen very diverse school systems in fourteen different states. In three of the systems she found so much recent change in the organization or turnover in evaluators or both that no clear role and stable set of relationships existed. In the other thirteen she identified four distinct patterns of in-house evaluator roles that she called technician, participant, management facilitator, and independent observer.

Patterns similar to these four are also evident in other kinds of people-changing organizations. Kennedy's typology is presented here with two caveats. The first is that any such classification really consists of what Weber (1978) called "ideal types"; they are an observer's conception of the pure pattern to which any specific person only conforms approximately. Most people actually share attributes of several types at various times, but may usefully be classified as predominantly of one type. The second caveat is that the comments on these types here reflect my impressions of them in a variety of people-changing organizations that I have known, and they may differ in some respects from Kennedy's account, although they are basically similar.

Technicians make only highly standardized types of in-house evaluations, and only when these are specifically requested by their superiors in the organization or mandated by law. They contribute little or nothing to management decisions on what programs or aspects thereof merit evaluation, the choice of research designs, or the interpretation of results. They are typically experienced MIS "number crunchers," efficient at routinizing the tabulation of data for standardized statistical reports. They also can be effective in making case record forms more efficient than they usually are when designed by clinicians. Their functions, which are essential, resemble those of the bookkeepers in an accounting department. If they are under enterprising evaluation researchers of other types, their efficiency can be applied to making the data in case records fit standardized categories that are demonstrated by research (such as that described in chapter 6) to be pertinent to routine but important case decisions. Tabulation of such data would greatly facilitate development and use of base-expectancy evaluation statistics, and decision guidelines.

Participants are evaluators who, Kennedy aptly asserts, "tend to serve people rather than issues, and . . . tend to take their clients' issues as their own" (1983:530). The "clients" that she refers to are the bosses of the evaluator, those higher up in the staff hierarchy, rather than the ultimate consumers of the organization's activities, such as students, patients, or prisoners. The participant type of valuator is typically a person who has been employed for some years at another job in the people-changing organization (for example, as a clinical psychologist or social worker). Some have studied research methodology while on that job by part-time enrollment in universities to qualify for civil service promotion. They are selected to direct evaluation research partly because higher officials know them well, believe them to be loyal, and attach great importance to having an evaluator who knows the organization rather than someone fresh from a university or from another agency.

Participants are often given managerial responsibilities, especially planning and budgeting, in addition to evaluation research. They usually are cautious about transmitting research findings to outsiders, and may be collusive with higher officials in suppressing data not favorable to management. This suppression usually is given a facade of legitimacy by their questioning the validity of findings that discredit current polices, although they accept evaluations equally weak or weaker that support the viewpoints of those in power.

Management facilitators are supervisors of evaluation who participate in executive policy making and agency monitoring with appreciable independence, and whose primary objective seems to be to help rationalize the organization in order to maximize its effectiveness. They can only be effective in an agency with leadership that shares these objectives, is secure in its position, and has clear authority in the staff hierarchy. They identify with such leadership, and Kennedy insightfully observes that they frequently use "we" when speaking of management policy making. They are eager to discuss the findings of their evaluation research and to take into account both favorable and unfavorable evidence on the merits of current policies. They are concerned with maximizing the organization's service of the public interest.

Independent observers are evaluators whose primary commitment is to scientific detachment and objectivity rather than to increasing the organization's effectiveness. They work hard at expanding knowledge for its own sake, and are even more careful than the management facilitators to present all of the qualifying or contrary evidence and inferences when they report their results. They are reluctant to take a stand on the practical implications of their findings, or to be identified with any side in policy disputes, for fear of appearing biased in their pursuit of the facts. As Kennedy observes, their image of themselves as maintaining an appropriate role "was more important to them than the services that were provided" (1983:540).

It is probable that the independent observers are at times more rigorously scientific and objective than the management facilitators, but it is unlikely that they are as influential in making an organization more effective. The optimum institutionalization of evaluative research in the guidance of a people-changing agency is a leadership that integrates top administrators and researchers into a collaborative policy-shaping team.

Linkage among Organizations and the Impact of Evaluation Research

The discussion of goals in chapter 2 pointed out the frequent contrast of latent and manifest goals in organizations. In particular, personal objectives often guide the work of many employees in a way that does not further the ultimate goals of their employer. One of the most obvious llustrations of such incompatibility of personal and organizational goals in people-changing agencies occurs when the employees make their work easier by keeping clients occupied primarily with games, television, and other time-killing activities. Thus, they avoid the hard work and frequent frustration involved in helping clients acquire new vocational skills, work habits, in-slights and relationships.

Adoption by officials of practices and policies that gratify in the short run, whether or not they are beneficial in the long run, occurs in many types of organizations. Christopher Stone (1975) points out that one of the problems in controlling crimes by corporations is that executives are promoted or go on to better jobs elsewhere on the basis of the impressions that they create by their short-run accomplishments. If their work increases sales or raises profits by violating antitrust, honest advertising or other business-crime laws, there is little prospect that the offender's company will be charged with the offenses, and if charged, it will only be prosecuted years later. In the unlikely event that the company is eventually penalized severely for these practices, the executive who first increased profits by committing offenses is likely to have advanced to a better job before the penalites are imposed, and will not be blamed for them.

In people-changing organizations, the long-run effects of staff practices in changing the conduct or abilities of their clients are too seldom known, because little or no research is done to assess these practices. When research provides knowledge, however, it still may not be reflected in agency policies, or if it leads to new policy formulations, the policies may not be carried out in practice. For example, regardless of directives, prison officials interested in easy management of the institution typically get skilled work done by assigning it to inmates with the most relevant preprison skill training and experience, rather than to the inmates whose postrelease employment prospects could be most improved by their developing a skilled trade in prison. Alternatively, after a prisoner receives trade training and experience while in maximum or medium custody, officials transfer him to unskilled work during the last portion of his confinement because he is then a safer risk for minimum custody placements where his skills are not needed; yet there is evidence that rates of postrelease utilization of prison-acquired trades diminish appreciably if the trade training ceases during the last several months before release (McKee 1978, 1985).

This failure of an agency's policy to be guided by the long-run goals of the larger organization of which it is a part reflects what has been called "loose coupling" or "weak linkage" among either the components of an organization, the several organizations comprising a larger system (such as the criminal justice or the mental health system), or such a large system and the rest of the society in which it exists. For example, within separate units of a prison or the separate wards of a mental hospital, staff are often highly autonomous in trying to make their jobs easier, independent of its effects on the institution. Also, courts and prisons affect each other but are so loosely coupled that court policies are made without considering consequences of prison crowdedness. Finally, these two criminal justice agencies and the police are not only poorly linked with each other, but none of them are guided adequately by feedback on the consequences of their practices for the total crime problem.

All organizations become more responsive to the interests of the larger whole in which they are nested only as their leadership becomes more aware of the impact of their policies and practices on the larger system, and their officials at every level are rewarded for contributing to the total system's functioning and discredited for impairing achievement of system objectives.

The purpose of evaluation research is to provide feedback on the consequences of policies and practices. This feedback is most influencial if it not only shows what policies and practices best serve intermediate or ultimate goals, but also shows *why* they are more effective than others. As chapter 4 detailed, understanding why methods worked or were ineffective in the past enhances the ability to design operations on the basis of valid theory, hence to achieve goals successfully in the future. Evaluation research must be continual, however, to determine how well practices still work, and to subject explanations to further tests that may lead to their improvement.

The greatest external validity in evaluation, chapter 4 argued, is probable if research is based on theories from the "pure" sciences that have been confirmed in many settings. The laws of learning from psychology and the law of sociocultural relativity from sociology and anthropology were cited as examples of such scientific principles having wide practical use. Other laws could be drawn from these and other disciplines, notably from economics. Less abstract theory is used in most applied research, but its prospects of being found valid are heightened if it is deducible from more general principles that have been widely confirmed. Chapter 4 illustrated this in reporting on the fruitfulness of reintegration theory to the Massachusetts Department of Correction in reducing recidivism.

Many academic researchers tend to be concerned with abstract rather than applied research, hence with testing the validity of a theory rather than the utility of a practice. These interests can be combined, however, by deducing from a theory the effects that a practice should have with a particular type of subject in a specific kind of setting or circumstance, then testing to see if it has these effects. Such research could be furthered by better communication among managers of people-changing agencies, their in-house researchers, and the faculty and graduate students of universities, if they are oriented to the problem of why some practices should achieve particular goals more successfully than other practices. This type of communication should be promoted by inviting presentations by in-house researchers at pertinent university seminars and by encouraging faculty and graduate students to explore research possibilities in people-changing agencies.

There are professional organizations in this country that bring such people from practice and research together. The Illinois Academy of Criminology and the Association for Criminal Justice Research (California) are two of many state groups established for this purpose, and the American Society of Criminology is one of several national organizations. George W. Fairweather, a great pioneer in theory-guided evaluation of mental health programs, with Louis G. Tornatzky (1977), propose that a center for experimental social innovation be established at every major state university to foster collaborative assessment of people-changing efforts in the state. Berk et al. (1985) urge national promotion of "social policy experiments." These could certainly be profitable investments for society.

Upper-level mental health officials in ten states and the federal government were each given a randomly chosen two of fifty abstracted mental health research reports by Weiss and Bucuvalas (1980), and all were asked to rate the reports by checking 5-point scales for twenty-six descriptors. Those of the 155 officials who were classified as decision makers were given three additional descriptors. Factor analysis showed that these descriptors cluster into five factors: *Research quality* descriptors ("objective, unbiased," "provides quantitative data," and so forth) were the most highly correlated with the officials' responses on whether they would use the research results ("Assuming your office had to consider the issues discussed ... how likely is it that you would take the ... results into account?" ($r = .54$). *Challenge to status quo* ("challenges existing assumptions and institutional arrangements," "implies need for major change in philosophy, organization or services") was next most correlated with use ($r = .26$), but almost identically related was *conformity to user's expectations* ("supports a position already held," "consistent with a body of previous knowledge") (r = .25). Less related to use were *action orientation* ("contains explicit recommendations," "analyzes effects of factors that decision makers can do something about" (r = .16), and *relevance* ("timely," "relevant to the issue your office deals with"), which was based on items only given to decision makers (r = .14).

These authors conclude that research must first of all convince practitioners of its validity, which is a strong argument for use of the most rigorous methods possible, including controlled experiments where feasible. It was somewhat surprising that truth was the first test of research usefulness rather than its focus on timely needs, with both research quality and conformity to user's expectations being tests of truth, but research quality most related to use.

The Stanford Evaluation Consortium, an interdisciplinary seminar that met intermittently for about six years, observed, according to its spokesperson: "Society has to act each year on the basis of its best present picture, risky though that process is. Evaluation checks on the contending beliefs rapidly and thus can reduce the short-run risk of ill-conceived action" (Cronbach et al. 1980:67). Such reduction of risk depends on communication between evaluators and those who decide on policies, and on their agreement as to the goals of policy and practice, as well as on the pertinent facts. Figure 9.1, based on a chart from this consortium, is an oversimplifed view of the relationship of such agreement to the basis for policy making.

If managers and researchers agree on agency goals and both accept re-

FIGURE 9.1
How Areas of Manager and Evaluator Agreement on Goals and Facts
Determine Four Bases for Policy Making
(based on Cronbach et al. 1980:92)

	Areas of Agreement	
	On goals:	
	Agree	Disagree
On facts:	The Bases for Policy Making:	
Agree	Rationality	Validated Facts But Divergent Goals
Disagree	Managers's Unvalidated Judgment on Facts Pertinent to Accepted Goals	Manager's Reactions to Most Persuasive Rhetoric and to Personal Impressions

search findings on facts, the ultimate in rationality is conceivable: policies and practices empirically and logically appropriate to maximizing goal achievement. Such consensus seems most probable with good in-house research, provided there is a close linkage among researchers, policy makers, and practitioners, so that each is highly responsive to the needs and knowledge of the others. Attainment of this ideal has been impressively close in the research-based systems of client classification in California, Michigan and Wisconsin (described in chapter 6), which now have been copied in most states, with or without the desirable local research on whether the import needs modification to fit the perhaps different circumstances where it is being adopted. Such guidelines quite literally routinize rationality in case decisions, and they could be developed for a large variety of fateful decisions in people-changing agencies of many types.

Wherever managers and researchers differ in the goals that concern them, their actions often reflect divergent objectives. Managers are usually more concerned with immediate goals, while evaluators—especially those from universities—focus on the ultimate ends of society in people-changing efforts. Only favorable political reactions to evaluations by outsiders are likely to pressure managers in such a situation to focus on societal concerns, but managers and researchers often share an interest in assessing the attainment of intermediate goals.

If there is agreement on goals, but mangement is not convinced of the facts as evaluators report them, policy will be based on the judgment of facts that managers respect most. This situation calls for improvement in the quality of research or in communication regarding its quality or both. If there is disagreement on goals as well as facts, the rhetoric and personal impressions most persuasive to managers will determine policy.

Levinger and Boruch (1983) compiled evidence to prove that in education, evaluation research has had a major influence on federal policies, legislation, and budgets. They show that many lower-level education adminstrators, as well as university professors of education, who have made sweeping generalizations to the effect that summative evaluations have no impact, have simply been unaware of the extent to which legislators and cabinet officials demand that their staffs compile the best available scientific evidence for their decisions. This impact may be greater in education than in criminal justice or mental health agencies because much more evaluation research has been done in education, aided by the fact that test and grade records provide more readily available, precise, and valid information for evaluation than can be procured in other fields. This should be a challenge to improve the data collected for guiding other types of people-changing efforts.

The Research and Planning Unit (known as "RPU") of the British

Home Office has in the 1980s achieved perhaps the world's best integration of in-house, academic, and independent organized research. Explaining how it retains a focus on immediate or intermediate goals, the RPU's "Research Programme, 1985-86" asserts:

> In developing . . . both in-house and external research, the RPU is guided by the customer-contractor principle: any project included in the programme must have a firmly identified 'customer' within the Home Office. This ensures that the programme remains in touch with administrative and management needs. When a research requirement is identified, the project is either commissioned from universities or other research bodies, or is allocated to internal staff. Occasionally, the RPU may use the external budget to buy-in fieldwork or other assistance for a study which has been planned by its own staff.
>
> . . . . It is important that this . . . does not stifle the growth of fresh ideas for research from outside the government and for this reason the RPU will continue to give careful consideration to research proposals which emanate from outside the Home Office.
>
> The RPU continues to value its links with academic researchers, many of whom help the Unit in its day-to-day activities by such means as consultances, seminars and in many other ways. (1985:(3-4)

In all governments—national, state and local—a close linkage among line staff, agency managers, both in-house and outside researchers, and top policy makers, enhances agreement on both goals and facts at every level of decision making. This book has been devoted to presenting ways of reaching such agreement, hence of making rational people-changing efforts more routine.

References

Aaronson, David E., Thomas C. Dienes, and Michael C. Musheno. 1978. "Changing the Public Drunkenness Laws: The Impact of Decriminalization." *Law and Society Review* 12 (Spring):405-36.

Ackoff, Russell L. 1978. *The Art of Problem Solving.* New York: Wiley.

American Child Health Association. 1934. *Physical Defects: The Pathway to Correction.* New York: the Association.

American Correctional Association. 1976. "The Use of Prisoners and Detainees as Subjects of Human Experimentation: Position Statement Officially Adopted." *American Journal of Correction* 38 (March):14.

American Psychological Association. 1973. *Ethical Principles in the Conduct of Research with Human Participants.* Washington, D.C.: the Association.

Andrews, D.A. 1980. "Some Experimental Investigations of the Principles of Differential Association Through Deliberate Manipulation of the Structure of Service Systems." *American Sociological Review* 45 (June):448-62.

Annas, G. J., L. H. Glanz, and B. F. Katz. 1977. *Informed Consent to Human Experimentation: The Subject's Dilemma.* Cambridge, Mass.: Ballinger.

Astin, A. W. and R. F. Boruch. 1970. "A Link System for Assuring Confidentiality of Research Data in Longitudinal Research." *American Educational Journal* 7 (August):615-24.

Babst, Dean V., Don M. Gottfredson, and Kelley B. Ballard, Jr. 1968. "Comparison of Multiple Regression and Configural Analysis Techniques for Developing Base Expectancy Tables." *Journal of Research in Crime and Delinquency* 5 (January):72-80.

Baird, Christopher S., Richard C. Heinz, and Brian J. Bemus. 1979. *The Wisconsin Case Classification/Staff Deployment Project: A Two-Year Follow-Up Report.* Madison, Wis.: Wisconsin Department of Health and Social Services, Division of Correction, Project Report No.14.

Bakwin, H. 1945. "Pseudodoxia Pediatrica." *New England Journal of Medicine* 232 (June 14):691-97.

Barber, Bernard. 1973. "Experimentation on Human Beings: Another Problem of Civil Rights." *Minerva* 11 (July):415-19.

_____.1980. *Informed Consent in Medical Therapy and Research.* New Brunswick, N.J.: Rutgers University Press.

Bartlett, C. J. and Calvin G. Green. 1966 "Clinical Prediction: Does One Sometimes Know Too Much?" *Journal of Counseling Psychology* 13 (Fall):267-70.

Baunach, Phillis Jo. 1980. "Random Assignment in Criminal Justice Research." *Criminology* 17 (February):435-44.

Beck, James L. 1979. "An Evaluation of Federal Community Treatment Centers." *Federal Probation* 43 (September):36-9.

Beha, James A. II. 1977. "Innovation at a County House of Correction and Its Effect Upon Patterns of Recidivism." *Journal of Research in Crime and Delinquency* 14 (January):88-106.

Berk, Richard A. 1983. "Recent Statistical Developments: Implications for Criminal Justice Evaluation." In *Handbook of Criminal Justice Evaluation. See* Klein and Teilmann.

_____. 1983. "An Introduction to Sample Selection Bias." *American Sociological Review* 48 (June):386-95.

Berk, Richard A., Robert F. Boruch, David L. Chambers, Peter H. Rossi, and Ann D. Witte. 1985. "Social Policy Experimentation: A Position Paper." *Evaluation Review* 9 (August):387-429.

Bernstein, Ilene Nagel and Howard E. Freeman. 1975. *Academic and Entrepreneurial Research.* New York: Russell Sage Foundation.

Bloom, Howard S. and Neil M Singer. 1979. "Determining the Cost-effectiveness of Correctional Programs: The Case of Patuxent Institution." *Evaluation Quarterly* 3 (November):609-28.

Bloomberg, S. A., and L. Wilkins. 1977. "Ethics of Research Involving Human Subjects in Criminal Justice." *Crime and Delinquency* 23 (October):435-44.

Blumstein, Alfred. 1967. *Task Force Report on Science and Technology, President's Commission on Law Enforcement and the Administration of Justice.* Washington, D.C.: U.S. Government Printing Office.

Blumstein, Alfred and Jacqueline Cohen. 1979. "Control of Selection Effects in the Evaluation of Social Problems." *Evaluation Quarterly* 3 (November):583-608.

Blumstein, Alfred, Jacqueline Cohen, and Daniel Nagin, eds. 1978. *Deterrence and Incapacitation: Estimating the Effects of Criminal Justice Sanctions on Crime Rates.* Washington, D.C.: National Academy of Sciences.

Bohnstedt, Marvin and Saul Geiser. 1979. *Classification Instruments for Criminal Justice Decisions.* Washington, D.C.: U.S. Department of Justice, National Institute of Corrections.

Boness, F. and J. F. Cordes. 1973. "The Researcher-Subject Relationship: The Need for Protection and Model Status." *Georgetown Law Journal* 62 (October):243-72.

Boruch, Robert F. 1976. "On Common Contentions About Randomized Field Experiments." In *Evaluation Studies Review Annual,* ed. G. V. Glass: No.1. Beverly Hills: Sage.

_____.1971. "Maintaining Confidentialty of Data in Educational Research." *American Psychologist* 26 (May):413-30.

Boruch, Robert F. and Joe S. Cecil, eds. 1983. *Solutions to Ethical and Legal Dilemmas in Social Research*. New York: Academic Press.

_____.1979. *Assuring the Confidentiality of Social Research Data*. Philadelphia: University of Pennsylvania Press.

Boruch, Robert F., David Rinckopf, Patricia S. Anderson, Imat R. Amijaya, and Douglas M. Jasson. 1979. "Randomized Experiments for Evaluating and Planning Local Programs: A Summary on Appropriateness and Feasibility." *Public Administration Review* 39 (Jan.-Feb.):36-40.

Bower, Robert T. and Priscilla de Gasparis. 1978. *Ethics in Social Research*. New York: Praeger.

Bradburn, Norman M., Seymour Sudman, and Edward Blair. 1979. *Improving Interview Methods and Questionnaire Design*. San Francisco: Jossey-Bass.

Brecher, Edward M. 1978. *Treatment Programs for Sex Offenders*. Washington, D.C.: U.S. Department of Justice, LEAA, Prescriptive Package.

Brodsky, Stanley, L. 1980. "Ethical Issues for Psychologists in Corrections." In *Who is the Client?*, ed. John Monahan: Washington, D.C.: American Psychological Association.

Brown, Peter G. 1975. "Informed Consent in Social Experimentation: Some Cautionary Notes." In *Ethical and Legal Issues of Social Experimentation. See* Rivlin and Timpane.

Buchanan, Robert A., Karen L. Whitlow, and James Austin. 1986. "National Evaluation of Objective Prison Classification Systems." *Crime and Delinquency* 32 (July):272-290.

California Youth Authority. 1985. *Youth Service Bureaus: Report to the Legislature*. Sacramento: the Authority.

Campbell, Donald T., Robert F. Boruch, Richard D. Schwarts, and Joseph Steinberg. 1975. "Confidentiality-preserving Modes of Access to Files and to Interfile Exchange for Useful Statistical Analysis." Appendix A to COFAER.

Campbell, Donald T. and Stanley C. Julian. 1966. *Experimental and Quasi-Exprimental Designs for Research*. Chicago: Rand McNally.

Campbell, Donald T. and H. Laurence Ross. 1968. "The Connecticut Crackdown on Speeding." *Law and Society Review* 3 (Fall):33-53.

Capron, Alexander Morgan. 1975. "Social Experimentation and the Law." In *Ethical and Legal Issues of Social Experimentation. See* Rivlin and Timpane.

Carney, Francis J. 1969. "Correctional Research and Correctional Decision-making: Some Problems and Prospects." *Journal of Research in Crime and Delinquency* 6 (July):110-22.

_____. 1967. "Predicting Recidivism in a Medium Security Correctional

Institution." *Journal of Criminal Law, Criminology, and Police Science* 58 (September):338-48.

Carter, Robert M., Daniel Glaser, and Leslie T. Wilkins, eds. 1985. *Correctional Institutions.* 3rd ed. New York: Harper and Row.

Clapp, Jane. 1974. *Professional Ethics and Insignia.* Metuchen, N.J.: Scarecrow Press.

Clear, Todd R. and Kenneth W. Gallagher. 1983. "Screening Devices in Probation and Parole." *Evaluation Review* 7 (April):217-34.

Coates, Robert B., Alden D. Miller, and Lloyd E. Ohlin. 1978. *Diversity in a Youth Correctional System: Handling Delinquents in Massachusetts.* Cambridge, Mass.: Ballinger.

COFAER (Committee on Federal Agency Evaluation Research). 1975. *Protecting Individual Privacy in Evaluation Research.* Washington: National Academy of Sciences.

Conner, Ross F. 1977. "Selecting a Control Group: An Analysis of the Randomization Process in Twelve Social Reform Programs." *Evaluation Quarterly* 1 (May):195-244.

Cook, Thomas D., and Donald T. Campbell. 1979. *Quasi-Experimentation.* Chicago: Rand McNally.

Cronbach, Lee J., and Associates. 1980. *Toward Reform of Program Evaluation.* San Francisco: Jossey-Bass.

Cullen, Francis T., and Karen E. Gilbert. 1982. *Reaffirming Rehabilitation.* Cincinnati: Anderson.

Diener, Edward and Rick Crandall. 1978. *Ethics in Social and Behavioral Research.* Chicago: University of Chicago Press.

Doshay, Lewis J. 1943. *The Boy Sex Offender and His Later Career.* New York: Grune and Stratton.

Douglas, Jack. 1979. "Living Morality vs. Bureaucratic Fiat." In *Deviance and Decency*, C, Klockars and F. O'Connor, eds. Beverly Hills, Calif.: Sage.

Duxbury, Elaine, Joachim P. Seckel, and James K. Turner. 1980. *Institutional Violence Reduction Project: The Impact of Changes in Living Unit Size and Staffing.* Sacramento: California Youth Authority.

Edsall, J.T. 1975. *Scientific Freedom and Responsibility.* Washington, D.C.: American Association for the Advancement of Science.

Edwards, Ward. 1980. "Multiattribute Utility for Evaluation: Structure, Uses, and Problems." In *Handbook of Criminal Justice Evaluation.* *See* Klein and Teilmann.

Edwards, Ward, and J. Robert Newman. 1982. *Multiattribute Evaluation.* Beverly Hills, Calif.: Sage.

Edwards, Ward, Marcia Guttentag, and Kurt Snapper. 1975. "A Decision-theoretic Approach to Evaluation Research." In *Handbook of Evaluation Research,* Elmer L. Struening and Marcia Guttentag, eds. Beverly Hills, Calif.: Sage.

Eisenstein, James and Herbert Jacob. 1977. *Felony Justice: An Organizational Analysis of Criminal Courts.* Boston: Little, Brown.

Ellickson, Phyllis and Joan Petersilia. 1983. *Implementing New Ideas in Criminal Justice.* Santa Monica, Calif.: Rand Corporation.

Empey, LaMar. 1980. "Field Experimentation in Criminal Justice: Rationale and Design." In *Handbook of Criminal Justice Evaluation. See* Klein and Teilmann.

Empey, LaMar and Maynard L. Erickson. 1972. *The Provo Experiment.* Lexington, Mass., : Heath.

Empey, LaMar and Jerome Rabow. 1961. "The Provo Experiment in Delinquency Rehabilitation." *American Sociological Review* 26 (October):679-96.

Fairweather, George W. with Louis G. Tornatzky. 1977. *Experimental Methods for Social Policy Research.* New York: Pergamon.

Federal Judiciary Center, Advisory Committee on Experimentation in the Law. 1981. *Experimentation in the Law.* Washington, D.C.: the Center.

Feeley, Malcolm M. 1983. *Court Reform on Trial.* New York: Basic Books.

Festinger, Leon. 1964. *Conflict, Decision and Dissonance.* Stanford, Calif.: Stanford University Press.

Fiedler, Fred E. and Arnold R. Bass. 1959. *Delinquency, Confinement, and Interpersonal Perception.* Technical Report no.6. Urbana, Illinois: University of Illinois Group Effectiveness Laboratory.

Flemming, Roy B., C. Kohfeld, and Thomas M. Uhlman. 1980. "The Limits of Bail Reform: A Quasi-Experimental Analysis." *Law and Society Review* 14 (Summer):947-76.

Fletcher, J. 1967. "Human Experimentation, Ethics and the Consent Situation." *Law and Contemporary Problems* 32 (Autumn):620-49.

Fogel, David. 1978. *We Are The Living Proof.* Cincinnati: Anderson.

Ford, Daniel and Annesley K. Schmidt. 1985. "Electronically Monitored Home Confinement." *NIJ Reports* (U.S. Department of Justice) SNI 194 (November):2-6.

Forst Brian, and William M. Rhodes. 1982. "Structuring the Exercise of Discretion in the Federal Courts." *Federal Probation* 46 (March):3-13.

Fost, N. C. 1975. "A Surrogate System for Informed Consent." *Journal of the American Medical Association* 233:800-03.

Fox, James A. and Paul E. Tracy. 1980. "The Randomized Response Approach and Its Applicability to Criminal Justice Research and Evaluation." *Evaluation Review* 4:601-22.

Freeman, B. 1975. "A Moral Theory of Informed Consent." *Hastings Center Report* 5:32-9.

Freund, Paul A., ed. 1970. *Experimentation With Human Subjects.* New York: George Brasiller.

Friedman, Lee S. 1977. "An Interim Evaluation of the Supported Work Experiment." *Policy Analysis* 3 (Spring):147-70.

Friedman, Neil. 1967. *The Social Nature of Psychological Research.* New York: Basic Books.

Gardiner, Peter C., and Ward Edwards. 1975. "Public Values: Multiattribute Utility Measurement for Social Decision Making." In *Human Judgment and Decision Processes*, Martin F. Kaplan and Steven Schwartz, eds. New York: Academic Press.

Geis, Gilbert. 1967. "Ethical and Legal Issues in Experimentation With Offender Populations." In *Research in Correctional Rehabilitation*, Joint Commission on Correctional Manpower and Training. Washington: the Commission.

Gendreau, Paul and Bob Ross. 1979. "Effective Correctional Treatment: Bibliotherapy for Critics." *Crime and Delinquency* 25 (October):463-89.

Gettinger, Stephen. 1982. "Objective Classification: Catalyst for Change." *Corrections Magazine* 8 (June):24-37.

Gilbert, John P., Bucknam McPeek, and Frederick Mosteller. 1983. "Statistics and Ethics in Surgery and Anaesthesia," In *Solutions to Ethical and Legal Dilemmas in Social Research, See* Boruch and Cecil.

Gillham, James, Carl Bersani, Darelene N. Gillham, and John Vesalo. 1979. "Workers Handling Errant Youth: A Field Experiment on the Effects of In-service Training." *Evaluation Quarterly* 3 (August):347-63.

Glaser, Daniel. 1987. "Classification for Risk." In *Classification and Prediction in Criminal Justice Decisions*, Vol. 9 of *Crime and Justice: An Annual Review of Research*, Don M. Gottfredson and Michael Tonry, eds. Chicago: University of Chicago Press.

_____. 1985. "Who Gets Probation and Parole? Case Study versus Actuarial Decision Making." *Crime and Delinquency* 31 (July):367-78.

_____. 1984. "Six Principles and One Precaution for Efficient Sentencing and Correction." *Federal Probation* 48 (November):22-8.

_____. 1980. "The Interplay of Theory, Issues, Policy and Data in Criminal Justice Evaluations." In *Handbook of Criminal Justice Evaluation. See* Klein and Teilmann.

_____. 1965. "Correctional Research: An Elusive Paradise." *Journal of Research in Crime and Delinquency* 2 (January):1-11.

_____. 1964. *The Effectiveness of a Prison and Parole System*. Indianapolis: Bobbs-Merrill (revised and abridged edition, 1969).

Goldenberg, Ira I. 1971. *Build Me a Mountain: Youth, Poverty, and the Creation of New Settings*. Cambridge, Mass.: MIT Press.

Gottfredson, Michael R. and Don M. 1980. *Decisionmaking in Criminal Justice*. Cambridge, Mass.: Ballinger.

Gottfredson, Michael R., Michael J. Hindelang, and Nicolette Parisi, eds. 1978 *Sourcebook of Criminal Justice Statistics—1977*. Washington: U.S. Department of Justice.

Gramlich, Edward M. and Larry L. Orr. 1975. "The Ethics of Social Experimentation." In *Ethical and Legal Issues of Social Experimentation. See* Rivlin and Timpane.

Gray, Charles M., ed. 1979. *The Costs of Crime.* Beverly Hills, Calif.: Sage.

Guttman, Evelyn S. 1963. *Effects of Short-term Psychiatric Treatment on Boys in Two California Youth Authority Institutions.* Sacramento, Calif.: California Youth Authority.

Hall, Reis, H., Mildred Milazzo, and Judy Posner. 1966. *A Descriptive and Comparative Study of Recidivism in Pre-Release Guidance Center Releasees.* Washington, D.C.: Bureau of Prisons, U.S. Department of Justice.

Hallowell, Lyle. 1985. "The Outcome of the Brojuha Case: Legal Implications for Sociologists." *Footnotes* (Newsletter of the American Sociological Association) 13 (9):1,13.

Harrison, Robert M. and Paul F. C. Mueller. 1964. *Clue-Hunting About Group Counseling and Parole Outcome.* Research Report no. 11 Sacramento: California Department of Corrections.

Higgins, Thomas. 1977. "The Crime Costs of California Early Minor Offenders." *Journal of Research in Crime and Delinquency* 14 (July):195-205.

Hoffman, Peter B. and James L. Beck. 1980. "Revalidating the Salient Factor Score: A Research Note." *Journal of Criminal Justice* 8:185-188.

Hoffman, Peter B. and Sheldon Adelberg. 1980. "The Salient Factor Score: A Nontechnical Review." *Federal Probation* 44 (March):44-52.

Hoffman, Peter B. and Barbara Stone-Meierhoefer. 1979. "Post Release Arrest Experiences of Federal Prisoners: A Six-Year Follow-up". *Journal of Criminal Justice* 7 (Fall):193-216.

Hogarth, Robin. 1980. *Judgment and Choice.* New York: Wiley.

Holland, Terril R. and Norman Holt. 1980. "Correctional Classification and the Prediction of Institutional Adjustment." *Criminal Justice and Behavior* 7 (March):51-60.

Holt, Norman and Daniel Glaser. 1985. "Statistical Guidelines for Custodial Classification Decisions" In *Correctional Institutions. See* Carter et al.

Holt, Robert R. 1978. *Methods in Clinical Psychology.* Vol.2. New York: Plenum Press.

Home Office Research and Planning Unit. 1985. *Research Programme, 1985-86.* London: The Home Office.

Horn, Wede F. and Joel Heerboth. 1982. "Single-Case Experimental Designs and Program Evaluation." *Evaluation Review* 6 (June):403-24.

Institute for Social Research. 1976. *Research Involving Human Subjects.* Report to the National Commission for the Protection of Human Subjects and Behavioral Research. Ann Arbor: University of Michigan.

Irwin, John. 1976. "An Acceptable Context for Biomedical Research." In National Commission for the Protection of Human Subjects, *Prisoners.* Washington, D.C.: National Institute of Mental Health, Publication (05)76-132.

Jesness, Carl. 1965. *The Fricot Ranch Study*. Sacramento: California Youth Authority.

_____.1971. "The Preston Typology Study." *Journal of Research in Crime and Delinquency*. 8 (January):38-52.

Joint Committee on New York Drug Law Evaluation. 1977. *The Nation's Toughest Drug Law: Evaluating the New York Experience*. New York: Association of the Bar of the City of New York.

Kant, Immanuel. 1938. *The Fundamental Principles of the Metaphysics of Ethics*. New York: Appleton-Century-Crofts.

Kantrowitz, Nathan. 1977. "How to Shorten the Followup Period in Parole Studies." *Journal of Research in Crime and Delinquency*.14 (July):222-36.

Kassebaum, Gene, David A. Ward, and Daniel M. Wilner. 1971. *Prison Treatment and Parole Survival*. New York: Wiley.

Kennedy, Mary M. 1983. "The Role of the In-house Evaluator." *Evaluation Review* 7 (August):519-41.

Kerlinger, Fred N. and Elazar J. Pedhazur. 1973. *Multiple Regression in Behavioral Research*. New York: Holt, Rinehart, and Winston.

Kershaw, David N. and Joseph S. Small. 1972. "Data Confidentiality and Privacy: Lessons From the New Jersey Negative Tax Experiment." *Public Policy* 20 (Spring):270-80.

Kitchener, Howard, Annesley K. Schmidt, and Daniel Glaser. 1977. "How Persistent is Post-prison Success?" *Federal Probation*. 41 (March):9-15.

Klein, Malcolm W. 1979. "Deinstitutionalization and Diversion of Juvenile Offenders: A Litany of Impediments." In *Crime and Justice: An Annual Review of Research*, Vol.1. Norval Morris and Michael Tonry, eds. Chicago: University of Chicago Press.

Klein, Malcolm W., and Katherine S. Teilmann, eds. 1980. *Handbook of Criminal Justice Evaluation*. Beverly Hills, Calif.: Sage.

Klempner, Jack. 1976. "Decision Making in a State Prison Reception and Guidance Center." Ph.D. diss., University of Southern California, Los Angeles.

Knight, Doug. 1971. *The Impact of Living-Unit Size in Youth Training Schools*. Sacramento: California Youth Authority.

Krisberg, Barry. 1980. "Utility of Process Evaluation: Crime and Delinquency Programs", In *Handbook of Criminal Justice Evaluation. See* Klein and Teilmann.

Langer, Ellen J. 1975. "The Illusion of Control." *Journal of Personality and Social Psychology* 32 (August):311-28.

LEAA (Law Enforcement Assistance Administration). 1970. *The St. Louis Detoxification and Diagnostic Evaluation Center*. Washington, D.C.: U.S. Government Printing Office.

LeClair, Daniel P. 1985a. "Community-based Reintegration." In *Correctional Institutions. See* Carter et al.

_____. 1985b. "Furloughs and Recidivism Rates." In *Correctional Institutions. See* Carter et al.

_____. 1981. *Community Reintegration of Prison Releasees: Results of the Massachusetts Experience.* Boston: Massachusetts Department of Correction, Publication no.12335.

_____. 1979. *Community-Base Reintegration: Some Theoretical Implications of Positive Research Findings.* Boston: Massachusetts Department of Correction, Publication no. 11625.

_____. 1977. *Development of Base Expectancy Prediction Tables for Treatment and Control Groups in Correctional Research.* Boston: Massachusetts Department of Correction. Publication no.9875-37-250-8/77-CR.

Leff, J. P. 1973. "Trials of Preventive Medication." In *Roots of Evaluation,* J. K. Wing and H. Haefner, eds. London: Oxford University Press.

Lerman, Paul. 1975. *Community Treatment and Social Control.* Chicago: University of Chicago Press.

Lerner, Kenneth, Gary Arling, and S. Christopher Baird. 1986. "Client Management Classification Strategies for Case Supervision." *Crime and Delinquency* 32 (July):254-271.

Levin, Martin A. 1977. *Urban Politics and the Criminal Courts.* Chicago: University of Chicago Press.

Levine, Robert. 1978. "The Role of Assessment of Risk-Benefit Criteria in the Determination of the Appropriateness of Research Involving Human Subjects." Appendix to the Belmont Report: *Ethical Principles and Guidelines for the Protection of Human Subjects,* Vol. 1. DHEW Publication no. (O.S. 78-0013). Washington, D.C.: U.S. Government Printing Office.

_____. 1975. "Proposed Rules on Ethics of Human Experimentation: Tensions Between the Biomedical Research Community and U.S. Federal Government." In *Social Science in Conflict with Law and Ethics,* Paul Nejelski, ed.. Cambridge, Mass.: Ballinger.

Levinger, Laura C. and Robert F. Boruch. 1983. "Contributions of Evaluation to Educational Programs." *Evaluation Review* 7 (October):563-98.

Lidz, Charles W., Alan Meisel, Zerubavel Eviatar, Mary Carter, Regina M. Sestak, and Loren H. Roth. 1984. *Informed Consent: A Study of Decision Making in Psychiatry.* New York: Guilford.

Lipsey, Mark W. 1984. "Is Delinquency Prevention a Cost-effective Strategy?" *Journal of Research on Crime and Delinquency* 21 (Novmber):279-302.

Lipsey, Mark W., David S. Cordray, and Dale E. Berger. 1981. "Evaluation of a Juvenile Diversion Program Using Multiple Lines of Evidence." *Evaluation Review* 5 (June):283-306.

Lipton, Douglas, Robert Martinson, and Judith Wilks. 1975. *The Effectiveness of Correctional Treatment: A Survey of Treatment Evaluation Studies.* New York: Praeger.

Littrell, W. Boyd. 1979. *Bureaucratic Justice.* Beverly Hills, Calif.: Sage.

Loftin, Colin, Milton Heumann, and David McDowall. 1983. "Mandatory Sentencing and Firearms Violence: Evaluating an Alternative to Gun Control." *Law and Society Review* 17 (2):287-318.

Loftus, Elizabeth F. 1979. *Eyewitness Testimony.* Cambridge, Mass.: Harvard University Press.

Los Angeles County Probation Department. 1982. *Differential Supervision Project: Preliminary Analysis of Harbor Adult Supervision Departures, October 1, 1980 to March 31, 1981.* Downey, Calif.: the Department.

Mannheim, Hermann and Leslie T. Wilkins. 1955. *Prediction Methods in Relation to Borstal Training.* London: Her Majesty's Stationery Store.

Martinson, Robert. 1974. "What Works? Questions and Answers About Prison Reform." *The Public Interest* 35 5(Spring):22-54.

Mayer, G. Roy and Tom W. Butterworth. 1981. "Evaluating a Preventive Approach to Reducing School Vandalism." *Phi Delta Kappan* 62 (March):498-99.

_____. 1979. "A Preventive Approach to School Violence and Vandalism: An Experimental Study." *Personnel and Guidance Journal* 57 (May):436-41.

Mayer, G. Roy, Tom Butterworth, Mary Nafpaktitis, and Beth Sulzer-Azaroff. 1981. "Preventing School Vandalism and Improving Discipline: A Three Year Study." California State University, Los Angeles.

Mayo, Elton. 1933. *The Human Problems of an Industrial Civilization.* Cambridge, Mass.: Harvard University Press (republished by Viking, 1960).

McCall, George J., and Jerry L. Simmons. 1966. *Identities and Interactions.* New York: Free Press.

McCleary, Richard, A. G. Gordon, D. McDowell, and M.D. Maltz. 1979. "How a Regression Artifact Can Make Any Delinquency Intervention Program Look Effective. *Evaluation Studies Review Annual.* Vol.IV. Beverly Hills, Calif.: Sage.

McCleary, Richard and Richard A. Hay, Jr. 1980. *Applied Time Series Analysis for the Social Sciences.* Beverly Hills, Calif.: Sage.

McGlothlin, William H., Douglas M. Anglin, and Bruce D. Wison. 1977. *An Evaluation of the California Civil Addict Program.* DHEW Publication no. (ADM) 78-558. Washington, D.C.: U.S. Government Printing Office.

McKee, Gilbert J. Jr. 1985. "Cost-benefit Analysis of Vocational Training." In *Correctional Institutions. See* Carter et al.

_____. 1978. "Cost-effectiveness and Vocational Training." In *Justice and Corrections,* Norman Johnston and Leonard E. Savitz, eds. New York: Wiley.

McKillip, Jack. 1979. "Impact Evaluation of Service Programs: Three Flexible Designs." *Evaluation Quarterly* 3 (February):97-103.

Mead, Margaret. 1970. "Research with Human Beings: A Model Derived from Anthropological Field Practice." In *Experimentation with Human Subjects. See* Freund

Meehl, Paul E. 1954. *Clinical vs. Statistical Prediction.* Minneapolis: University of Minnesota Press.

Meehl, Paul E., and Albert Rosen. 1955. "Antecedent Probability and the Efficiency of Psychometric Signs, Patterns or Cutting Scores." *Psychological Bulletin* 52 (May):194-215.

Merton, Robert K. 1957. *Social Theory and Social Structure.* Rev. ed. New York: Free Press.

Mills, M. and Norval Morris. 1974. "Prisoners as Laboratory Animals." *Transaction* 11 (July/August):60-9.

Mishan, E. J. 1976. *Cost-Benefit Analysis.* Rev. ed. New York: Praeger.

Mitford, Jessica. 1973. *Kind and Usual Punishment.* New York: Knopf.

Monahan, John. 1981. *Predicting Violent Behavior: An Assessment of Clinical Techniques.* Beverly Hills, Calif.: Sage.

Morris, Norval. 1981. "Punishment, Desert, and Rehabilitation." in *Sentencing.* Hyman Gross and Alexander von Hirsch, eds. New York: Oxford University Press.

_____. 1974. *The Future of Imprisonment.* Chicago: University of Chicago Press.

_____. 1966. "Impediments to Penal Reform." *University of Chicago Law Review* 33 (Summer):646-653.

Murray, Charles A. and Louis A. Cox, Jr. 1979. *Beyond Probation: Juvenile Corrections and the Chronic Delinquent.* Beverly Hills, Calif.: Sage.

Murphy, Terrence H. 1980. *Michigan Risk Prediction: A Replication Study.* Lansing: Michigan Department of Corrections.

Musheno, Michael, Dennis Palumbo, and James Levine. 1976. "Evaluating Alternatives in Criminal Justice." *Crime and Delinquency* 22 (July):265-83.

Muthen, Bengt and George Speckart. 1983. "Categorizing Skewed Dependent Variables." *Evaluation Review* 7 (April):257-270.

Nagel, Stuart S. 1983 "Nonmonetary Variables in Benefit-Cost Evaluation." *Evaluation Review* 7 (February):37-64.

National Academy of Sciences. 1975. *Academy Forum: Experimentation and Research With Human Values in Conflict.* Washington, D.C.: National Academy of Sciences.

NCPHSBBR (National Commission for the Protection of Human Subjects of Biomedical and Behavioral Research). 1976. *Research Involving Prisoners.* Washington D.C.: U.S. Government Printing Office.

National Conference on Parole. 1957. *Parole in Principles and Practice* New York: National Probation and Parole Association.

National Institute of Justice. 1984. *Jailing Drunk Drivers: Impact on the Criminal Justice System.* Washington, D.C.: U.S. Department of Justice.

_____. 1981. *Exemplary Projects*. Washington: U.S. Department of Justice.

Nejelski, P. and H. Peyser. 1975. "A Researcher's Shield Statute: Guarding Against a Compulsory Disclosure of Research Data." Appendix B to *Protecting Individual Privacy in Evaluation Research. See* COFAER.

Nejelski, Paul, and Lindsey Miller Lerman. 1971. "A Researcher-Subject Testimonial Privilege: What to do Before the Subpoena Arrive?" *Wisconsin Law Review* (4):1048-85.

Nelson, Carl W. 1975. "Cost-Benefit Analysis and Alternatives to Incarceration." *Federal Probation* 39 (December):45-50.

Nimmer, Raymond T. 1978. *The Nature of System Change: Reform Impact in the Criminal Courts*. Chicago: American Bar Foundation.

Ohlin, Lloyd E. 1951. *Selection for Parole*. New York: Russell Sage Foundation.

Ostrom, Charles W., Jr. 1978. *Time Series Analysis: Regression Techniques*. Beverly Hills, Calif.: Sage.

O'Sullivan, Elizabeth Ann. 1985. "Decision Support Systems: An Introduction for Program Evaluators." *Evaluation Review* 9 (February):84-92.

Palmer, Ted. 1978. *Correctional Intervention and Research*. Lexington, Mass.: Heath.

_____. 1974. "The Youth Authority's Community Treatment Project." *Federal Probation* 38 (March):3-20.

Palumbo, Dennis J., Steven Maynard-Moody and Paula Wright. 1984. "Measuring Degrees of Successful Implementation." *Evaluation Quarterly* 8 (February):45-74.

Parsons Talcott. 1970. "Research with Human Subjects and the Professional Complex", In *Experimentation with Human Subjects. See* Freund.

_____. 1951. *The Social System*. New York: Free Press.

Patton, Michael Q. 1980. *Qualitative Evaluation Methods*. Beverly Hills, Calif.: Sage.

_____. 1978. *Utilization-Focused Evaluation*. Beverly Hills, Calif.: Sage.

Paul, Gordon L. 1967. "Insight versus Desensitization in Psychotherapy Two Years After Termination." *Journal of Consulting Psychology* 31 (August)333-48.

Pawlak, Edward J. 1977. "Differential Selection of Juveniles for Detention," with comments by Lerman and Empey. *Journal of Research in Crime and Delinquency* 14 (July):152-76.

Poister, Theodore H. 1982. "Performance Monitoring in the Evaluation Process." *Evaluation Review* 6 (October):601-23.

Reynolds, Paul Davidson. 1979. *Ethical Dilemmas and Social Science Research*. San Francisco: Jossey-Bass.

Rivlin, Alice A. and Michael P. Timpane, eds. 1975. *Ethical and Legal Issues of Social Experimentation*. Washington, D.C.: Brookings Institution.

Rosenfeld, Albert. 1981. "Hard Time for Prison Research." *Science* 81 (January):14,18.

Rosenthal, R. 1967. "Experimenter Expectancy and the Reassuring Nature of the Null Hypothesis Decision Procedure." *Psychological Bulletin* 70 (6, part 2) (July):30-47

_____. 1967. "Covert Communication in the Psychological Experiment." *Psychological Bulletin* 67 (May):356-67.

Ross, H. Laurence. 1984. *Deterring the Drinking Driver*. Rev. ed. Lexington, Mass.: Heath.

_____. 1975. "The Scandinavian Myth: The Effectiveness of Drinking-and-Driving Legislation in Sweden and Norway." *Journal of Legal Studies* 4 (June):285-310.

_____. 1960-1961. "Traffic Law Violation: A Folk Crime." *Social Problems* 8 (Winter):231-40.

Ross, H. Laurence, Donald T. Campbell, and Gene V. Glass. 1970. "Determining the Social Effects of a Legal Reform: The British 'Breathalyser' Crackdown of 1967." *American Behavioral Scientist* 13 (March-April):495-509.

Rossi, Peter H., Richard A. Berk, and Kenneth L. Lenihan. 1980. *Money, Work, and Crime*. New York: Academic Press.

Rutstein, David R. 1969. "The Ethical Design of Human Experiments." *Daedalus* 98 (Spring):523-41.

St. Pierre, Robert G. 1982. "Management of Federally Funded Evaluation Research: Building Evaluation Teams." *Evaluation Review* 6 (February):94-113.

Sassone, Peter G. and William A. Schaffer. 1978. *Cost-Benefit Analysis*. New York: Academic Press.

Sawyer, Jack. 1966. "Measurement *and* Prediction, Clinical *and* Statistical." *Psychological Bulletin* 66 (September):178-200.

Scheff, Thomas J. 1966. *Being Mentally Ill*. Chicago: Aldine.

Seckel, Joachim. 1965. *Experiments in Group Counseling at Two Youth Authority Institutions*. Sacramento: California Youth Authority.

Shover, Neal. 1974. "Experts and Diagnosis in Correctional Agencies." *Crime and Delinquency* 20 (October):347-58.

Simon, Frances H. 1971. *Prediction Methods in Criminology*. London: Her Majesty's Stationery Store.

Simon, Herbert A. 1965a. *Administrative Behavior*, 3rd ed. New York: Free Press.

_____. 1965b. *The Shape of Automation for Men and Management*. New York: Harper and Row.

Singer, Richard G. H 1979. *Just Deserts: Sentencing Based on Equality and Desert*. Cambridge, Mass.: Ballinger.

Skogan, Wesley G. 1986. *Evaluating Neighborhood Crime Prevention Programs*. The Hague: Netherlands Ministry of Justice, Research and Documentation Centre.

Snortum, John R. 1984. "Controlling the Alcohol-Impaired Driver in Scandinavia and the United States: Simple Deterrence and Beyond." *Journal of Criminal Justice* 12 :131-48.

Solberg, Ann. 1983. "Community Posthospital Followup Services." *Evaluation Quarterly* 7 (February):96-109.

Sonquist, John A. 1970. *Multivariate Model Building*. Ann Arbor, Mich.: University of Michigan, Institute for Social Research.

Steadman, Henry J., and Joseph J. Cocozza. 1974. *Careers of the Criminally Insane*. Lexington, Mass.: Heath.

Steiner, Zanaleen. 1985. *First Annual Report on Research Progress, Youth Work Project*. Los Angeles: Foundation for People.

Stone, Christopher. 1975. *Where the Law Ends: The Social Control of Corporate Behavior*. New York: Harper and Row.

Stromsdorfer, Ernst W. and Teh-wei Hu. 1978. "Control Group Selection." In *Conference Report on Youth Employment: Its Measurement and Meaning*. Washington, D.C.: U.S. Department of Labor.

Sudnow, David. 1965. "Normal Crimes: Sociological Features of the Penal Code in a Public Defender's Office." *Social Problems* 12 (Winter):255-76.

Tabor, John G. 1978. "The Role of the Accountant in Preventing and Detecting Information Abuses in Social Program Evaluation." In *Evaluation Studies Review Annual*. Vol.3. Thomas D. Cook, Marilyn L. Del Rosario, Karen M. Hennigan, Melvin M. Mark, and William M. K. Trochim, eds. Beverly Hills, Calif.: Sage.

Thalheimer, Donald J. 1975. *Cost Analysis of Correctional Standards— Halfway Houses*. 2 vols. Washington, D.C.: U.S. Department of Justice, National Institute of Law Enforcement and Criminal Justice.

Thompson, Mark S. 1980. *Benefit-Cost Analysis for Program Evaluation*. Beverly Hills, Calif.: Sage.

Thornberry, Terence P. and Joseph E. Jacoby. 1979. *The Criminally Insane: A Community Follow-up of Mentally Ill Offenders*. Chicago: University of Chicago Press.

Tittle, Charles K. 1973. "Punishment and Deterrence of Deviance." In *The Economics of Crime and Punishment*. Simon Rottenberg, ed. Washington, D.C.: American Enterprise Institute.

Tracy, Paul E. and James A. Fox. 1981. "Validity of Randomized Response." *American Sociological Review* 46 (April):87-200.

U.S. Departments of Justice and Commerce. 1977. *Trends in Expenditure and Employment Data for the Criminal Justice System, 1971-1975*. Washington, D.C.: Bureau of the Census.

Veatch, Robert M. 1978. "Three Theories of Informed Consent: Philosophical Foundations and Policy Implications." Appendix to the Belmont Report: *Ethical Principles and Guidelines for the Protection of Human Subjects*. DHEW Publication no. (O.S.) 78-0014, Vol.2. Washington: U.S. Government Printing Office.

_____. 1975. "Ethical Principles in Medical Experimentation." In *Ethical and Legal Issues of Social Experimentation. See* Rivlin and Timpane.

Vera Foundation for Criminal Justice. 1970. *The Manhattan Court Employment Study.* New York: the Foundation.

von Hirsch, Andrew. 1976. *Doing Justice: The Choice of Punishment.* New York: Hill and Wang.

von Winterfeldt, Detlof and Ward Edwards. 1986. *Decision Analysis and Behavioral Research.* New York: Cambridge University Press.

Wainer, Howard and Anne M. B. Morgan. 1982. "Robust Estimation of Parole Outcome." *Journal of Research in Crime and Delinquency* 19 (January):84-109.

Warner, S. L. 1965. "Randomized Response: A Survey Technique for Eliminating Evasive Answer Bias." *Journal of the American Statistical Association* 60 :63-9.

Webb, Eugene J., Donald Campbell, Richard D. Schwartz, and Lee Sechrest. 1966. *Unobtrusive Measures.* Chicago: Rand McNally.

Weber, Max. 1978. *Economy and Society* 2 vols. Berkeley: University of California Press.

Weiss, Carol H. 1972. *Evaluating Action Programs.* Boston: Allyn and Bacon.

Weiss, Carol H., and Michael J. Bucuvalas. 1980. "Truth Tests and Utility Tests: Decision Makers' Frames of Reference for Social Science Research." *American Sociological Review* 45 (April):302-13.

Wiederanders, Mark R. 1983. *Success on Parole.* Sacramento: California Youth Authority.

Wilkins, Leslie T., Jack M. Kress, Don M. Gottfredson, Joseph C. Calpin, and Arthur M. Gelman. 1978. *Sentencing Guidelines: Structuring Judicial Discretion.* Washington, D.C.: U.S. Department of Justice, National Institute of Law Enforcement and Criminal Justice.

Wilson, James Q. 1980. "'What Works?' Revisited: New Findings on Criminal Rehabilitation." *The Public Interest* (Fall):3-17.

Winick, Bruce J. 1981. "A Preliminary Analysis of Legal Limitations on Rehabilitative Alternatives to Corrections and on Correctional Research." In *New Directions in the Rehabilitation of Criminal Offenders,* Susan E. Martin, Lee B. Sechrest, and Robin Redner, eds. Washington, D.C.: National Academy of Sciences.

Wolfgang, Marvin E. 1981. "Confidentiality in Criminological Research and Other Ethical Issues." *Journal of Criminal Law and Criminology* 72 (Spring):345-61.

_____. 1976. "Ethical Issues of Research in Criminology," In ed. *Social Research in Conflict With Law and Ethics.* Paul Nejelski, ed. Cambridge, Mass.: Ballinger.

Wolfgang, Marvin E., Robert M. Figlio, and Thorsten Sellin. 1972. *Delinquency in a Birth Cohort.* Chicago: University of Chicago Press.

Wright, G. N., L. D. Phillips, P. C. Whalley, G. T. Choo, K. Ng, I. Tan, and A. Wisudha. 1978. "Cultural Differences in Probabilistic Thinking." *Journal of Cross-Cultural Psychology* 9 (September):285-99.

Wright, George. 1984. *Behavioral Decision Theory*. Beverly Hills, Calif.: Sage.

Wright, K. N., T. R. Clear, and P. Dickson, 1984. "Universal Applicability of Probation Risk Assessment Instrument." *Criminology* 22 (February): 113–34.

Zeisel, Hans. 1983. "Reducing the Hazards of Human Experiments through Modifications in Research Design." In Solutions to Ethical and Legal Dilemmas in Social Research. See Boruch and Cecil.

Zimring, Franklin E. and Gordon J. Hawkins. 1973. *Deterrence: The Legal Threat in Crime Control*. Chicago: University of Chicago Press.

Index